CUBA
and the UNITED STATES
Long-Range Perspectives

CUBA
and the UNITED STATES
Long-Range Perspectives

JOHN PLANK *editor*

essays by

HENRY WRISTON

ROBERT F. SMITH

TAD SZULC

J. WILNER SUNDELSON

KALMAN H. SILVERT

RAYMOND ARON & ALFRED GROSSER

RAYMOND CARR

LEON LIPSON

HANSON W. BALDWIN

BAYLESS MANNING

THE BROOKINGS INSTITUTION

Washington, D.C.

THE BROOKINGS INSTITUTION is an independent organization devoted to nonpartisan research, education, and publication in economics, government, foreign policy, and the social sciences generally. Its principal purposes are to aid in the development of sound public policies and to promote public understanding of issues of national importance.

The Institution was founded December 8, 1927, to merge the activities of the Institute for Government Research, founded in 1916, the Institute of Economics, founded in 1922, and the Robert Brookings Graduate School of Economics and Government, founded in 1924.

The general administration of the Institution is the responsibility of a self-perpetuating Board of Trustees. The trustees are likewise charged with maintaining the independence of the staff and fostering the most favorable conditions for creative research and education. The immediate direction of the policies, program, and staff of the Institution is vested in the President, assisted by the program directors and an advisory council, chosen from the professional staff of the Institution.

In publishing a study, the Institution presents it as a competent treatment of a subject worthy of public consideration. The interpretations and conclusions in such publications are those of the author or authors and do not purport to represent the views of the other staff members, officers, or trustees of the Brookings Institution.

Foreword

We in the United States have always had a "Cuban prob-
lem." Over the years that run from Jefferson's time to our own, the problem has taken on different forms, but at bottom it has always been the
same. Generations of our statesmen have had to ask themselves, "What
can be done to ensure that Cuba, which lies athwart the trade routes to
the Panamanian Isthmus and a few score miles from our own territory,
does not become a base from which extracontinental powers hostile to
the United States can mount attacks against us?" It is *that* question, not
the thrust toward Manifest Destiny or the assumption of a White Man's
Burden, that historically has largely determined our Cuban policy.

The prospect we had dreaded materialized with the accession of Fidel
Castro and the subsequent identification of his regime with the Communist states of the world. Not only was a Western Hemisphere government now allied with our declared antagonists in the cold war; a stra-
tegically and militarily important outpost in this part of the world had
been opened to extracontinental powers. Public alarm over this turn of
events was—and continues to be—widespread. Although the extreme
fears caused by the introduction of Soviet missiles into Cuba have now
receded, anxiety about Cuba is still deeply felt.

The purpose of the present volume is to consider various aspects of
the Cuban situation within a long-range framework in order to provide
a sounder basis for thinking about future United States policy toward
the troubled island.

John Plank, the editor of this volume, is a member of the Brookings Senior Staff. He was formerly Director of the Office for Research and Analysis for American Republics in the Bureau of Intelligence and Research of the U.S. Department of State, and Professor of Latin American Affairs at the Fletcher School of Law and Diplomacy. He has also taught at Harvard University and Northwestern University.

The work is organized as a symposium in order to take advantage of diverse interests, skills, and experience. The Institution considers itself fortunate to have been able to enlist so able a group of authors, whose backgrounds are described at the beginning of the chapters. Those who participated as advisers, either in helping to plan the book as a whole or in reviewing individual manuscripts, are Philip W. Bonsal, Armand Boucher, William Butler, John Dreier, Michael Deutch, John P. Hoover, Peter T. Jones, Charles Loring, Edward G. Miller, Jr., Teodoro Moscoso, Maurice Mountain, Forrest D. Murden, Jr., W. L. McKee, John E. Rielly, and Bryce Wood. Their assistance is gratefully acknowledged. Mrs. Adele J. Garrett edited the manuscript and prepared the index.

The views expressed in the chapters, however, are entirely the responsibility of the authors and do not purport to represent the views of the advisers just listed or of the Trustees, officers, or staff members of the Brookings Institution.

Special thanks are due Dean Bayless Manning of the Stanford University Law School, who played a key role in helping to plan the project, recruit the authors, and review the manuscripts. His challenging essay, the concluding chapter of the book, is both an able summation of what precedes it and a bold look toward the future.

The Institution also wishes to express its gratitude to the Ford Foundation and the Rockefeller Foundation for their special grants which supported the project.

ROBERT D. CALKINS
President

June 1967
Washington, D.C.

Contents

Introduction

JOHN PLANK

This book was conceived at a time when Cuba was very much in the public's mind. Memories of the missile crisis of October 1962 were still fresh, Castro's efforts to export his revolution through insurgency to other Latin American countries were mounting in intensity, Cuban refugee groups were making frequent, if sporadic and futile, forays against the island, the United States government was working assiduously to secure an effective quarantine of Cuba by the Western world. Moreover, Cuba was a major domestic political issue. In the Congress and in the press discussion of Cuba and Cuban policy was heated and sustained.

In the early 1960's the public was deluged with information about Cuba, some of it reliable, much of it based on rumor, some of it balanced and objective, much of it warped and politically slanted. The careful reader with sufficient time, energy, and interest could thread his way through the voluminous literature of press stories, congressional statements, journal articles, pamphlets, and books and could reach a reasoned position of his own. But the average concerned citizen, without much time, without access to a full range of opinion and fact, and without substantial background knowledge, was in a difficult position to assess and evaluate what he heard and read about Cuba.

It was to help the concerned citizen that the Brookings Institution decided to commission the series of essays brought together here. The objective was to provide a context, historical and global, within which a reader could interpret the unfolding Cuban story. Those who were asked to contribute to this book responded ably to their difficult assignments, basing their essays upon the best knowledge available to them and preparing essays that transcended the immediate and contingent. It was not the intention of the authors to write with an eye on yesterday's headlines. Rather, their purpose was to give sober thought and judgment to the enduring aspects of the Cuban situation in its many dimensions.

The essays themselves were submitted at various times between late 1963 and late 1965. It is a tribute to their quality that the passage of time has detracted so little from their pertinence to the Cuban situation today.

Undoubtedly, were the book being planned today, it would be noticeably different. Greater account would be taken, for example, of the increasingly serious split between the Soviet Union and Red China, and of the implications of that split for Castro's Cuba. Attention would be paid to the strained relations between Havana and Peking, to the divergence in tactics and strategy between Havana and Moscow with regard to the advancement of the purposes of Communists in the Western Hemisphere, and to the Tri-Continental Congress of January 1966.

Also, the Vietnam conflict does not figure in these pages; but increasingly heavy United States involvement in Vietnam bears indirectly on our Cuban policy. Correspondingly, the rotund fiascos of the Red Chinese in Indonesia and Africa would presumably call for some comment: those events have affected Castro's hemispheric posture and prospects.

Clearly, events in the Dominican Republic during the spring and summer of 1965 would have been dealt with, however summarily, for the fear of "another Cuba" was high among the factors that motivated United States intervention there.

Basically, though, the interpretations our authors gave of Cuba's internal situation and of its position vis-à-vis the United States, in the hemisphere, and in the world, remain valid. Castro is still very much in command in Cuba and the regime shows no signs of imminent collapse; Castro is still unalterably hostile to the government of the United States; the United States is still unremitting in the economic and political pressures it is bringing to bear against Castro's govern-

ment; the hemispheric pretensions of Castro's revolutionary movement have not been abandoned (nor have they in any way been realized); the Soviet Union is still keeping Cuba economically and militarily afloat, and Castro's dependence upon the Soviet Union is as
great today as ever it has been; the Europeans, or most of them, are
still faintly bemused by United States Cuban policy and continue to
be reluctant to cooperate with us in implementing that policy; the
Cuban refugee community in the United States, while larger than
two years ago, is still badly divided; and the United States public is
still subjected to a flow of usually superficial and frequently suspect
Cuban information. What has altered, of course, is the focus of public
attention: with the intensification of the conflict in Vietnam, most of
us are looking away from Cuba toward Asia. Cuba remains a latent
concern for us, lurking never far below the level of consciousness; but
today it is not the almost constant preoccupation that it was several
years ago.

At this time of comparatively reduced public excitement about
Cuba, it is especially appropriate to present this book to thoughtful
citizens. Late or soon, through conscious design or through the play
of contingent events, the contours of the United States-Cuba problem
will change, and options at present not realistically open to us as a
people will emerge. But it is realistically open to us now—and indeed
is incumbent upon us as citizens—to think soberly and responsibly
about how we would respond to such options. Such thinking is greatly
aided by the kind of judicious and informed interpretation and analysis this book provides.

HENRY WRISTON, author of *Executive Agents in American Diplomacy* (1929), *Diplomacy in a Democracy* (1956), *Strategy of Peace* (1944), and other books, is a former president of Lawrence College, Brown University, the Council on Foreign Relations, and the American Assembly.

A Historical Perspective

HENRY WRISTON

For present purposes Cuba is discussed in isolation from other nations. It is a useful device but artificial. The relations between the United States and Cuba interpenetrate many other foreign relations. Separate consideration of one country may produce serious distortions. For example, Cuban governments seem unstable, but political instability is a common characteristic of the world. There have been many coups d'état in the Arab world; in Central and South America revolutions have been endemic; coups are common in parts of Africa and Asia.

Fundamental changes occur not only in respect to Cuba but also in respect to areas where stability seems inherent. In ethical values, for instance, there have been dramatic changes. Statesmen long took positions that would today be regarded as morally outrageous, yet acted in the conviction that their motives were pure. No president, even in private conversation, would now refer with patent disdain to Cubans as "dagoes." Yet that was the term used by one president who laid great stress on moral values.

For a long time imperialism—now an anathema—seemed natural. Later a client status became normal; it was formalized in the mandates of the League of Nations and the trusteeships of the United Nations. Even the Cuban patriot José Martí, deeply as he desired independence, was fearful that the formal status would not mean full freedom and that it might require time, preparation, and a subsequent revolution of a different sort.

1

The great powers long arrogated to themselves authority to direct
lesser nations financially, politically, and otherwise. A "show of force,"
a few shells from a gunboat, would usually suffice. Even a minatory
tone or a threat of action might produce the desired compliance. Those
days are gone, and in retrospect it is easy to see that the identification
of power with moral superiority was wrong. Now the great nations are
often hectored in the United Nations—and elsewhere—by new states
that lack essential qualities of nationhood and cannot govern their own
territories effectively. It ought to be obvious that weakness is no better
guarantee of moral superiority than was power.

Ministers of the Gospel approved of slavery, which seems unbeliev-
able after a sea change in the ethical atmosphere. Slavery was ardently
defended in the United States as part of an inviolable right to hold
property—even human chattels. The laggard abolition of slavery in
Cuba affected its people and political life. The aftermaths of slavery in
the economic, political, and social structure of the United States have
influenced our international relations.

Economic theory has undergone complete revision during the period
of contact between Cuba and the United States. It is reflected in trade
relations, in finance, and in the concept of underdevelopment and what
to do about it.

The divergent intellectual orientation of the Cuban and American
cultures has great significance. Though many of Karl Marx's ideas have
been unconsciously absorbed into the American point of view, his formal doctrines evoke a violently negative reaction. In Cuba, Marx's
views have been widely accepted by intellectuals, and they saturate the
outlook of students. Thus events receive contrary interpretations in the
two countries, and mutual understanding becomes difficult.

The processes of change affect all these as well as other factors, but
at different times, at varying paces, and often with contrary effects. Strategic concepts may be out of harmony with economic interest. Either or
both may be out of key with the political, social, cultural, ethical, or
other phases of international relationships. History is infinitely complex; though it is continuous, it never moves in a straight line. Historical analysis makes clear, therefore, that no mere extrapolation of past
experience will suffice as a guide for the future.

Moreover, a policy that seems adequate at the moment of its adoption may have secondary effects that negate the initial gains and pro-

duce unhappy aftermaths. Cuba was ideally situated to grow sugar cane, and heavy commitments were made in its production. It became the key to Cuban solvency, but adverse terms of trade in that commodity brought severe hardship. When the United States agreed to buy large quantities at a price above the world market, it seemed a stabilizing factor in the Cuban economy. The secondary consequence, however, was to make an economy already dominated by sugar dependent upon the sugar policy of the United States. To that extent the United States retarded the diversification essential to genuine economic independence and perpetuated a client relationship, which is always inherently unstable. That fact is fundamental to subsequent relations not only with Cuba but also with Panama and other "banana republics" of Central America—and elsewhere. To maintain a longtime client relationship requires a far tougher policy than the American public is likely to support. Even the Soviet satellite states have shown restlessness, particularly since the ruthless policies of Stalin were modified.

History as Mentor

Historical method has characteristic limitations. The issues that engage a historian's mind are usually those which concern his own era. Other things may be more important for the future without having yet been recognized. A historian also writes from his own position in space and subconsciously tends to make that locus appear at the center. To the mainlander Cuba has normally been at the margin of interest; relations with it have been subordinate to European concerns. For the Cuban his own nation is at the core of the drama, and its relations with the United States engross his attention.

Two illustrations must suffice. By its basic treaty with Cuba the United States had the right not only to Guantánamo but also to a naval station near Havana. Elihu Root decided that it would not be "reasonable" to keep an armed force "in immediate juxtaposition to the capital and chief commercial city." Nevertheless, the Cuban revolution of 1912 saw a U.S. attempt to do just that. In the perspective of our history, the incident is so trivial that few American books mention it. From the Cuban point of view it was vital.

The Isle of Pines offers the second illustration. An agreement to turn it over to Cuba was signed on February 23, 1903, but the Senate, despite a favorable report from its Committee on Foreign Relations, failed to give its advice and consent. Not until twenty-two years later, after the treaty had been "mislaid," was consent to ratification finally voted. A matter of great importance to Cuba was treated with casual neglect by the United States.

The historian, however, has some advantages. He can isolate the problem and reflect upon it dispassionately, free of demands for speed of decision and action. The statesman, on the contrary, has many simultaneous perplexities pressing upon him. He does not have time to garner all the facts, much less leisure to reflect upon them. Frequently he has to shoot from the hip, so to speak. The historian can offer criticisms with a good deal of assurance, for he knows the outcome—a benefit denied the statesman at the moment of decision. However, there is no proof that the historian's "second guess" would have produced better results, since his judgment cannot be put to the acid test.

The statesman is called upon to "settle a matter," to "solve a problem." The historian knows that no large issue is ever really settled; it merely assumes a different form. His discipline habituates him to the expectation of continuous change. He sees peace as a dynamic process rather than a fixed status.

The historian, moreover, can never regard events as governed by logic. Men are reasonable—sometimes—but surely an era that has seen Hitler, Mussolini, Perón, and Castro should not expect reason always to control. Deeply embedded in the historical process are the charisma of leaders, ancient and modern, and the readiness of many people, burdened by their personal cares and confused by the world's complexities, to surrender and follow blindly.

Up to a point, nationalism represents a rational attitude, but ultranationalism may be quite irrational. Passion replaces logic, and a nation follows courses not in accord with its own true interests. This sometimes occurred in Cuban upheavals with profound effects on relations with the United States. A historical approach can take account of such psychological forces, which are often vastly more potent than logic.

Geography

Geography seems unalterable, but that appearance conceals significant realities. In the contacts between the United States and Cuba, even the physical reality has been modified—for instance, when the Panama Canal brought fundamental changes.

Political geography is just as fundamental as the physical. Cuba is only 90 miles off our coast, and in a position to dominate both entrances to the Gulf of Mexico as well as a passage between the Atlantic Ocean and the Caribbean Sea, and it is one of the principal routes to the Panama Canal. Historically, however, the location of Cuba was politically irrelevant to the United States for many years. Its strategic importance developed slowly so far as the United States was concerned. It was not until 27 years after the Declaration of Independence that Jefferson concluded the Louisiana Purchase, which gave us our first land on the Gulf of Mexico. Florida was not acquired until 43 years after the Declaration, when it was still sparsely inhabited and when, in those days of sailing ships and cannon with a three-mile range, 90 miles was a very respectable distance. It was 70 years before the acquisition of Texas completed our holdings on the Gulf, and the Panama Canal was not finished until 138 years after 1776.

Nor are the changes in political geography complete. Cuba's physical and political relations with the United States will be further modified by air, missile, and other technological developments. Many American citizens realized for the first time in 1962 that Cuba was situated not merely where we could use it for our strategic purposes, but also where it could be exploited to our disadvantage—a fact appreciated by statesmen much earlier.

The political geography of Cuba depended upon who controlled it and who sought dominion over it. As long as Spain was master of the Caribbean and most of South America, we could regard other issues as more urgent. As Spain's grip on Latin America loosened and our self-confidence increased, we sought to assert a reversionary right to some of Spain's possessions—the two Floridas, for example.

However, Napoleon set up his brother as ruler of Spain. Had that proved a stable arrangement, we would have faced an aggressive neighbor. But Napoleon's troubles in Spain multiplied, and in 1809 Thomas Jefferson thought the French Emperor might let the United States have Cuba "to prevent our aid to Mexico and the other provinces. That would be our price, and I would immediately erect a column at Cuba's southernmost limit, and inscribe upon it a *ne plus ultra* as to us in that direction."

Jefferson's hoped-for bargain was never struck. The Bourbons re-

turned to the throne in 1814, and by 1821 all of Spain's American possessions, save Cuba and Puerto Rico, passed out of Spain's control. Their
insular character had been a factor in partially shielding these two
islands from the forces that won the mainland. Thereafter Cuban revolutionaries always looked abroad for help. This was a fundamental fact,
for therein lay seeds of clientage that were sure to mature.

Other nations coveted Spain's colonial possessions. George Canning,
the British Foreign Secretary, having recognized the independence of
several former Spanish colonies, wrote on December 17, 1824: "The
deed is done, the nail is driven, Spanish America is free, and if we do
not mismanage our affairs badly, she is English." Such sentiments did
not pass unnoticed. Our nation had begun to think in hemispheric terms
—as the Monroe Doctrine dramatized. Jefferson expressed a revised
view in 1823: "The control which, with Florida Point, this island [Cuba]
would give us over the Gulf of Mexico and the countries and isthmus
bordering it, as well as all those whose waters flow into it would fill up
the measure of our well-being."

John Quincy Adams' expectations were explicit: "The apple, severed
from its tree, must fall to the ground. Cuba severed from Spain, and
incapable of self-support, can gravitate only towards the North American Union, which by the same law of nature cannot cast her off from its
bosom." This candid statement contains two points of particular interest. First, the phrase "incapable of self-support" became the thesis on
which future policy was to rest; the seeds of clientage were already
sprouting. Second, the statement was an explicit proclamation of Manifest Destiny, though the phrase was coined later.

Adams was suspicious of Canning and was determined "not to come
in as a cock-boat in the wake of the British man-of-war." His view was
reinforced by Henry Clay, his Secretary of State, who asserted: "We
could not consent to the occupation of those islands [Cuba and Puerto
Rico] by any other power than Spain under any contingency whatsoever." Clay was equally opposed to Cuban independence, and so instructed the United States delegates who were appointed to, but never
reached, the Pan American Congress of 1825. This attitude impaired
the influence of the United States with Latin America—a situation
which Canning was quick to exploit. In March 1826 he said: "Neither
England nor France could see with indifference the United States in
occupation of Cuba." He still hoped to inherit Spain's American domin-
ions. Adams' suspicions were justified.

Two decades later the Polk administration made an informal offer of $130,000,000 for Cuba. This was not unreasonable, since in 1836 the Spanish queen had offered Cuba to Louis Philippe, and the sale was almost consummated. The American offer, however, was brusquely refused. Soon thereafter Britain and France suggested that the United States join in a tripartite convention never to acquire Cuba. Edward Everett, Secretary of State for President Fillmore, declined, asserting that the future of Cuba was an American question.

Everett's attitude was the precursor of the famous boast of Secretary of State Richard Olney that the United States "is practically sovereign on this continent." Cuba and indeed the whole Caribbean came to be claimed as an exclusive American "sphere of interest," though we sedulously eschewed the tainted phrase.

Client Status

Under the Spanish colonial system the entire bureaucracy consisted of Spaniards. Cubans had no opportunity to gain understanding of the problems, or to learn the art, of government. Economically, the island and its inhabitants were exploited rather than developed. Even the Church was served by priests brought from Spain. No body of Cuban clergy supplied local leadership or instructed Cubans. The level of literacy was low, and was deliberately kept so. Taxes were burdensome and viciously unfair. The principal business enterprises were not only owned but managed by Spaniards, and Cubans had little opportunity to acquire capital or gain managerial skills. Slavery and the slave trade continued after both had disappeared from most of Europe's possessions.

The Spanish government was unstable, slow almost to the stalling point, and grossly inefficient. The nation had dynastic crises, incompetent royalty, fitful civil war, brief attempts at republican government, a relapse into monarchy with a series of constitutions, and occasionally feeble representative institutions. All the inefficiencies of the metropolitan power were reflected—and magnified—in Cuba. There were ample reasons for revolt, but the chances of success for an indigenous revolution were negligible. Leadership and resources were both lacking.

By President Polk's time the optimism of Jefferson and the patience of John Quincy Adams no longer prevailed. Because of the slavery issue, which was poisoning domestic politics, the North had lost any ardent desire for annexation of territories while the South became more avid. The annexation of Texas in 1845 and the Gadsden Purchase in 1853 were symptomatic. The Mexican War of 1846-48 had carried us to the Pacific, and Buchanan, Polk's Secretary of State, had wanted to annex all of Mexico. He still had Jefferson's dream of going to the southernmost tip of Cuba, and he again offered to buy Cuba.

During the Pierce administration the slavery question assumed even greater importance. The American ministers to Spain, France, and Britain joined in a confidential report to Secretary of State Marcy, on October 15, 1854. Possession of Cuba seemed to them so necessary for the perpetuation of slavery in the United States that they urged a fresh attempt at purchase and a resort to force if refused: "By every law, human and divine, we shall be justified in wresting it from Spain." Though the misnamed "Ostend Manifesto" was repudiated by Secretary Marcy, the damage had been done.

Southerners encouraged filibusters (military adventures), lest Spain make Cuba "another Haiti" by freeing the slaves. These professional revolutionaries have often been pictured as heroic and romantic figures. Most could better be described as ruthless soldiers of fortune seeking their own ends. Narciso López was a notable example. He had held high office in Spain and in Cuba, but after conviction for a plot against Spain he came to the United States and devoted himself to filibustering, making three expeditions. The first, from New York, proved a fiasco; neutrality laws were enforced. He found impressive support in New Orleans, set out again in 1850, failed, and fled to Key West. The third time he landed at Bahía Honda. He was captured and executed. There is a straight line of succession from López to the Bay of Pigs expedition and the cabals that operate from southern Florida even now. Expeditions usually were badly planned and inadequately fitted out, and ended in a futile waste of life. The invaders' hope for a rising of the people has always ended as it did for López and the Bay of Pigs misadventure.

The Civil War absorbed the energies of both North and South. When times returned to normal, filibusters—and liberators such as José Martí —operated from the United States. There was no longer much public support for armed intervention, and the neutrality laws were better enforced. Nevertheless, there was a good deal of latitude for propaganda, fund-raising, and action short of violence.

Cuba's Ten Years' War for independence (1868-78) illustrated all these things. American sympathy was with the rebels; without the restraining influence of Secretary of State Hamilton Fish, President Grant might well have accorded them recognition. The United States made a futile effort to bring the fighting to an end in 1875. One result of the rebellion was ultimately to eliminate remnants of slavery; another was to open the way for American capital to buy out bankrupt sugar planters. The whole tragic episode showed that native revolt could not win independence and that the metropolitan nation could not suppress rebellion. The war ended with Spain's empty promises of reform: even assuming good faith, there was neither energy nor competence available to fulfill the promises.

One custom guaranteed trouble: American citizenship was easy to acquire, and it was sought by Cuban refugees. Many became good American citizens; others gained citizenship for ulterior ends. Their basic loyalty was still to a "free Cuba." They did not hesitate to engage in activities hostile to Spain, and when they got into trouble they relied on their American citizenship to escape punishment.

Near the end of the century events moved toward the inevitable. European subsidies on beet sugar and the American panic of 1893 combined to affect sugar prices disastrously, and the tariff of 1894 made the situation worse. Insurrection flared, and in February 1895 a "republican government"—a name appealing to Americans—was set up in Eastern Cuba while a junta in New York poured out propaganda and sought money for the rebels. General Valeriano Weyler, the Spanish Governor, was pictured as "the butcher," and not without warrant. Naturalized American citizens were abused.

Even after Weyler was recalled and a moderate installed as governor of Cuba, the United States was in no position to act wisely. President McKinley lacked firmness, and the Department of State was in charge of a Secretary bordering on senility. The situation needed only a spark to start a conflagration. The explosion on the warship *Maine*, with the loss of hundreds of lives, was precisely the kind of episode that, properly exploited, would bring war. Moreover, there was a strong humanitarian impulse to make Cuba free. Elihu Root, who later was Secretary of War and Secretary of State for almost ten years, spoke of the attitude of the American public at the time as "altruistic and sentimental." It was, but, as President Cleveland had observed, our economic interests were very substantial.

By a resolution in April 1898, Congress asserted that "the people of Cuba are, and of right ought to be, free and independent." To effectuate those ends, the President was authorized to use the armed forces. Impulsively, without debate or roll call, the Teller Amendment was added to the resolution. It contained a self-denying clause disclaiming any intention "to exercise sovereignty, jurisdiction and control"; it promised "to leave the government and control of the island to its people." Spain's answer was a declaration of war.

There were a few sharp engagements on land, in some of which the Cuban army played an effective part, but one principal result was a growing contempt for the Cubans on the part of the Americans, somewhat as British regulars were scornful of American colonials. In this period the term "dagoes" gained the currency that explained its later use in the White House. Most of the fighting, however, was naval. American casualties came more from poor training, faulty logistics, and inadequate sanitation than from fighting. By August hostilities were ended. The Treaty of Paris, signed on December 10, 1898, provided that the "civil rights and political status" of the island should "be determined by the Congress" of the United States. Spain hoped the United States would annex the island. Significantly, President McKinley had never recognized a Cuban government; therefore no Cuban signed the treaty. The client status of the island was dramatically emphasized, and inevitable tensions began to develop.

The United States set up a military government. It was extraordinary that it worked at all. The departing Spaniards had looted and gutted public buildings, going so far as to rip out plumbing and plug drains. They left a mostly illiterate, poverty-striken population, living amid indescribable filth and suffering from disease. The new rulers had no past experience to guide them in dealing with an alien culture, which, in any case, seemed to them in a state of advanced decay. At the very start contacts were clumsy. Cuban leaders had planned a great celebration on the termination of Spanish sovereignty, but the American general would not let the Cuban army into Havana to march in the parade, and the celebration was canceled. An indecisive President postponed crystallizing policy; the commanding general tended to wait for such a clear policy definition; the Secretary of War was discredited and of no help; subordinate generals undercut their superior and competed to replace him; Congress seemed unable to refrain from meddlesome interference; and speculators abounded. Despite all these handicaps, General John R. Brooke, as military governor, made a brave attempt to have Cuban leaders participate in government operations in order to give them experience. He also had the Cuban flag flown, as evidence that independence was to be real.

At the end of 1899 there was a new Secretary of War, Elihu Root, and a new military governor, General Leonard E. Wood. To achieve rapid results in a desperately bad situation, Wood used autocratic methods. He also made less use of Cuban colleagues than had his predecessor, Brooke, and thus curtailed training for true independence. The occupation reorganized the finances, made a determined and successful assault on yellow fever, and otherwise improved public health. A census was taken, and local government was organized. The administration of justice was speeded up. Schools were set up, staffed by Cubans, many of whom had short courses of special training in American universities.

Wood was convinced that annexation was the only solution. A good many members of Congress were of the same view, and ingenious arguments were concocted to explain away the Teller Amendment. However, the anti-imperialists were active, vocal, and numerous, and Secretary Root remained adamantly opposed to annexation. He admitted that the Cubans were "wholly ignorant of the art of self-government," but hoped to give them a "fair and favorable" start, "to help them avoid the conditions which have subjected Hayti, San Domingo, and the Central American Republics to continuous revolution and disorder."

Secretary Root later commented that there were "not a dozen men in Cuba who believed that the United States was going to keep faith with them" and abide by the Teller Amendment. Many in the United States shared that skepticism and had reason to do so. Partly because of that doubt, partly because the Cuban army had not been paid, and for many other reasons, there was imminent danger of guerrilla warfare against the United States, such as occurred in the Philippines. The tragedy of rebellion in Cuba was avoided through the temperate leadership of the principal Cuban general, who was at odds with the civilian

Cuban Assembly; the payment, long overdue, to Cuban soldiers who returned to civilian status; and firm American administration.

The Foraker Act forbade granting any franchises during the occupation. Like the Teller Amendment, it was designed as a self-denying ordinance and aimed at preventing speculative exploitation or the establishment of permanent economic domination. It failed: in order to build what was regarded as an essential railroad, the Act was circumvented. Moreover, whatever the Foraker law might say, capital and top management would have to be found abroad. In the circumstances, both were sure to come from the United States. Many Americans hoped that economic interests would lead Cuba ultimately to ask for annexation, a view that accorded closely with Wood's hopes.

Everything was done at top speed in order to set up the new republic at the earliest possible moment. On July 25, 1900, a constitutional convention was ordered. Elections were held. Despite a limited suffrage designed to restrict voting to "responsible elements," nearly all elected delegates belonged to radical revolutionary groups—a result not pleasing to American administrators. Nonetheless, the convention met between November 1900 and February 1901 and framed a constitution.

The Constitution contained no reference to the relations between the new government and the United States. Secretary of War Root now made it clear that American control would continue until such provision was made, though earlier he had taken a more liberal position. The Cubans took no initiative in drafting an acceptable provision, so the Platt Amendment (drafted by Senator Orville H. Platt) was passed by the Senate and attached as a rider to an Army appropriation bill. It required Cuba to sell or lease lands to the United States for naval stations, limited Cuba's treaty-making power and its capacity to contract debts, and gave the United States the right to intervene to preserve independence and to maintain law and order.

The constitutional convention refused to accept these terms until a committee went to Washington and got reassurance. Secretary Root said: "It is a question of purely internal constitutional limitations." The Constitution of the United States, he pointed out, limited the powers of our own Congress. The proposed limitations "concern Cuba alone, and will be executed by Cuba, and by Cubans exclusively." Senator Platt added that "the Amendment was carefully worded so as to avoid any possible thought that acceptance . . . would tend to establish a protectorate or a suzerainty, or any form of meddling with the independence or sovereignty of Cuba." On the basis of these promises, the Platt Amendment was incorporated into the new Constitution on June 2, 1901. The occupation ended on May 20, 1902, and Cuba was formally independent. Each country had adopted the Platt Amendment unilaterally. In May 1903 it was incorporated into a "permanent" treaty between the two nations.

Why did the United States insist upon such unwelcome demands? First, Theodore Roosevelt wanted to teach the "cheating, mañana lot" to behave decently. This attitude reflected a fatal defect of the occupation itself—a basic lack of respect for the Cuban population, its temper, its culture, and its legal system. In retrospect it seems astounding that there should have been such an arrogant assumption that the way to reverse the downward trend of "a declining race" was to Americanize them—in education, in law, in government, in economic life, and in cultural values. Yet that was the clear, if unproclaimed, objective. This fact has particular importance because Cuba supplied precedents used in deciding to supervise other Caribbean countries, and the Roosevelt Corollary to the Monroe Doctrine came partly from Cuban experience.

The votes for the Platt Amendment in Congress represented many shades of opinion regarding Cuba's future. Several senators were glad to support it in the hope that it would put a final quietus on the idea of annexation. Others voted for it in the confident expectation that it offered a means of circumventing the Teller Amendment and opening the way for annexation.

There were also international reasons for a determination to provide against governmental collapse in Cuba. The United States had been through the Boxer Rebellion in China—a recent and painful experience with a government unable to protect foreign nationals, even those with diplomatic status. We wanted nothing more to do with impotent governments. Both Roosevelt and Root were suspicious of Germany. Bismarck had denounced United States "arrogance" in 1897; Admiral Dedrich had behaved badly in Manila; Germany had interfered in Haiti. There was fear that impotence in Cuba might supply an excuse for a German foothold in the Caribbean.

Economic reasons also played a significant part. Even the "anti-imperialists" who opposed annexation were eager for economic expansion, while those who desired incorporation of Cuba into the Union believed that economic dominance would advance that cause. Capital was looking for outlets, and speculators and entrepreneurs saw great opportunities—if the government was stable. The Platt Amendment, they thought, would assure that.

In perspective the really astonishing fact is not that the United States attached leading strings to the new nation but that it withdrew its troops so soon and formally gave Cuba independence. Asia and Africa were being carved up, and spheres of influence were established where there was not outright annexation. The United States, newly conscious of its status as a world power, and led by a bold, vigorous president, nevertheless declined to join the rush—even regarding an island which at an earlier time we had urgently wanted to annex, and which was wholly in our hands.

American Guidance

The Platt Amendment dominated Cuban-American relations for over thirty years. Senator Platt hoped his Amendment would "settle what may be called the Cuban question satisfactorily to the people of Cuba, and satisfactorily to our own people." It was a fatal confusion of benevolence with wisdom, two radically different things. Theodore Roosevelt said somewhat later that the people of the Caribbean area "will be happy . . . if only they will be good." Perhaps it was too much to expect the exponent of "the strenuous life" to understand inhabitants of the tropics who had little or no education, and even less governmental experience. Senator John T. Morgan of Alabama, who opposed the Platt Amendment, was a better prophet: "We will keep a sort of Sunday school down there with an army at any time and every time that they do not do exactly what we want them to do."

From start to finish the Cubans resented the paternal attitude of the United States. They insisted that the Platt Amendment "did not grow out of the need for protection but rather engendered that need for the future." In the light of the way the great powers were then gobbling up territories, the first half of the assumption was clearly wrong. The independence of a small, weak state in a strategic location and devoted to a valuable world crop needed a protective shield. The success with which they were protected made it seem to them that protection was unnecessary. The second half of the complaint, however, was correct, for tutelage, long continued, retards the development of a sense of responsibility. Clientage can become a habit that continues even after the occasion for it has passed. What to the United States seemed a generous gesture of friendly guidance in launching a new nation successfully, seemed to the Cubans merely a curtailment of their full independence.

Dislike of the Amendment, however, did not prevent Cuban politicians who denounced it publicly from exploiting it privately. They provoked threats of intervention and then advised acquiescence in American suggestions on the ground that "it was better to accept than to suffer intervention." From time to time they agreed to "reform," lest domestic violence signal intervention. Cosme de la Torriente was correct when he wrote: "Certain people will always be disposed to appeal to a foreign power, alleging that their lives are in danger, their property insecure, their liberties disregarded." Unhappily, the things they feared were sometimes very real: lives were destroyed, property rights were violated, and political freedom was trespassed upon scandalously, not once but many times.

In retrospect, it is difficult to see how the United States could responsibly have turned the new nation loose without some help. Yet the incorporation of such guidance in the Cuban constitution and in the basic treaty between Cuba and the United States had a fatal flaw: the absence of any promise that guardianship would ever end. No goal was set toward which Cuba could work. The American Ambassador reported to the Secretary of State thirty years later that the treaty had become "both irksome to Cuba and useless, if not actually harmful, to the United States."

In addition to the Platt Amendment of 1901, a reciprocity treaty was negotiated in 1902. It provided for a mutual reduction of tariffs, and it opened Cuba to American exports and America to Cuban goods. Under it and successive agreements, a quarter of a century later Cuba was ahead of every other Latin American country in both export and import trade with the United States. Secretary Root had insisted that the treaty must be "for the protection and furtherance of Cuban interests, and not . . . for the furtherance of United States interests as against Cuba." He had to face powerful beet sugar interests in his own country and did not get as favorable treatment for Cuba as he had wished. It was the opening round of a struggle that had to be fought not only then but recurrently.

The Cuban government did not prove to be viable. The first President, Tomás Estrada Palma, rigged his own reelection, faced a revolt that he could not suppress, and resigned. The Vice President refused the presidency, and the Cuban Congress provided no successor. In 1906 the executive power collapsed. Secretary of War Taft and Acting Secretary of State Bacon went to Havana to mediate. It was a frustrating experience. Taft wrote: "This has been the greatest crisis I ever passed through and some of the sleepless nights I passed I hope I may not have to pass again. I am anxious to get away from here and out of this atmosphere which is only of disappointment, intrigues, and discouragement."

Mediation failed. The situation came down to a choice between intervention and civil war. Both sides wanted intervention, and Taft took over as Provisional Governor. Nonetheless, his proclamation sought to open the way for the recovery of independence: "Insofar as is consistent with the nature of a provisional government established under the authority of the United States, there will be a Cuban government, conforming as far as may be, to the constitution of Cuba." He directed that the Cuban flag should fly over all government buildings. Having set the tone of the provisional administration, he turned over the post of governor to Charles E. Magoon. The new man became intensely unpopular. Though accusations of graft and corruption were unfair, he lacked the subtlety and skill needed to settle the family quarrels of the Cuban politicians. Perhaps no one could have done so.

The easy "solution" would have been annexation, for which many Spanish merchants and many American citizens in Cuba were eager, but again the temptation was firmly rejected. The occupation ended on January 28, 1909. Root's final counsel was characteristic: we should not ask the new Cuban government to pay the cost of the occupation, since it would produce no money and would further exacerbate bad feeling.

Three years later new troubles led to a warning of intervention and to an agreement among the disputants to avoid "justification for any intervention in our internal affairs." However, Philander Knox, the new Secretary of State, had neither the patience, the restraint, nor the deftness of Root. His "preventive" policy regarding revolt left the shadow of intervention hanging perpetually over the island.

In 1916 a new revolt arose over a "rigged" reelection of a president.

Secretary of State Robert Lansing threatened to treat those "under arms against the Government of Cuba" as enemies of the United States, "and to deal with them accordingly." In the face of such a threat the rebels knew their case was hopeless. General Enoch Crowder was sent to "investigate" and "adjust" the election question. Political parties in Cuba were induced to unite in asking him to assist in drawing up a new electoral law, which he did.

Amid expressions of dissatisfaction with a new election, General Crowder was sent back to Havana by President Wilson, as his personal representative, at the end of 1920. He remained for approximately two years and made a valiant attempt to correct gross abuses. Cosme de la Torriente expressed a Cuban viewpoint: "The Platt Amendment was constantly invoked as an excuse for intervening in every problem, whether political or economic." It was a comment that found substance in a series of fifteen memoranda by General Crowder famous for their detailed criticism of the administration of Cuba and specific proposals for reform. If they could have been made effective they would have been of great benefit, but some were out of harmony with the temperament and tradition of the Cubans. In 1925 Secretary of State Charles Evans Hughes effectively abandoned the "preventive" policy.

Ambassador Harry F. Guggenheim summed up the record in 1933: "There has been a *laissez-faire* policy and there has been a tutorial policy; there have been lectures, admonitions, and threats; there has been a policy based on a strict construction of the Platt Amendment; and there has been a policy based on a broad construction."

The concept of public office as a public trust is a highly sophisticated democratic ideal, never perfectly realized, and dependent upon long years of growth. Unhappily, it was an ideal alien to the Cuban environment. Corruption was a normal way of life to the Cuban politician. Land reform, fiscal responsibility, and personal freedom were sacrificed to illegal profits from the lottery, self-perpetuation in power, or revolution. Ambassador Guggenheim described the situation in these terms:

The franchise was suddenly bestowed upon the Cuban masses who for centuries had been under the influence of the "twin evil spirits of autocracy and exploitation." The new voter . . . has been taught to believe that he has an inalienable right to sell his vote in a free market, and when that market is closed, as in periods of the suppression of political liberties, he is more sympathetically inclined to revolutionary movements.[1]

[1] Harry F. Guggenheim, *The United States and Cuba* (Macmillan, 1934), p. 160.

It was the only way the voter could restore the cash value of his franchise.

Administrations came and went in Havana. Meanwhile, each party put out a stream of propaganda. The American Embassy caught it from both angles—one side claiming support, the other asserting that the Cubans in power were puppets of the United States. For a Cuban to defend the Platt Amendment would have been tantamount to political suicide; the denunciation of "Yankee imperialism" was perenially popular. In the end it was clear that "intervention" had become more a gambit in Cuban politics than an effective instrument of American policy. Amidst all the activity the masses of the people remained in a state of abysmal poverty and ignorance.

The protectorate was also disruptive of American opinion. There was a flow of statements by senators, representatives, and business interests. Editorial writers and magazines denounced successive administrations in Washington for "supporting dictators" and "encouraging" the suppression of freedom, or for undertaking to "dictate" the kind of government an independent nation should have.

Ambassador Guggenheim concluded that "the difficulty in our relations with Cuba was not to be found in the policy of strict neutrality we were then pursuing, which was less objectionable than any other we might follow or that had been followed under the Permanent Treaty. The difficulty was with the Treaty itself." He recommended renegotiation "contingent upon certain constitutional reforms and the reestablishment of truly representative government in Cuba."[2] There is sharp irony in that qualification; it involved a last attempt to use the Platt Amendment to do once and for all what it had failed to do in thirty years.

As 1933 dawned, a new administration was shortly to take office, with Cordell Hull as Secretary of State. President Franklin D. Roosevelt wanted to try for Cuban peace once more and sent Sumner Welles to attempt a political settlement. Welles did his best to get reform. But Cuba's President Machado was stubborn. In August 1933 he was ousted by the army, to be succeeded by the transient Céspedes administration (less than a month), which could not possibly provide stability.

The substance of power came into the hands of Sergeant Fulgencio Batista in September 1933, though he did not take political office at

[2] *Ibid.*, p. 236.

once. Ramón Grau San Martín was appointed as provisional president. The new revolution used the slogans of extreme nationalism. Welles regarded Batista as "ultraradical" with Communist leanings. Again intervention was considered. The decision against it reflected new and determined efforts to woo the rest of Latin America rather than any satisfaction with the new Cuban regime. To display our dissatisfaction, however, recognition was withheld from Grau San Martín, who held the office of president by grace of Batista's other preoccupations. In January 1934 Batista ousted Grau San Martín. Carlos Mendieta was installed as provisional president, and he was promptly recognized by the United States. Batista, it was felt, had taken "a turn to the right."

In May 1934 a new treaty replaced the permanent treaty of 1903; the Platt Amendment was dropped, save for the provision regarding Guantánamo. Cuban politicians were deprived of their private asset and public whipping boy. Also, a new Reciprocal Trade Agreement in 1934 gave tariff relief for Cuban sugar. A law was passed providing for sugar quotas, which, though not wholly to Cuba's liking, served partially to stabilize the price of a vital element in the island's economy. Provision for an Export-Import Bank completed the trilogy of measures designed to put relations on a new and better basis.

The Platt Amendment in Perspective

Considering Cuba apart from the rest of the Caribbean area is valid only if there is frequent reference to the total picture. Otherwise the issues are drawn so badly out of perspective that they cannot be understood. The Platt Amendment raises the problem in a peculiarly acute form. It is often blamed for all the difficulties that have beset our dealings with Cuba and the ills that have afflicted the island. But there is no evidence to support the view that without the Platt Amendment there would have been harmonious relations and no intervention.

Intervention in weak states by the great powers was a common occurrence in the early years of this century. Theodore Roosevelt's Corollary to the Monroe Doctrine sought to preclude European intervention that might ripen into possession:

Chronic wrongdoing, or an impotence which results in a general loosening of the ties of civilized society, may in America, as elsewhere, ultimately require intervention by some civilized nation, and in the western hemisphere the adherence of the United States to the Monroe Doctrine may force the United States, however reluctantly, in flagrant cases of such wrongdoing or impotence, to the exercise of an international police power.

This arrogation to ourselves of international responsibility occurred at a time when there was a scramble to grab territories. The United States purchased the Virgin Islands, lest some great power snap them up for a coaling station or naval base that could threaten the Panama Canal, which years before President Hayes had called "part of our coastline."

Now that Western empires are in the final stages of dissolution, such sensitiveness to this danger seems overdrawn, but at that time the Kaiser, having dismissed Bismarck, was engaging in adventures that helped precipitate World War I.

We sought to make the Caribbean a *mare nostrum* in order to guarantee the security of the Canal. Between 1895 and 1933, according to a publication of the Committee on Foreign Affairs of the House of Representatives, we intervened no less than thirty times in countries within the Caribbean area, in addition to our actions in Cuba. Such intrusions occurred in Nicaragua many times, and in Colombia, Panama, Honduras, Haiti, the Dominican Republic, Guatemala, Mexico, and Costa Rica. With none of these did we have, at the first intervention, anything like the equivalent of a Platt Amendment, though we reached the substance of such an agreement with Panama and Nicaragua, and after the occupation of Haiti and the Dominican Republic in 1915 and 1916 we made treaties that were in some respects even more sweeping. In 1912, the Solicitor of the Department of State remarked that no nation "has with more frequency . . . used its military forces for the purpose of occupying temporarily parts of foreign countries."[3] Our intervention in Cuba had set a pattern.

One of the most drastic acts was the promotion of revolution in Panama, which broke the state loose from Colombia. Colombia was trying to make the most of its bargaining position as possessor of Theodore Roosevelt's favorite canal route. But Roosevelt was impatient with haggling over terms. Any conceivable question that the separation of Panama from Colombia was achieved through United States connivance was dispelled when he bluntly asserted: "I took the Canal Zone

[3] Quoted in D. A. Graber, *Crisis Diplomacy* (Public Affairs Press, 1959), p. 21.

and let Congress debate, and while the debate goes on the Canal does also." No wonder that when President Roosevelt sought to justify his action in a Cabinet meeting, Philander C. Knox is said to have exclaimed sardonically: "Oh, Mr. President, do not let so great an achievement suffer from any taint of legality."

Armed intervention was not the only method employed. No Platt Amendment justified appointing fiscal officers to supervise the collection of customs and the expenditure of funds in Haiti and the Dominican Republic. The process was repeated in other states under the Corollary.

No Platt Amendment existed to give legal basis for the new recognition policy. Jefferson had set the classic American policy: recognition followed the "will of the nation substantially declared" even if by force. In practice, *de facto* recognition was also *de jure*. Like other classic policies it was eroded in time by incidents that were dealt with *ad hoc*. Its destruction was completed by Woodrow Wilson, who enunciated as a principle the refusal to recognize governments erected by force on the ruins of their predecessors. He was convinced that dictatorships were inherently unstable, and he withheld recognition from presidents whom he considered incompetent or untrustworthy. He pursued the will-o'-the-wisp of "constitutionality" and its twin, "stability." American recognition was so important to governments in the area that withholding it often toppled presidents from office; it brought about the elevation of others who were regarded as more desirable by the President of the United States.

Wilson went so far as to say he was ready to violate the sovereignty of these nations in order to teach them democracy. His efforts to transfer the preceptorial system from Princeton to the Caribbean were unsuccessful. "Constitutional legitimacy," in the role of operative principle, proved as ineffective in the Caribbean as the monarchist, antirevolutionary doctrines of the late eighteenth century in strangling the infant United States.

The Platt Amendment was no more disastrous than like policies pursued in other Caribbean countries based essentially on its principles. The key to the weakness of the policy is that all intervention, whether physical or moral, involves an identification of power with virtue. We were big enough to impose our will, and we rationalized our acts by assuming that our morals and our institutions were superior. Theodore

Roosevelt's assumption in the Corollary that we were a "civilized" nation carried the unmistakable implication that "the dagoes" were not; it
was an assumption that was bitterly—and properly—resented. Moralistic pronouncements and interventions reached their zenith with Wilson.

Power, however great, cannot suppresss resentment and anger; indeed, it is more likely to stimulate them. This proved to be true in the
Caribbean. Latin America caught, in virulent form, the nationalistic
fever and began to press for the abandonment of intervention and for a
change in recognition policy so that it could no longer be employed
to exert pressure.

In 1930, Cosme de la Torriente, who was a jurist of international reputation, an effective ambassador, and a Foreign Minister in a Cuban
government, wrote:

> Evils will only be aggravated in the future if Washington continues to
> pursue the mistaken policy of not recognizing such governments in Latin
> America as proceed from revolutionary movements, regardless of the merits
> of the revolutions. It is the habit of all self-perpetuating governments on our
> continent to cloak their abuses of the rights of citizens under irreproachably
> legal forms and under language of the profoundest respect for democratic
> principles, morality and justice. *The continuance of this policy will result
> in the establishment of despotisms in several of our republics,* since few
> people will venture to struggle against the power of despots who rule over
> them combined with the refusal of Washington to recognize revolutionary
> governments.[4] (Italics supplied.)

In the same year, the Mexican Secretary of Foreign Relations, Señor
Estrada, adverted to the fact that Mexico had suffered as had few
other nations from American recognition policies based on the doctrine
of constitutional legitimacy. He declared that thenceforth the Mexican
government would issue no "grants of recognition, since . . . such a
course is an insulting practice and one which . . . implies that judgment
of some sort may be passed upon the internal affairs of those nations by
other governments."

Franklin Roosevelt, in response to the obvious failure of intervention
by force, by fiscal control, or by nonrecognition, gave up the Platt
Amendment and permitted his Secretary of State to join in a protocol
which agreed: "The High Contracting Parties declare inadmissible the
intervention of any one of them, directly or indirectly, and for what-

---

[4] Cosme de la Torriente, "The Platt Amendment," *Foreign Affairs*, VIII, 3 (April
1930), 375.

ever reason, in the internal or external affairs of any other of the Parties." The Senate gave its advice and consent. Thus the United States was committed to what amounted to absolute nonintervention on a unilateral basis. There were also commitments to take action only as part of a joint endeavor agreed to by the other American countries. At least in form, this remained the basic policy of the United States in the area.

The Batista Regime

Disillusionment with "running a Sunday school" with our armed forces was followed by a period during which the basic American policy in Cuba was "hands off." It was of a piece with taking—at long last—a hands-off policy regarding the Mexican revolution, a decision which showed more satisfactory results than earlier efforts at "guidance toward democracy."

The quarter-century after 1933 was mostly dominated by Fulgencio Batista, whether or not he held an official title. His two coups d'état were both bloodless. When he first took over, he did not choose to hold political office, though he was a dominant figure in the country. Subsequently he was elected President and served from 1940 to 1944. The next two presidencies were opposed to him—the second administration of Grau San Martín (1944-48) and the administration of Prío Socarrás (1948-52). The latter was overthrown in 1952 by Batista, again without firing a shot. During the period that he was out of the presidency, Batista was elected Senator from Las Villas province, though he was living in Florida and did not visit the province until after his election.

During his first successful revolt he had taken a strongly nationalist line, but once settled in power he took a more "conservative" tack, and those with interests in Cuba heaved a sigh of relief. He took care not to abuse American rights of property or person grossly. There were also valued gestures of cooperation, such as the declaration of war in World War II. Moreover, some officials were men of great ability and high integrity.

During his first administration as President, he appointed Communists to high-level posts in his Cabinet. Two of these men became prominent in the Castro regime. Batista subsequently explained these appointments; he said that they were made during the war, when Russia was an ally, and that they were in accord with the spirit of cooperation between Russia and the United States. However, he also permitted Communists a strong position in the labor movement and indeed protected and used Communists to the end of his career in Cuba. The Communists worked both sides of the street: they collaborated with Batista on the one hand and opposed him as a dictator on the other. Therefore one must say that Sumner Welles's original fears were not without foundation. It should be noted that both Grau and Prío also collaborated with the Communists. Profession and practice were often contradictory. Castro did not initiate the use of Communists but gave them power far beyond earlier practice.

Over the years there was marked deterioration in the character of the Batista regime. Graft and corruption, inhuman cruelties, gross misuse of government power, and many other manifestations of tyranny became conspicuous. There were numerous occurrences that would have led to intervention in earlier periods. In the late 1950's it became highly likely that Batista's dictatorship could not survive. Topography facilitated guerrilla activities, since the rugged mountains of Eastern Cuba provided convenient cover. The sugar economy made it relatively easy for hit-and-run raids to burn cane fields and destroy mills. The proximity of the island to areas in the Caribbean from which personnel and resources could come added other advantages to rebel action. Revolution was attempted several times—by naval officers, by political opponents, by guerrillas.

Adherence to the policy of nonintervention did not make mutual relations simpler, or the United States more popular. The pursuit of the Good Neighbor policy in Latin America often took precedence over specific annoyances with Cuba; the State Department made a sincere effort to make the "Colossus of the North" seem less menacing. Nevertheless, the nearness of Cuba, the depth and scope of the penetration of American investment, the conspicuous presence of Guantánamo, all united with the long history of clientage to make every gesture assume greater significance than may have been intended.

When arms were sold to Cuba for use in "hemispheric defense," dissident juntas and later the guerrillas would shriek to high heaven that the real purpose was to help the dictator perpetuate his power. These plaints were echoed in Congress and by portions of the press in the

United States. If, on the other hand, arms were withheld from delivery to the government, it was taken as evidence that the demonstrated friendliness of the government of Cuba for the United States was being repaid with "help for the rebels, who were probably Communists."

Whatever was done either positively or negatively, there was always someone eager to inflate its significance and insist that it constituted meddling or "indirect intervention." The last U.S. Ambassador to Cuba in the Batista regime reported that suspending the sale of arms "had a devastating effect upon those supporting the government of Cuba" and "gave a great psychological uplift to the Castro followers."[5] He agreed with Batista that there was inadequate enforcement of our neutrality laws; that in the United States fund-raising for rebellion went virtually unchecked; and that antigovernment propaganda was vigorous and men and materials found their way to the rebels.

No policy could undo in twenty years what forty years had built up. Long after the American public had forgotten the early annexationist desires—even after disenchantment with imperialism was complete (as revealed in the grant of independence to the Philippines at an earlier time than stipulated)—the memory of tutelage lingered among Latins. Ending the Platt Amendment, abandonment of the protectorate over Panama and Haiti in 1936, and the discontinuance of controls over the Dominican Republic five years before the treaty was due to expire, were all greeted with satisfaction, salted with skepticism that the actions represented any real change of policy. Concern for the protection of the Panama Canal and worry about Communist infiltration led to acts that occasionally seemed to validate the skepticism.

Several domestic forces retarded attainment of understanding between the United States and Cuba. Some Americans, who were influential in molding opinion, hated all dictators so bitterly that they demanded that we encourage their overthrow, without concern regarding those who would replace the current tyrant or what the successor's policy was likely to be. They overlooked the historical fact that the successor of a bad man may be a worse one. Pursuit of dogmatic "democracy" produced as much intolerance on one side as insistence upon the status quo on the other. Some were so profoundly concerned with the threat of Communism that they were ready to see any anti-Communist regime hold power, no matter what its other qualities might be. All

[5] Earl E. T. Smith, *The Fourth Floor* (Random House, 1962), pp. 118, 119.

who promoted extreme views helped prevent the development of the public consensus essential to consistent policy. Some encouraged revolution out of utopianism; others made ultimate revolution more violent by tying down the safety valve in the interest of "stability" or the "defeat of Communism."

Meanwhile, two other factors complicated matters. During World War II covert operations became a structural part of the United States government. After the tyrannous character of the Cuban regime was fully revealed, the clandestine arm of our government sought to promote Batista's overthrow. Sometimes the coordination between the ambassador and officers of the Central Intelligence Agency faltered, even though these officers were in the Embassy and part of the "country team" under the ambassador. The ambassador later testified that the court-martial of some Cuban naval officers who had participated in an abortive revolt revealed that a CIA officer in the Embassy had inadvertently created the impression that, if the revolution succeeded, the new government would be recognized by the United States.[6]

This kind of dual participation in foreign relations is common practice in many nations. It grates harshly upon American sensibilities, long unaware of the prevalence of such practices; more particularly, it distresses a nation that has been led to expect a large element of morality in its public policy. In any event, public awakening to clandestine operations has brought a serious disadvantage in its train: official pronouncements now are greeted with skepticism because they represent only the overt policy of the government, while its covert policy may be different.

A second factor also tended to becloud our foreign policy. It has become customary to denigrate the status of the chief of mission by visits from his superior officers. Ambassadors have always protested this kind of impairment of their standing. Even more exasperating have been instances when a private citizen with an informal appointment from the President or Secretary of State supplanted the Ambassador in some of his functions. This happened in Cuba. As it became clearer that the Batista regime was doomed because of military defections, the alienation

---

[6] *Communist Threat to the United States Through the Caribbean,* Hearings before the Subcommittee of the Senate Judiciary Committee to Investigate the Administration of the Internal Security Act and Other Internal Security Laws, 86 Cong. 2 sess., Aug. 30, 1960, Pt. 9, pp. 694, 698.

of the Cuban public, and the progress of the rebels, it was decided to make an effort to have Batista yield control to a junta composed of some of his more moderate opponents. It was hoped that they would take charge during a transition to a new regime. The Ambassador was called to Washington "for consultation." Meanwhile he had learned from a distinguished Cuban that the Department of State and the CIA had decided to send a private emissary to induce Batista to yield to a junta (the name of the envoy and the time of his mission were unknown to the Ambassador).

A "private citizen" went to Cuba and unsuccessfully urged Batista to yield. Subsequently, before the Senate Judiciary Committee, William D. Pawley testified: "I offered him an opportunity to live at Daytona Beach with his family, that his friends and family would not be molested; that we would make an effort to stop Fidel Castro from coming into power as a Communist, but that the caretaker government would be composed of men who were enemies of his."[7] The emissary felt that his mission failed because his authority was limited!

Meanwhile the Ambassador remained in the dark regarding the emissary, his instructions, or the results. It would be difficult to describe diplomatic shenanigans less likely to lead to desired ends. If the Department of State had lost confidence in the Ambassador, he should have been recalled; after he learned of the maneuver, he should have tendered his resignation.

The political situation in Cuba continued to deteriorate. Batista left the country, and Fidel Castro took over on January 1, 1959. There is no consensus as to whether a different policy would have prevented Castro from attaining power. There is also no agreement as to whether he was known to be a Communist or merely had Communist support. Nearly every account, including that published by the Department of State in its White Paper titled "Cuba,"[8] reveals a strong bias. Understatement probably reached its apogee in an official reference to the Bay of Pigs disaster as "April 17-19 Cuban patriots fail in an attempt to redeem the independence of their homeland."[9] One fact emerged with crystal clari-

[7] *Communist Threat to the United States Through the Caribbean*, Hearings, 86 Cong. 2 sess., Sept. 2 and 8, 1960, Pt. 10.
[8] April 3, 1961.
[9] *Events in United States–Cuban Relations: A Chronology, 1957-1963*, prepared by the Department of State for the Senate Committee on Foreign Relations, 88 Cong. 1 sess. (1963), p. 20.

ty: the hands-off policy had collapsed. In retrospect it seems equally clear that when the hands were off they were not far away.

The political record, however, is only part of Cuba's experience. Even in the midst of political turmoil such as marked Cuba's history in the twentieth century, there were marked efforts at diversification of the economy. The process was begun in earnest as early as Machado's presidency in the last half of the 1920's. In the 1950's it gained momentum and speed; the economy was being "Cubanized" to a striking degree. Perfectionists will insist that the progress was too slow and too little, but the difficulty our own South has experienced in diversifying the economies of the older cotton-growing states offers evidence that considerable time as well as intensive effort are required to produce impressive results. Despite all the difficulties, Cuba became a leader among the Latin American countries in economic diversification.

Cattle raising, important in colonial days, had suffered disastrously as a result of the revolt of 1868-78 and again during the War of Independence (1895-98). In the twentieth century it made a sharp recovery. The number of cattle rose from less than 400,000 at the end of the War of Independence to over 5,500,000 in the late 1950's; the stock was of high quality and being improved. Cuba, indeed, became the leader of the whole world in the number of cattle per hectare—having, for example, four times the United States average. This led to the development of a dairy industry, canning, homogenizing and pasteurizing milk, and the manufacture of cheese and butter.

The establishment of poultry farms made Cuba independent of imports of poultry products. Pigs increased from 850,000 in 1940 to 3,400,000 in 1956; and sheep from 141,000 to 380,000. A number of foods that had been imported began to be grown in amounts large enough to make Cuba self-sufficient. Even where achievement did not go so far, there were marked increases in the cultivation of rice, coffee, potatoes, corn, beans, and pineapples.

There was also industrial diversification: Leather, shoes, textiles, fibers, and several derivatives of the sugar industry, such as paper and boxes from bagasse, were manufactured. Other products were chemicals for fertilizers, cement, flour, and feed for cattle and poultry. Mineral deposits were exploited more aggressively.

Despite the smallness of the country, Cuba stood fourth among all Latin American countries in the total amount of cement used; only

Venezuela, Uruguay, and Argentina were ahead. In total electric energy generated, Cuba stood fourth, and also had the fourth largest per capita use of electricity—behind Uruguay, Argentina, and Chile. Its electric power consumption rose from less than 700,000,000 kwh in 1950 to 1,620,000,000 in 1959.

The National Bank was organized in 1950, and Cuba established its own currency. Bank deposits rose from 650,000,000 pesos to 815,000,000 between 1950 and 1955. Moreover, the ownership of the banks was moving into the hands of Cubans. Whereas, in 1950, 45 percent of the banks were Cuban-owned and 55 percent foreign-owned, by 1955 over 60 percent were Cuban and less than 40 percent foreign. Clearing-house operations had increased from $4 billion to nearly $7 billion.

Even in the sugar industry, ownership was being steadily transferred to Cubans. In 1940 American ownership amounted to 55 percent of total production and Cuban ownership to only 22 percent, the rest being divided between Spaniards, Canadians, British, French, and Dutch. By 1958, the Canadian, British, and Dutch holdings had been liquidated; French capital amounted only to a minuscule fraction; and Spanish investment had shrunk to negligible proportions. Meanwhile, the United States had only 37 percent of total production, whereas the Cubans had 62 percent. However, the United States was still the dominant market.

There was an impressive gross increase in American investment, which rose from $642 million in 1950 to $955 million in 1959. Despite this increase, however, the growth of the Cuban control of its own economy was such that the percentage of American ownership was steadily—and rather rapidly—falling.

The trade of Cuba with the United States was very old, dating back before the American Revolution. After Spain had formally opened Cuban ports to international trade in 1818, the United States speedily became the supplier of more than half of all Cuban imports.[10] Before Castro took over, Cuba was third in trade with the United States among all Latin American countries, following only Venezuela and Brazil in imports and Mexico and Venezuela in exports.

Under the impulse of economic growth and diversification, Cuban per capita income increased to become the highest of any Latin Ameri-

[10] R. F. Smith, *What Happened in Cuba* (Twayne, 1963), p. 22.

can country. There was not a corresponding improvement in the spread of the benefits, and an unhealthy social imbalance remained. One group had conspicuous wealth; at the other extreme there was intense poverty, unemployment and partial employment, and only limited opportunity for education and advancement. Even so, a substantial middle class was growing with considerable rapidity. In this matter Cuba did better than most Latin American countries, though not well enough to provide a stable basis for democracy in American terms.

The Castro Era

Though the understanding of events since Castro came to power has been clouded in controversy, some points are clear:

1. After several failures it did not seem likely that Batista could be overthrown by moderates; the task fell to men of violence.

2. Castro had no training or experience in broad policymaking or administration. He knew how to fight ruthlessly and with shrewd skill. He is a charismatic rabble-rouser, able to take his cue from his emotions and transmit them to the multitudes. He has never gained the self-discipline that would enable him to develop an orderly or a comprehensive plan of administrative action. Administrative tasks fell, inevitably, to a disciplined group of trained and dedicated Communists, operating behind his messianic control of public opinion.

3. It is now fruitless to discuss precisely when Castro became a Communist. As late as November 1959, the Deputy Director of the Central Intelligence Agency declared:"The Cuban Communists do not consider him [Castro] a Communist Party member, or even a pro-Communist," but "they are delighted with the nature of his government which has allowed the Communists opportunity, free opportunity, to organize, to propagandize, and to infiltrate." They regard Castro as "representative of the bourgeoisie." From the Communist viewpoint a "bourgeois-democratic revolution precedes a Communist rise to power." They were nervous when, during his trip to the United States, "he showed evidence of a friendly attitude" toward this country.[11]

4. It is certain that Communists were among his close associates in the rebellion. However, in war one does not always choose one's allies.

[11] *Communist Threat to the United States Through the Caribbean*, Hearings, 86 Cong. 1 sess., Nov. 5, 1959, Pt. III, pp. 162, 163.

The United States accepted Stalin as a "loyal ally" in World War II. In the light of Khrushchev's revelations, some of the descriptions of Stalin by Presidents Roosevelt and Truman now sound incredible, though they were doubtless sincere.

5. At the end of a revolution it is almost standard practice—and probably necessary—to purge some wartime associates who want to go in different directions. Castro not only shot longtime opponents but cast off former supporters who deviated from his leadership. He destroyed those who, speaking relatively, were moderates; he kept those with Communist zeal. His own early selections, President Urrutia and Prime Minister Miró Cardona, became political casualties—the Prime Minister in six weeks, the President in about six months. Meanwhile, men like Osvaldo Dorticós, Che Guevara, and Raúl Castro gained in power.

6. Castro broke many promises. Examples of nonfulfillment include the promised restoration of the Constitution of 1940, freedom of information, individual rights, honest democratic elections. Even after accession to power, he repeatedly promised elections. Each iteration, however, set the date further into the future, until finally the whole idea was abandoned.

7. The United States promptly granted recognition and attempted to woo the new master of Cuba. The record shows official assurances that the United States appreciated the depth and meaningfulness of the revolution, the pressing need for genuine land reform, and the right to expropriate property (with prompt and fair compensation). Arrangements were initiated to assure the new government adequate financing during the difficult transition period. When relations began rapidly to deteriorate, all officials of the United States government, from the President down, sought improvements in mutual understanding. Whether those efforts were carried as far as they might have been or were as skillful as was desirable are debatable points.

8. The judgment of John Quincy Adams was again vindicated; Cuba was not independently viable under the new regime. The government, conspicuously short of skilled administrators, took over and undertook to manage complex economic enterprises. Ineptitude in their operation made nonviability certain.

9. The nation therefore had to have a new sponsor. Geography and the availability of capital and management suggested that the role be

assumed once more by the United States. However, the United States was rejected as guide, counselor, or even friend. Cuba had long been an American client, and Cuban politicians, while profiting from the relationship, had made a career of denouncing the giant "imperialist" neighbor. They could hardly accept the sponsorship of a government that had, according to the new masters, kept Batista in power.

10. The eagerness of the Soviet rulers to gain a base of operations in the Western Hemisphere, new means of communication and transport, the absolute necessity for Cuba to find arms and technical help, and the predisposition of the dominant group around Castro—all combined to make the Soviet Union the logical choice.

As dependence upon the Soviet Union became heavier and more and more American property was seized, the diplomatic strain became acute. Cuban officials showed no disposition to ease relations. Instead, the old hate record was played repeatedly and more stridently than ever before. Denunciations of the United States increased in frequency, length, and bitterness. Meanwhile, the American government sought amelioration of the situation through bilateral diplomacy, the Organization of American States, and the United Nations.

The patience of a great power in the face of deliberately provocative words and acts was striking. It is true that arms shipments were halted, the sugar quota was reduced and then eliminated, and other economic leverages began progressively to be employed. Nevertheless, two years passed by before there was a break in relations, and it was initiated by Cuba. In January 1961 Castro demanded that the personnel of the American Embassy in Havana be reduced to eleven persons within 48 hours. Relations were terminated immediately.

11. It became progressively clearer that the displacement of the Castro regime was the only way to prevent Soviet domination of Cuba.

Then ensued the ultimate tragedy of American policy. It arose from undue reliance upon clandestine means to achieve the overthrow of Castro. However, the covert character of the preparation for invasion fooled no one—unless it was the American public. The arms, the ships, the planes were all supplied by the United States, a fact well known. The Cuban Brigade was trained under American supervision and in part at least by American officers. Before the expedition set out, some magazines and newspapers gave several particulars of the preparation.

Certainly each step in readying the enterprise was reported to Castro, whose spies had no difficulty in infiltrating the "freedom fighters." When the invasion was finally mounted, it contained no serious element of surprise. Not only was Castro prepared militarily, but he had had time to arrest thousands of persons of doubtful loyalty to his regime, thus eliminating the danger of a popular uprising. The underground enemies of the regime had not even been notified of the Bay of Pigs invasion and had no opportunity for diversionary activity.

Denials that the United States was planning an invasion put this nation in an equivocal position. In the United Nations, Cubans asserted that an invasion was planned. "Monstrous distortions and downright falsehoods" was the American answer. One arm of the government said one thing, apparently with sincerity, while another was preparing to do the reverse. The assertion that "there were no Americans in any actions inside Cuba" may have been technically correct; if so, it was telling the truth with the intention to deceive. The invasion attempt, inadequate as it was, could not have been mounted without American support, and all well-informed persons knew it. Given the free press and the fact that the CIA is the best-publicized "secret" operation in the world, it is clear, in retrospect, that this enterprise was much too large for an American clandestine operation, and much too small to achieve its objective.

What was attempted was intervention by deputy while avoiding responsibility for the act. In pursuit of that policy, the expedition was deprived, at the last moment, of essential air cover; and disaster, already almost inevitable, was ensured. The damage done, the President accepted "sole responsibility for the events of the past days." A great power conceded, in effect, that it had violated the spirit and probably the letter of international agreements into which it had freely entered; it had winked at the violation of its own neutrality laws.

There is one absolute requirement for intervention by a great power in a small nation: it must be done skillfully enough and on a large enough scale to guarantee its success. In this instance there was greater need than usual for special care. Two weeks before the invasion the Department of State issued a pamphlet, apparently prepared in the White House, giving in some detail the large amounts of Czech and Soviet military equipment in Cuba. It also emphasized that the Castro regime had, save for the United States, "the largest ground forces in the hemisphere," estimated at between "250,000 and 400,000." Such an official document should have left no illusions regarding the hazards inherent in such an adventure.

Total failure seriously damaged American prestige and impaired its influence in other sensitive situations. It increased the danger that small states would not again cooperate as fully as they had in this instance, lest they find themselves embarrassed by another fiasco. The disaster enhanced the prestige of Castro. The man who had bested the "Colossus of the North" became a hero to many and was made to appear a good deal larger than life size. Castro, who had denounced all intervention, engaged actively in the infiltration of other nations. The frustration of the American gambit facilitated those efforts and advanced the very cause it had been intended to defeat. Moreover, failure impaired the standing of the United States not only in this hemisphere, but also with its major allies, some of whom were still smarting from our participation in halting their Suez adventure.

Before the year 1961 was out, Castro declared: "I am a Marxist-Leninist and will be a Marxist-Leninist until the last day of my life." He also asserted that he had concealed his convictions earlier because, had they been known, "all the social classes that are making war on us would have been doing so from that time on." It is not necessary to believe this statement about his earlier commitment, nor is it strictly relevant; neither truthfulness nor consistency has marked his pronouncements. However, this confession did encourage the Foreign Ministers of the American Republics at Punta del Este to exclude Cuba from participation in the inter-American system. Cuba was shortly barred from discussion of hemispheric defense. The United States virtually declared economic war on the Castro regime.

Cuban dependence on Moscow constantly intensified. In 1962 Soviet technicians and soldiers began secretly to install rockets capable of a nuclear strike against much of the United States and Latin America. There is no means of knowing how far such adventurism was stimulated by a feeling that the American administration was indecisive, as indicated by efforts to avoid overt commitments before the Bay of Pigs invasion. Such considerations may have encouraged a belief that the United States would not respond decisively to a challenge to its hegemony in a vital area. What is abundantly clear is that if the Bay of Pigs intervention had been successful, no basis would have existed for such an acid test of American will, though there might well have been grave problems in living with any government of Cuba that succeeded Castro.

The Soviet Union must have realized that news of the installations would reach the United States from Cuban sources, though neglect of early warnings may have encouraged a hope that they would not be taken with adequate seriousness. Photographic reconnaissance was known to be under way, though somewhat infrequently. American capacity to interpret the photographs accurately was also known. The stealth and speed with which the installations were constructed may have given Khrushchev hope that rockets would be in place before the United States had solid confirmation of his intent, and thus make the logistics of resistance formidable and the decision to resist more difficult.

In October 1962, we faced in Cuba precisely what James Madison had feared a century and a half earlier—namely, that some great power "might make a fulcrum of that position against the commerce and security of the United States." What had seemed absolutely incredible even a few years before, because of our overwhelming power, had come to pass. The menace was not alone to our physical security but also to our ideology. The threat in this respect was far more serious than that of monarchism, "the European system," which Madison, Monroe, and Adams had felt was hostile to our institutions. The Soviet Union offered a fundamental challenge to the political philosophy of the whole hemispheric system.

Response was prompt and firm: the rapid assembling in large numbers of men and matériel ready for action on sea or land and in the air. Notice was given that ships bearing arms would be intercepted. Vigorous and stern diplomacy, rare but welcome unanimous support from the Organization of American States, and the mediation of the Secretary General of the United Nations—combined with a clear and explicit warning that the United States would act—induced the Soviet Union promptly to withdraw offensive weapons. At a more leisurely pace, the size of foreign armed forces in Cuba was reduced.

The face-down did much to restore American prestige, though failure to follow through on inspection, which had been termed essential, dimmed the impact somewhat. Defeat of Russia's spectacular gamble correspondingly impaired Russia's standing, and demonstrated that the threat to the hemisphere was real and not merely "another instance of American hysteria regarding the aggressive intentions of Communism."

Still another consequence was to knock Castro from his pedestal. He was exposed as a Soviet client, and his influence in Latin America was severely damaged, though his success in preventing inspection salvaged some of his standing. The United States stepped up the effort to achieve the economic and, so far as the Americas were concerned, the political isolation of Cuba. Castro was made dependent on the Soviet Union to the extent of perhaps a million dollars a day. Cuba's client status was not eased by the fact that the Soviet government may have made a profit by the resale of sugar bought from Cuba. Men were diverted to military, as opposed to productive, labor; military costs were disproportionately large; economic progress was slowed, perhaps put in reverse. Castro was in no position to fulfill promises of social and economic betterment.

Revelation to all the world of his client status made Castro sullen. He refused to abide by stipulations regarding inspection of rocket removal to which Khrushchev had virtually agreed on his behalf. Not all the wily diplomacy of Mikoyan could move him. As usual, he resorted to television to expound his "divergencies" from Moscow. Red China became a fellow critic of Moscow and denounced Khrushchev's two mistakes: "the error of adventurism" and "the error of capitulation." The breach between Castro and Khrushchev was not fully healed despite a trip to Moscow by the Cuban leader and the customary honeyed words appropriate to such occasions. In a sense, each was a captive of the other. China could supply only part of the enormous amounts of aid needed by Cuba, and Khrushchev could not casually abandon his base in the Western Hemisphere. Cuba offered the only established center for Communist infiltration in the hemisphere.

Conclusion

What conclusions does a historian reach as a result of reflection on our relations with Cuba?

All naïve expectations of an easily swallowed effective foreign-policy capsule must be abandoned. Senator Platt's idea that he could settle the Cuban question was folly. Even Elihu Root, the most sophisticated American involved in launching the new nation, thought that giving

Cuba a "good start" would avoid the disastrous record of Haiti and the Dominican Republic. The bitter experiences of more than two generations of relations with Cuba should by now have demonstrated beyond challenge that there is no simple or single formulation that applies to all contingencies. Yet expectations of settling some enormously complicated matter with one application of wisdom still regularly appear in Senate speeches and resolutions.

It is absurd, moreover, to hold a stopwatch on events and demand quick decisive results. Yet this, also, is a temptation to which members of the Congress sometimes yield. If progress does not maintain the pace or follow the desired direction, legislative action is proposed. We have come a long way from Jefferson's dictum that foreign policy is "executive altogether." President Kennedy, in the speech he would have delivered but for the assassin's bullet, protested severe legislative restrictions on his management of foreign policy. President Johnson, in his first speech to the Congress, repeated the plea for freedom from legislative hobbles. It is not a new problem. Woodrow Wilson once went so far as to direct the Secretary of State, in writing, to disobey a congressional stipulation on the ground that it was a legislative trespass upon executive responsibility.

If we are to play an effective role in a sensitive and complicated world, it is essential that members of the Congress have a care for what they say. The effect of sensational statements is sometimes disastrous. There are large congressional responsibilities in foreign affairs that should not and cannot be curtailed, but the sensitiveness of other nations "craves wary walking." Certainly in our dealings with Cuba, from the beginning of agitation for American intervention to the present moment, the Congress has played a large, often constructive but sometimes destructive, role.

In matters of foreign relations, even when events seem to be conclusive, the result may often turn out to be only an evanescent mirage. Again and again it was asserted that the Cuban constitution had been "vindicated," and "stability" assured. In every instance the appearance proved deceptive—or at best transitory. Expectation of satisfactory definitive results in Cuba was particularly unrealistic because of the volatile Cuban temperament. The United States, in seeking to serve as guide, was working against the leverages of three centuries of a different culture, political institutions wholly unlike our own, and an economy in sharp contrast with ours. Because of underestimation of the difficulties inherent in our special relations with Cuba, the United States never developed an expert staff who had fundamental understanding of Cuban institutions and the Cuban legal system, or genuine appreciation of the Cuban people, their characteristics, their strengths, and their weaknesses. Too many were ready to accept as ultimate truth Leonard Wood's dogma: "Nothing more idiotic can be imagined than the attempt to establish a liberal government under Spanish laws."[12]

Historically, perhaps because of long isolation, American sensitiveness to our impact on other cultures around the world has too often been deficient. It was futile to expect the Cubans to regard us as wholly benevolent and to respond with gratitude. Though there was an element of genuine altruism in American policy and action, there was also a very large admixture of economic, strategic, and political self-interest. We should have learned by now that gratitude is a rarity in international relations. In the future the American public, the Executive, and the Congress all need to show far more sophistication in this respect.

One evidence of such sophistication will be a tardy recognition that there are no safe havens into which diplomatic novices can be sent with the rank of ambassador to enjoy the social and other benefits that still adhere to that sadly depreciated title. It is no less than reckless to commit American relations in sensitive areas to the care of men wholly unprepared for the task, and all areas are now sensitive. We have given up the type of political generals who maneuvered shamelessly for position during the Cuban occupations. No one would suggest putting a military tyro in charge of a major military operation. It is just as foolish to expect diplomatic skill from a party donor. There is a proper place for nonprofessional diplomats, but they should be chosen with care for their special abilities, not for party service or as patronage.

When a former amateur ambassador to Cuba testified before a Subcommittee of the Senate Judiciary Committee that "the American Ambassador was the second most important man in Cuba; sometimes even more important than the president,"[13] he made, unwittingly, a fatal confession of latent imperialism. It was far too reminiscent of the attitude of Senator Platt and his associates, who thought that they could

[12] Quoted in David F. Healy, The United States in Cuba, 1898-1902 (University of Wisconsin Press, 1963), p. 183.
[13] Communist Threat . . . Through the Caribbean, Hearings, Pt. 9, p. 700.

manage an independent country by remote control and with only a margin of their attention.

The assumption that the correlative of "problem" is "solution" is a fatal transfer of a mathematical concept to the alien environment of politics, where it has no relevance. Under the illusion of its validity, there is always a temptation to assume that when a policy does not "succeed" it must have been "wrong," and that if a policy "fails," its opposite would have succeeded. In many situations no policy can be a "success," even though it is legally correct, morally right, and thoroughly rational. A nation may be dominated by ignorance, by xenophobia, by hatred resting on baseless myths, or it may be under the domination of a charismatic leader who makes all qualities save his own seem irrelevant. Under such circumstances sensible policies are as though caught up in a cyclone, wholly out of control. Surely, on several occasions this was the situation in our relations with Cuba.

We must purge our minds of the notion that if the United States had behaved generously and wisely all would have been well. The hidden assumption in that proposition—namely, that the United States is omnipotent—needs only to be mentioned to expose its absurdity. Despite our enormous power we are far from all-powerful, since the human spirit is the most refractory material in creation. If our performance in Cuba had been flawless, it might still have proved futile because of Cuban unwisdom. Reform can be encouraged but cannot be managed from the outside. The effective impulse and the necessary determination for reform must be domestic. We managed the finances, police, and sanitation of Haiti and the Dominican Republic for years; to what a state have they fallen!

The idea of public office being a public trust was alien to the experience of Cuba as a colony and as a nation. It is tragically clear that many leaders lacked dedication to the public interest and sought personal wealth or power or both. The appalling record of graft and corruption demonstrates what should be a patent fact—that it takes two parties to succeed but only one to ensure failure. Cubans had talents (and ultimately training) enough to have made the island politically and economically viable. But such a development would have required a reversal of historical tradition. It was unrealistic to expect the nation to achieve political maturity and self-discipline in six decades.

We made a grand gesture of good neighborliness in dropping the Platt Amendment and pursuing a hands-off policy at a time when our power in the area was beyond challenge. It seemed that we were through with attempts at remote control of other nations. But when the zone of acute danger shifted to Asia, the United States (however reluctantly) again resorted to intervention—in Korea and South Vietnam— and we have not been able to escape responsibility for violent changes in their governments. Such instances remind us once again that our relations with Cuba did not in the past and will not in the future occur in the sterile vacuum of a laboratory vessel. Our total foreign policy must be interpreted in that light.

Cuba is now caught in one of the worst situations of the cold war. It has become dependent upon the Soviet Union, though insofar as its leaders have an ideological bent they seem to lean toward Red China. Meanwhile the island is squeezed by the continued existence of the naval base at Guantánamo, American economic and political pressure, and growing Latin American resentment at the export of terrorists to harass other countries.

Efforts of the United States to bring about the collapse of the Castro regime by isolating Cuba economically are almost certain to fail. The experience of the League of Nations with economic sanctions revealed how ineffectual such measures are in the face of determination on the part of the pressured country on the one hand, and the divergent interests of the participants in economic sanctions on the other. When there is a powerful sponsor of the pressured nation, failure of economic sanctions is almost inevitable. Moreover, while hemispheric solidarity is a mouth-filling phrase, its substance is both slight and fragile. We should pursue it with unflagging zeal, but with modest expectations. Inevitably Mexico, Brazil, Argentina, and other countries of the hemisphere will fail to give full support to a drastic policy of economic isolation for Cuba.

Canada and our other allies in Europe are certain to take advantage of the suspension of American economic relations with Cuba to strengthen their own position. They will not stand idly by while the Russians gain a virtual monopoly in a potentially lucrative market. The effort of the United States to hold other nations to quarantine measures would require energy and concessions disproportionate to the effective economic pressure upon Cuba. In the light of our reaction to Marxism, there is irony in American reliance on Marxist economic determinism to dislodge Castro.

The United States is in a veritable thicket of thorns with regard to its Cuban policy. There are many more things we cannot do than those we can. The time for direct unilateral intervention is past; we made firm treaty commitments against such an action. Moreover, intervention would not be supported by the Latin American states and would rouse the ire of the Afro-Asian bloc, now a majority in the United Nations. We can no longer make Olney's boast that "the United States is practically sovereign on this continent" and that "its fiat is law upon the subjects to which it confines its interposition." It was an unwise piece of bombast and contributed to stimulating fear of the "Colossus of the North." Though our power is now infinitely greater relative to our neighbors than it was in 1895, the "fiat" has become incredible as a doctrine of American foreign policy.

The United States cannot again place major reliance on Cuban exiles to achieve our purposes—or theirs. Some are corrupt politicians eager to return to lucrative office; others, of a much higher type, became disillusioned by the Bay of Pigs fiasco. Even in their desperation the exiles have shown no power of cohesion, no capacity for agreement on leadership, no program that would appeal to broad segments of the Cuban people. The personal factionalism and the splintering of groups that bedeviled the Cuban government for two generations is evident among those who fled the Castro regime.

While the United States deprecates "power politics," it does not, and cannot, wholly eschew such tactics. Guantánamo offers a prime example. Our right to be there rests upon a treaty freely negotiated after abandonment of the Platt Amendment. Indeed, the American presence was welcomed. In 1940 Cosme de la Torriente, often a sharp critic of our policies, wrote: "If the United States Government should ever decide to abandon the Guantánamo Station, Cuba might have to ask the United States to stay. Otherwise, enemy forces might occupy Cuban soil to the peril not only of Cuban independence but the security of the United States."

Now Castro demands that the United States leave. We cannot comply, for the stakes are too high. We would not be willing to let the Soviet Union gain a major naval base in addition to an ideological foothold in this hemisphere. That we would not tolerate such an event became evident when we risked war to force the withdrawal of the Soviet rockets. Furthermore, the interests of the nations in the great arc that extends from Venezuela to Mexico are deeply involved. Even when those nations do not support us they are tacitly glad that the United States has Guantánamo.

In the interdependent era, no nation, however great, is completely master of its fate. Small states inevitably feel the gravitational pull of greater powers despite the dogma of equality in international law. In the excitement and uproar over the passing of colonialism, the residual clientage of many states tends to be overlooked—for example, in the relations of France to some of its former African colonies. The status of Korea, Laos, Vietnam, Taiwan, and many other nations illustrates the point. Even within NATO, the Scandinavian nations are so sophisticated that they accept a limited role, as do the Benelux countries.

Cuba and the United States will, in the long run, have to find ways to cooperate. Geography, economics, and the shared desire of Cubans and Americans for freedom all make the same demand. Yet there is no simple, clear, open road to a restoration of normal friendly relations. The first, and vital, requirement is patience, one of the most difficult of all political virtues to acquire. The second need is alertness to seize any favorable opportunity. The situation is like a game where the best strategy is to "play for the breaks" and capitalize on them promptly and with skill. When the opening comes, the United States must make a conscious endeavor to avoid any resumption of a full client status for Cuba. Every effort must be made to diversify its economy, to share its trade with other nations, and to avoid tying its sugar revenue to American policy. As a prelude—and as practice—we could well make serious efforts to reduce overaccent on clientage in our relations with Panama and other nations of Central America.

We must abandon expectations that other nations will adopt our pattern of democracy. This involves no surrender of our goals. The glowing words of Woodrow Wilson are still in our hearts, but they must be recognized as ideals. He tragically underestimated the difficulties not only in the Americas but around the world. His program faltered, then failed. Many nations turned to Communism, Fascism, Nazism, dictatorship, and one-man rule under various guises. Some of these systems of government proved ephemeral; others appear to move toward permanence.

The nations that have attained the democratic ideal as we interpret it are few indeed. Sukarno called for "guided democracy." Ayub Khan planned for "basic democracy" coming from the villages. Many nations have only a single party; opposition is reduced to terrorism, or to guerrilla fighting, physical or political. Cuba enjoyed the substance of democracy, as we conceive it, for only very brief periods. Nearly everywhere parliamentarism is in trouble. The many blocs that frustrated government in France opened the way for de Gaulle to declare: "In our age nations need greater direction by their governments. . . . This is a necessity of our times. There is no escape."[14] The instability of many governments is obvious. To call one-party rule, or trading among splinter blocs, or personal government "democratic" is to stretch the meaning of words beyond their elastic tolerances.

Trying to keep what we consider a "good" or a "democratic" government in power may be self-defeating; it may raise the cry "Yankee puppet" and injure the cause we seek to support. Efforts to dislodge a "bad" or "military" regime evokes the shout "Yankee imperialism," with the result of helping those we would like to see replaced.

As a part of adjustment to realities, public understanding must be clarified regarding our policy on recognition of foreign regimes, because democratic control of the broad strategy of our foreign policy is essential. To that end there must be clear guiding principles to which the public can refer. Ever since 1898 Cuba has been an important testing ground for recognition policies; these were subsequently applied elsewhere, particularly in the Caribbean. Woodrow Wilson enlarged on Theodore Roosevelt's moralistic pronouncements and taught the American people that the grant of recognition reflected a moral judgment and was a proper means of exercising decisive influence on the life of other nations. That policy was a failure; Franklin Roosevelt and Cordell Hull sought to abandon it. Nevertheless, recognition and approval are still indissolubly linked in the public mind—and in the minds of many members of the Congress. It is a fatal confusion.

Some policymakers do not want either democratic control of foreign policy or a set of principles clearly understood by the public. Recognition is conceived by this group as a "flexible instrument" to be used empirically as each situation develops. Such a concept raises a fundamental issue: whether the experts like it or not, public opinion will ultimately be dominant. That is the reason why, after bitter experience, the Constitution so firmly established civilian control of the military (the

[14] *New York Times,* Nov. 23, 1963.

only experts then in government service) in our political structure. The Department of State could make no more fundamental error than to leave the public mind confused regarding a basic element in foreign policy—namely, recognition—to which, in the current political flux, there must be frequent resort. Now is the time—before any change occurs in Cuba—to rally public support to an explicit doctrine regarding recognition.

The final lesson from the Cuban experience is that, at all costs, the United States must not again impair its own integrity. There seems to be something about airplanes that leads to confusion between the Department of State and the Central Intelligence Agency. It might have been thought that the U-2 episode of 1960 would have been enough to warn against any repetition. Not so; at the United Nations Ambassador Stevenson showed a photograph of a plane which he assured his hearers was Cuban, though it was known in some parts of our government to be American and shortly was revealed to all the world as American. The effectiveness of a difficult and delicate mission was dealt a needless blow. Abolition of clandestine operations is impossible, but they should never again be allowed to impair the status of our own spokesmen.

ROBERT F. SMITH, of the University of Connecticut, is the author
of The United States and Cuba: Business and Diplomacy, 1917-1960
(1960), What Happened in Cuba? A Documentary History of
U.S.–Cuban Relations (1963), and Background to Revolution:
The Development of Modern Cuba (1966).

Castro's Revolution: Domestic Sources and Consequences

ROBERT F. SMITH

The revolution led by Fidel Castro was not an illogical or
unnecessary historical "sport" foisted on Cuba by some accident or con-
spiracy. It was a product of fundamental instabilities. The revolution
had its roots in the problems, hopes, and frustrations of a Cuba that has
rapidly emerged into the world of industrial technology with relatively
little advance preparation. The groups that exercised political power in
Cuba after 1902 were generally unable or unwilling to make the kind of
adjustments necessitated by these rapid changes, and the resulting dis-
integration had already produced a revolutionary situation by the late
1920's. Revolution aimed at the reorganization of Cuban society came
in 1933, but after its abortion in 1934 the island fell back into the traditional ruts. Some reforms were enacted, and subsequent developments
did moderate some of the problems. But the basic problems were not
solved, and Cuban society between 1934 and 1959 was characterized
by violence, instability, and movements symptomatic of a continuance
of revolutionary conditions.[1] Thus, Castro crystallized a revolutionary
process that had been in existence for about three decades, and the revolution still in progress can only be understood as a part of long-range

[1] E. S. Stokes, "National and Local Violence in Cuban Politics," Southwestern
Social Science Quarterly, XXXIV, 3 (Sept. 1953), 57-63.

45

historical developments. As such, the Castro revolution is a phase in the overall evolution of Cuban society, which will in turn be modified and shaped by the basic conditions peculiar to Cuba.

Between 1868 and 1929 the relatively stable socioeconomic pattern of colonial Cuba was completely disrupted by a combination of factors. The struggles to overthrow Spanish rule between 1868 and 1898 resulted in much destruction of property and loss of life. Coinciding with these struggles was the introduction of industrial technology into the sugar economy. This development involved the small mill owner and farmer in a desperate battle for survival with those who had the capital needed for modern mills, rail transportation, and expanding landholdings. All these factors disrupted the traditional pattern of rather widespread ownership of land and the means of producing sugar. In the process of this change, many Cubans were reduced to a landless or dependent status (as in the case of those called *colonos*, who grew cane but were dependent on the mill owner for credit, transportation, and markets). Between 1877 and 1899 the number of sugar mills declined from 1,190 to 207.[2]

This process was accelerated after the Spanish-American War, as North Americans took advantage of depressed land prices and general economic chaos to buy sugar mills and land. At the same time the large corporation was replacing the individual entrepreneur in the sugar industry—a trend that reached a new level in the 1920's, when North American banks moved into the sugar industry. The elimination of individually owned sugar mills leveled off after 1915 (there were 170 in 1915 and 161 in 1959), but these mills were steadily consolidated into the structure of the large corporations. By 1926 the industrialization of the sugar industry had reached a peak.

This relatively rapid economic transition had a variety of effects on Cuban society. The revolution in land tenure produced a high concentration of landownership and rendered landless or dependent an important segment of the rural population, creating the conditions for an agricultural class not of peasant farmers but of a rural wage-earning proletariat. Between 1899 and 1933 the number of farms declined, and from 30 to 40 percent of the total arable land of Cuba passed into the hands of sugar companies. These companies rented or leased additional

---

[2] Lowry Nelson, *Rural Cuba* (University of Minnesota Press, 1950), p. 94.

land, further increasing their direct control of the island's arable lands.[3] Some of those uprooted by war and industrialization became wage laborers on the sugar centrals, while others drifted to the rapidly growing cities and towns.

Another element in the disruptive process was the rapid growth of slavery during the nineteenth century. This not only added thousands of new inhabitants to the population, but also resulted in a more dehumanized relation between whites and blacks, as the old Spanish slave code was steadily eroded by the new relationships created by the sugar plantations. The abolition of slavery in the 1880's added thousands of Negroes—including many who had been in Cuba only a short time—to the growing numbers of displaced Cubans searching for some kind of social status and for a productive role in the economy. This problem was further compounded between 1912 and 1924, when approximately 230,000 contract laborers were imported from Haiti and Jamaica.[4]

The wealth of the island was increasing, but at the same time the gap between upper and lower classes was widening.[5] So long as the sugar industry was expanding and prospering, the tensions in Cuban society remained below the boiling point, but when the industry began to stagnate after 1926 the fact that large numbers of Cubans had not been integrated into the new order became readily apparent. Loyalties to the new institutions were, for many Cubans, either weak or nonexistent. The dominant feature of the economy, the sugar *latifundios*, did not possess even the traditional ties of the feudal land systems in other parts of Latin America, and capitalism—with its preponderant foreign control—was to many Cubans synonymous with the new *latifundio* system.

In the first quarter of the twentieth century Cuba had a highly "invertebrate" society. Social cohesion was minimal, since the institutions

[3] Raymond L. Buell et al., *Problems of the New Cuba: Report of the Commission on Cuban Affairs* (Foreign Policy Association, 1935), p. 51; U.N. Economic and Social Council, Economic Commission for Latin America, *Economic Survey of Latin America, 1959 Preliminary Report* (United Nations, 1960), p. 132; Nelson, *op cit.*, p. 116.

[4] Sidney W. Mintz in the Foreword to Ramiro Guerra y Sánchez, *Sugar and Society in the Caribbean* (Caribbean Series No. 7; Yale University Press, 1964), pp. xi-vliv.

[5] Nelson, *op. cit.*, pp. 96-97, 103-4; Buell et al., *op. cit.*, pp. 3-8; Mancur Olson, Jr., "Rapid Growth as a Destabilizing Force," *Journal of Economic History*, XXIII, 4 (Dec. 1963), 529-52.

that normally perform the unifying function—such as the Church, army, nation, or other forms of conscious social groupings—had either been severely weakened or were new creations. During the nineteenth century, when other Latin American countries were struggling to build independent societies, Cuba was experiencing the full brunt of colonial rule and the destructive force of a prolonged and violent conflict to end Spanish rule. The one-time stable Cuban society, based on widespread ownership of land and Spanish indifference, was destroyed. Thus Cubans were faced, at the beginning of the twentieth century, with the difficult task of molding a social order out of the undigested products of the previous century—a task complicated by foreign tutelage and the nature of the economy.[6]

AFTER 1926 THE CUBAN ECONOMY entered a period of stagnation. Some changes took place during World War II and the Korean war, but by 1959 the island's economy was still based largely on a declining share of the world's sugar market. Instability was a consequence, as the life of the island oscillated between the *tiempo muerto* and the grinding season, and between the periods of high and low sugar prices. Some industrial diversification was accomplished during World War II, but many factories were abandoned after 1945. Between 1950 and 1959 industrialization was renewed as North American investments in manufacturing other than sugar doubled, mainly through large-scale subsidiaries of North American corporations.[7]

The industrial progress of the post-World War II period, however, did not alter the basic economic patterns of the country sufficiently to overcome the problems of waste, maldistribution, and fluctuation. Between 1948 and 1954 the Cuban gross national product, though growing, was sufficient to allow the 1947 standard of living to be maintained in only five of the seven years included in the period. Moreover, if real per capita income is calculated on the basis of the United States and Havana wholesale price indexes, the result shows a drop from 204 pesos (one peso equal to one dollar) in 1947 to 180 pesos in 1954. Na-

[6] The concept of the "invertebrate society" has been presented by José Ortega y Gasset, *Invertebrate Spain* (Norton, 1937). See also Roberto Ortigueira, "La Desintegración, Estado Normal de Paises en Desarrollo," *Journal of Inter-American Studies*, V, 4 (Oct. 1963), 471-94.

[7] Wyatt MacGaffey and Clifford R. Barnett, *Cuba: Its People, Its Society, Its Culture* (HRAF Press, 1962), p. 73.

tional income reached the highest levels in Cuban history during this period, but rising prices (especially for imports) and a steadily increasing population (over one million between 1943 and 1953) helped to prevent any major changes in the overall standard of living.[8]

Economic instability and erratic fluctuation were weightier elements in the revolutionary situation than dire poverty as such. One of the major causes of the unstable conditions was the relationship of sugar to the overall economy of Cuba. The International Bank for Reconstruction and Development issued a *Report on Cuba* in 1950 which clearly indicated the nature of the problem:

> In the last quarter century, national income, while extremely unstable, has experienced hardly as much over-all growth as the growth of population, even though the latter has slowed down somewhat since 1925. This would seem to be the picture of an economy which has lost its pre-1925 "dynamic" and has not yet found a new dynamic.[9]

In 1956 the U.S. Department of Commerce described much the same situation:

> While exports contribute between 30 and 40 percent of the national income, they play a role of considerably greater magnitude since almost all the activities of the island are geared to the rise and fall in the volume and value of export crops. When demand and prices abroad are favorable, all sectors of the Cuban economy are prosperous, but when conditions abroad are unfavorable, the economy has very little to cushion the adverse effects.[10]

A decided majority of the Cuban working population were wage laborers, who were highly vulnerable to market fluctuations. Cuba had a chronic unemployment rate of about 9 percent of the total working population.[11] The approximately 42 percent of the work force engaged in agriculture (70 percent of this force consisted of wage workers in

[8] U.S. Department of Commerce, *Investment in Cuba: Basic Information for United States Businessmen* (Government Printing Office, 1956), pp. 6-7, 184. An economic upturn began in 1955, by 1957 the 1952 national income level had been passed, and another recession began in 1958. U.S. Department of Commerce, World Trade Information Service, *Economic Developments in Cuba, 1957*, Economic Reports, Pt. II, No. 58-25 (Government Printing Office, 1958), p. 1; and *ibid.*, Pt. I, No. 59-42, p. 1. See also Dudley Seers *et al.*, *Cuba: The Economic and Social Revolution* (University of North Carolina Press, 1964), pp. 6-17.

[9] Economic and Technical Mission to Cuba, *Report on Cuba* (International Bank for Recontruction and Development, 1951), p. 42.

[10] U.S. Department of Commerce, *Investment in Cuba*, p. 7. The average yearly increase in the birth rate jumped from 1.7 percent for 1931–43 to 2.3 percent for 1943–53.

[11] *Ibid.*, p. 23. See also Economic and Technical Mission to Cuba, *op. cit.*, pp. 47-57.

sugar production) were especially hard hit by economic fluctuation, but workers in other industries were affected as well.

Although the Cuban government made sporadic attempts to alleviate the economic instability of the country, the path of least resistance was to continue the sugar system—an easy source of national income and foreign currency, and the economic base of the power structure of the island. Thus Cuba did little about the vast waste in labor, land, and capital which the system encouraged. During the prosperous year of 1952, one-fourth of the working population worked less than forty weeks.[12] Though 80 percent of the total area of Cuba was considered to be arable, in 1945 only 22 percent of the arable land was under cultivation, owing to the concentration of land in sugar *latifundios* and cattle ranches.[13] According to the U.S. Department of Commerce, "few countries carry a heavier overhead of under-utilized productive facilities."[14] Included in the list of such facilities were sugar mills, railroads, and ports. Wealthy Cubans tended to invest their capital in real estate or foreign holdings. In 1955 the U.S. Treasury Department estimated Cuban investments abroad at $312 million, with at least $150 million in south Florida real estate.[15] This capital outflow was complicated by the presence of heavy foreign investment—mainly North American—in the Cuban economy, ranging from 90 percent control in the telephone and electric services to about 37 percent in sugar (see J. Wilner Sundelson's chapter, pp. 98-116). Profits made on these foreign investments were sometimes reinvested in the island, but often were not, and significant repatriation of capital abroad could produce at any time a condition of net disinvestment in the Cuban economy.[16]

Thus pre-Castro Cuba had a solid modern infrastructure of roads and communications, a developed agricultural industry in sugar, and a capital-generating economy. In comparison with other Latin American countries, Cuba was relatively well off.[17] With appropriate allocation of

---

[12] U.S. Department of Commerce, *Investment in Cuba*, p. 23.
[13] *Ibid.*, pp. 30-32. In 1946, 7.9 percent of the farms controlled 71.1 percent of the land; 69.6 percent of the farms controlled 11.2 percent of the total land in farms.
[14] *Ibid.*, p. 6.
[15] *Ibid.*, pp. 14-15.
[16] Cuba had a net investment deficit of $65.6 million in 1957, and $47.9 million in 1958. MacGaffey and Barnett, *op. cit.*, p. 346.
[17] In 1959 per capita income in Cuba was fourth highest among the countries of Latin America. Only Argentina, Venezuela, and Uruguay stood above it. See United Nations, *The Economic Development of Latin America in the Post-War Period* (United Nations, 1964), p. 51.

resources, the output of the economy could have increased considerably. But many Cubans were living on the margin of existence, especially in rural areas. And many of the rest lived in a twilight zone of semipoverty, fluctuating between degrees of quasi-affluence and hard times. Cubans were living in a consumer-market cash economy, and their appetites were conditioned by the prosperous periods. Even those at the bottom of the economic ladder generally had enough contact with society at large to see that poverty was neither inevitable nor immutable. Cubans could see about them a paradox of "progress and poverty." New expectations and frustrations, brought about by Cuba's development and economic fluctuation, produced greater dissatisfaction than the centuries-old conditions of abject poverty.

RESPONSIBLE LEADERSHIP was at a minimum among the more powerful elements in Cuban society. Such leadership could not have solved all the problems of the republic, or remedied all the difficulties that flowed from a one-crop export economy, but it might have contributed to the creation of a greater degree of social cohesion on the island. The opposite took place, and social disunity was a significant component in the revolutionary situation that emerged.

The Cuban upper class had wealth and time to devote to leadership, but it lacked the ability to govern effectively. The upper class had undergone changes in composition and loyalties between 1868 and 1929. Independence from Spain reduced the power and influence of the old pro-Spanish *Criollos* (Cuban-born Spaniards) and led to the elevation of some of the leaders of the independence movement. A new element in the upper class was composed of men who had made fortunes through association with foreign business—such as José Miguel Tarafa and Gerardo Machado. At the same time, many Spaniards in Cuba continued to hold posts of influence in the Church and in commerce. Disparate in socioeconomic interests and in identification with rival foreign countries and ideas, the ruling groups found it difficult to act together, to inspire a national unity, and to maintain their influence.

The upper class retained the colonial view of social relationships and conceived of their countrymen as divided between the ruler and the ruled, the rich and the poor. This view grossly oversimplified Cuban society and made cooperation between the classes difficult. In this scheme of things the rising middle sectors had little status. The aristo-

cratic aversion to work was a part of this view; it affected not only relations with other classes but also the use of resources. At a time when
Cuba was developing a more complex industrial economy, many of
those in positions of power held to ideas, aspirations, and social goals
that were incompatible with the new order of reality.

Stimulated by European radical thought, the Cuban workers of the
1890's initiated the Cuban trade union movement. As early as 1892 a
thousand delegates to the first National Workers Congress stated in a
resolution: "The Congress recognizes that the working class cannot
emancipate itself unless it adopts the ideas of revolutionary Socialism,
and therefore urges Cuban workers to study and adopt its principles."[18]
Major organizational activity, however, did not begin till the mid-
1920's, when the harsh antilabor policies of President Machado combined with growing economic depression to infuse the labor movement
with a militant outlook. The general strike of August 1933 was an effec-
tuating force behind the overthrow of the dictator. Agitation and unrest
continued to mount as workers seized numerous sugar centrals, took
over the Bethlehem Steel mines, staged massive demonstrations, and
even formed several short-lived soviets. One observer in Cuba noted:

> We have so many strikes that it is useless to talk about them. . . . Every-
> body puts on demonstrations. . . . The only thing they all agree on is "Down
> with the Americans."[19]

Inevitably, the class consciousness of Cuban labor was tinged with
dislike for North American business in the island. Machado's antilabor
policy had received the full approval of these business interests, who
had labeled every act of Cuban labor since 1919 as "Communist-in-
spired." The Communists did gain some influence in the labor movement, especially after 1935, but the attitudes of Cuban workers were
molded by factors other than Communist agitation. In fact, the Communists demonstrated their lack of real influence by their opposition to
the revolutionary government of Ramón Grau San Martín which held
power from September 1933 to January 1934. As a result the party was
overhauled in 1934-35 and subsequently gained substantial power in
the labor movement. During the late 1930's Fulgencio Batista drew on
Communist support in an effort to control the labor movement.

---

[18] As quoted in Phillip Foner, *A History of Cuba and Its Relations with the
United States* (International Publishers, 1963), Vol. II, p. 303.
[19] R. Hart Phillips, *Cuba: Island of Paradox* (McDowell, Obolensky, 1959), p. 79.

During the 1930's a number of measures to protect the workers were enacted by the Cuban government, and the labor movement became, in effect, an arm of the government. By the 1950's the movement had lost much of its earlier militancy, and some factions, especially among skilled workers, became defenders of a status quo that gave rigid job protection to the more privileged unions. In the process, some unions adopted such tight admission requirements that membership was almost on a hereditary basis. In spite of minimum-wage laws, many other workers were still highly vulnerable to the instability of the Cuban economy. The mass of unskilled casual workers in the cities and the wage laborers on the sugar centrals generally found themselves in an insecure position. A lack of confidence in the economic system was common in almost all segments of Cuban labor, and even the members of the "aristocratic" unions owed more loyalty to the organization than to the system. As the U.S. Department of Commerce stated in 1956:

Collectively . . . the Cuban workers are likely to be intransigently opposed to any mechanical or organizational improvements that would appear to threaten their jobs. Frequently, little mutual confidence is found between the industrial worker and his employer and much skepticism exists regarding the ability of Government and private initiative to create an expanding and dynamic economy in Cuba.[20]

The Negro in Cuba did not experience the same kind of discrimination as his counterpart in the southern United States, but much subtle discrimination did exist. Color was a factor in the Cuban social hierarchy, and few Negroes attained high positions in the government. The Negro struggle for status in modern Cuba led to the race war in 1912, in which 3,000 Negroes were killed, and there was some racial conflict during the 1933 revolution. The old racial attitudes of the upper class were fortified by contact with North Americans. Conditions improved in later years, but the color line continued to be a divisive factor. Since most Cuban Negroes were in the lower income group, the categorization of "rich and poor" was reinforced. Many Negroes felt that they were not really part of modern Cuba—an attitude reflected in the remark of a proud member of Castro's militia: "I wasn't a man before. I was a nigger, only the whites were men."[21]

Thus the lower class of Cuba, plagued by illiteracy (which actually

[20] U.S. Department of Commerce, *Investment in Cuba*, p. 24.
[21] Victor Franco, *The Morning After* (Praeger, 1962), p. 63

increased between 1931 and 1950), economic instability, and frustrations born of abortive reforms, was generally cynical about the existing
order. As the sociologist Lowry Nelson found, the lower-class people of
the 1940's possessed a "desire for better schools, better roads, and a
better life in general." He wondered at the persistence of such ideals in
"the face of repeated frustrations," but it was just this combination of
factors that helped to create a revolutionary situation.[22]

SOME OBSERVERS HAVE DOUBTED that a middle class existed in Cuba,
and this is probably a clue to the dilemma of people who were economically in the middle.[23] In sociopsychological terms, middle-class
self-identification was weak, and there existed a strong tendency for
members of the middle sectors to identify either with the upper class
or with the lower class. The lack of economic opportunity and the
nature of Cuban higher education prevented the middle sectors from
playing a significant role in the new republic. As a result, many turned
to politics, government service, the professions (especially law), and
teaching as a means of attaining upper-class status.

In purely economic terms there might have been a middle class but in
terms of self-identification and bourgeois culture values a middle class
scarcely existed. Instead, there were what the Cubans themselves describe
as the *capas medias*. There was no strong bourgeois tradition to offset the
rentier mentality which was one of the main legacies of the *criollo* plantoc-
racy. Neither anticlericalism nor anti-Americanism gave homogeneity to
these groups, whose factionalism was the bane of Cuban politics.[24]

Young Cubans from the middle sectors came away from Havana
University determined to build a stable, unified Cuba and reform its
socioeconomic system. In their writings, they led the way in criticizing
the situation. They articulated a strident, if nebulous, nationalism.
Many tried the path of reform, but, finding the way blocked by the socioeconomic power structure, came to accept the status quo in return
for admission to some level in the ranks of power and the privilege of
using governmental graft as a means of gaining the accoutrements of
upper-class status. Others made limited compromises and continued to
agitate for change. Frustrated reform and frustrated ideals constituted
a leading element in the development of the revolutionary situation

[22] Nelson, *op. cit.*, p. 252.
[23] *Ibid.*, pp. 159-61.
[24] C. A. M. Hennessy, "The Roots of Cuban Nationalism," *International Affairs*, 39,
3 (July 1963), 351.

and men from the middle sectors were often the most determined voices of these frustrations.

The first major wave of middle-sector reforms emerged in the 1920's. Some tried to work through the Veterans and Patriots Movement to reform the government, while others brought the University Reform Movement to Havana University in 1924.[25] The university became a center of the "regenerative movement," and the students carried the movement to the lower class through extension classes in the Universidad Popular José Martí. These movements, however, had little effect on Cuban society. As Gerardo Machado became increasingly dictatorial, many of the young reformers adopted other policies. Some went into exile, some formed underground terrorist groups, and others turned to Marxism. The young poet Juan Marinello and the intellectual Julio Antonio Mella were representative of those who found in Communism what they believed to be the solution for Cuba's ills. But the growth of the Communist party during this period caused a serious schism in the ranks of the reformers as a result of the party's insistence on internal discipline and noncooperation with other groups.

The "generation of the thirties"—the name given to these reformers—had its moment of triumph in the revolution of September 1933. Professor Ramón Grau San Martín and his Student Directorate at Havana University proclaimed a number of sweeping reforms and announced the nationalist motto "Cuba for the Cubans." The revolution was aborted in January 1934, when Colonel Fulgencio Batista allied the army with the conservative upper class. Some of the young revolutionaries—such as Antonio Guiteras, the leader of *Joven Cuba*—went underground, and fought against Batista and his puppet presidents until the general strike of March 1935. After the bloody suppression of that outburst the "generation of the thirties" was scattered. A survivor later wrote: "Henceforth it was to be an 'absent' generation, as whoever remained alive went wandering through life like one removed from everything around him."[26] Some survivors went to fight in the Spanish Civil War, and others went into exile. Some returned to Cuba in later years to pursue diverse paths. The later careers of Carlos Prío Socarrás, Ramón Grau San Martín, Raúl Roa, and Herminio Portell Vilá, to name but a few, reveal much about this diversity.

[25] *Ibid.*, p. 352.
[26] Teresa Casuso, *Cuba and Castro* (Random House, 1961), p. 77.

Grau San Martin and Prío Socarrás were elected president in 1944 and 1948, respectively, but these "tired radicals" of an earlier time did little to change the basic power structure. Both supported some reform measures, but neither attacked the problem of land reform or tried to implement the more radical sections of the 1940 Constitution. In addition, both accepted the system of organized political corruption and used it in the traditional manner of helping their supporters climb the socioeconomic ladder. Neither really attacked the upper class, yet both were damned as Reds by that class and by the business elements. Batista's return to power by a coup d'état in 1952 was welcomed by the upper class as a means of saving Cuba from the "socialist miasma."[27]

A new generation was reaching maturity in the late 1940's. Disillusioned with the failure of the old generation, this group formed the Ortodoxo party in 1947. The dramatic suicide of its leader, "Eddie" Chibás, in 1951 was symptomatic of a growing despair among young Cubans with the existing system and with the traditional methods of governing Cuba and traditional ways of trying to change it. The rootlessness and lack of orientation of many students and intellectuals found expression in terrorism and gang warfare during the 1930's and 1940's. These activities had little real direction. They were outbursts of the kind that often characterizes groups having weak social loyalties and no vital movement with which to identify. The second period of Batista rule gave this generation a symbol on which to focus—first for their hopes and later for their frustrations. During the 1950's Fidel Castro, with his extraordinary charismatic personality, emerged as the inheritor of generations of revolutionary aspiration.

Since 1920 a revolutionary "myth" had been in the process of development in Cuba. Such a "myth" is a necessary ideological element in any social revolution. It is compounded out of the historical experience of a country. The Cuban version, only partly formed at the time of the 1933 revolution, continued to develop over the next three decades.

A major ingredient in the revolutionary "myth" was the theme of United States imperialism. With an overwhelming sense of national frustration, many Cubans saw the United States as a chief source of Cuba's failure to establish a unified, stable nation. They also accused

<hr/>

[27] Editorial in *Cuba Económica y Financiera,* April 1952, p. 3.

the Cuban upper class of cooperating in the foreign exploitation of Cuba. To the revolutionists, this alliance explained the frustration of Martí's dreams of a truly independent Cuba, the failure of the 1933 revolution, and the instability of the Cuban economy. Thus many equated true socioeconomic reform with national economic independence, both to be gained by reshaping the existing system and eliminating foreign influence.

Oversimplified and hyperemotional though it was, this "myth" was a predictable reaction of sensitive inhabitants of a weak country living under the ever-present influence of a strong power. The predominant economic position of North American business, the naval base at Guantánamo, the history of past interventions, and the periodic meddling in Cuban politics to ensure a United States version of order and stability were all factors involved in the Cuban reaction. In addition, Cuban intellectuals protested vigorously against what they regarded as the attempt by the United States to deny—or to rewrite—the historical heritage of the republic. Cuban historians produced many volumes aimed at establishing pride in the Cuban historical tradition and building national sentiment. In the process the United States emerged as the principal enemy of Cuban sovereignty.

The Cuban nationalistic historians were especially angry over the fact that the United States had taken over their War of Independence and named it the Spanish-American War. Historians such as Emilio Roig de Leuchsenring and Herminio Portell Vilá wrote numerous books describing the role of the Cubans in the achievement of independence and criticizing the activities of the United States. In a multi-volume work published in the late 1930's, Portell Vilá stated that the United States was responsible for Cuba's failure to attain independence prior to 1898, and had vastly limited Cuban sovereignty during the subsequent years.[28] This side of Cuban nationalism has been poorly understood in the United States, but perhaps we can imagine a similar reaction if, in a world dominated by France, the French had called the American Revolution the Franco-British War, had relegated George Washington to the level of bushwhacker and baggage carrier, and had retained a permanent naval base at the Brooklyn Navy Yard.

[28] Herminio Portell Vilá, *Historia de Cuba en sus relaciones con los Estados Unidos y España* (Havana: Jesús Montero, 1938-41); Emilio Roig de Leuchsenring, *1895 y 1898: Dos guerras cubanas, Ensayo de revaloración* (Havana: Sociedad Cubana de Estudios Históricos y Internacionales, 1945).

This group of Cuban scholars formed an organization in the early 1940's which held annual congresses. Out of these came streams of papers and resolutions attacking United States imperialism and the status quo in Cuba. One of these congresses voted to rename the war of 1898 the "Spanish-Cuban-American War," and this was officially approved by the Congress of Cuba. Other events in Cuban history were interpreted in a similar manner, and Grau San Martín titled his explanation of the 1933 revolution "The Cuban Revolution Against America."[29]

The emotional supporters of Cuban nationalism were not confined to the intellectuals. In 1922 a relatively conservative newspaper stated that "the day will have to arrive when we will consider it the most sacred duty of our life to walk along the street and eliminate the first American we encounter."[30] Cuban mobs screamed anti-U.S. slogans in 1933, and these same sentiments could be found in Cuba in later years if one left the tourist circuit and business circles.

Thus defensive nationalism became a principal part of Cuba's revolutionary "myth." Many of the young men who made the revolution after 1959 were weaned on this tradition, and it was symbolic that the first book to explain the Castro revolution to the peoples of Latin America echoed the theme of United States imperialism as a cause of Cuba's problems.[31]

By the 1950's Cuba contained many of the elements that students of social movements have identified as characterizing a society pregnant with revolution. In fact, Cuba did not have an effectively working society. A working society must create a sense of status and unity for most of its members, and it must uphold a set of ideals that appeal to its people as generally acceptable and practicable.[32] Cuban society was highly fragmented, even within nominally cohesive groups, and loyalties to national systems, institutions, or goals were weak or nonexistent. The Cuban intellectual class was disaffected with the existing order. Sporadic violence permeated many aspects of life. The organizations usually identified as traditional conservative forces—the Church and the army—were relatively weak. The Church did not have enough priests,

---

[29] Alberto Arrendondo, *Cuba: Tierra indefensa* (Havana: Editorial Lex, 1945).

[30] *New York Times,* June 22, 1922.

[31] Armando Giménez, *Sierra Maestra: La revolución de Fidel Castro* (Buenos Aires: Editorial Lautaro, 1959).

[32] Richard M. Haywood, *The Myth of Rome's Fall* (Crowell, 1958), pp. 149-51; Crane Brinton, *The Anatomy of Revolution* (Random House, 1960), pp. 28-29.

and those who were in Cuba were generally Spaniards concentrated in the cities. The army had been divided and reorganized several times since 1909, and violent political conflict within the officer corps seriously weakened it. Political life was characterized by *personalismo*, corruption, and cynicism. Many Cubans agreed with the comment made by a Cuban woman: "Cubans will not work together; they don't trust each other; they are afraid someone will get more benefit from such a project than they will."[33] A historical pattern of frustrated dreams and ideals made Cuba ripe for a mass movement.

SYSTEMATIZED AND REGULAR PRESSURE from an upper class can apparently be tolerated by a society almost indefinitely, but irregular, corrupt, and violent intrusions by a ruling group eventually become intolerable. Against the background of general conditions just described, the sporadic tyranny and gross ineffectiveness of the Batista regime provided the catalyst that made it possible for a messianic leader to bring together the various disaffected groups in Cuban society. Between 1956 and 1959 the Batista regime alienated almost all sectors of Cuban society. By 1958 the society had completely disintegrated. Cubans turned against Batista for various reasons: some because he became overly corrupt, some because of his terrorism, and some out of their hopes for a revitalized Cuba. All these factors had their effect on the Cuban army. When it refused to fight and melted away—through negotiated surrender and desertion—Batista's last vestige of power was gone.

On January 1, 1959, Fidel Castro walked into Havana without firing a shot—just as Batista had done in 1952. The actions of revolutionary groups played a dominant role in undermining Batista's position, but Castro's victory did not come about through sheer preponderance of numbers. The downfall of Batista's personal power marked the preliminary stage of the revolution. The confusion that followed obscured for many the fact that the Cuban revolution possessed all the ingredients that have characterized the major socioeconomic revolutions of the Western World. A mass of people with hopes, frustrations, and weak institutional loyalties had been converted (or were potential converts) to a revolutionary mystique that promised some kind of new and better

[33] Nelson, *op. cit.*, p. 246; Hugh Thomas, "The Origins of the Cuban Revolution," *The World Today*, 19 (Oct. 1963), 454-56.

order. This environment of aroused hopes and almost messianic expectations (the emotional propellant of revolution) had long been in the process of being generated. An organized, hard-core leadership had emerged, imbued with the revolutionary "myth," a sense of mission, and a determination to bring about some kind of radical revolution. Fidel Castro had already become the symbol of the revolutionary mystique, and he quickly moved to consolidate his position as the leader of the organized power structure of the revolution—an unusual dual role perhaps indicating the continuing importance of *personalismo* in Cuba.

Fidel Castro has been described as an eternal rebel, a romantic idealist, a messianic zealot burning to reform the world regardless of cost. He has been able to convey this mystique to others in emotionally intelligible and dramatic forms. He has been able to symbolize hope, national pride, and self-dedication—in part through his own faith in the righteousness of his cause. The true believers of the revolution look to Castro as the founder of the faith. Castro has articulated this faith within the framework of Cuban culture by drawing on Christian symbolism, the hagiography of Simón Bolívar and José Martí, and even the romantic gaiety of song and dance. A cha-cha band playing "*Cuba sí, Yanqui no!*" is an apt symbol of the unique Cuban revolutionary aura which Castro personifies.

Militant personal leadership is a key element in the Cuban revolutionary dynamic, but there is also a peculiar internal logic—compounded of emotions, expectations, and opposition forces—to the revolutionary process, which in turn influences the leadership. The peculiar combination of these factors helped to shape the course of the revolution after its earliest days.

The first provisional government, set up in January 1959, was relatively conservative. The reform plans announced in January called for such measures as profit sharing and division of unused lands, which were to be purchased. This pace was much too slow for the radicals, and Castro began to mobilize public support for more drastic moves. During March and April a variety of measures were promulgated: The Rent Law instituted reductions ranging from 30 to 50 percent, according to the renter's income bracket; a decree of March 20 reduced the price of medicines; the Installment Purchase Law reduced monthly payments by 50 percent and doubled the payment period with no increase in interest; the Vacant Lot Law not only wiped out speculative profits above 15 percent on unimproved real estate but also provided for compulsory sale at reduced prices. Low-cost housing projects were started, and construction was begun on schools, roads, and hospitals. The final act in this phase of the revolution was the Agrarian Reform Law, promulgated on June 2, 1959.

During this period the Cuban government was subjected to a variety of pressures. There were signs that the old problem of social fragmentation was once more threatening Cuban stability. Groups demanded concessions for their support in the struggle against Batista. The Church asked for religious instruction to be established in the public schools; the conservatives called for an end to drastic reforms; the Communists agitated for greater wage increases; and the restaurant and hotel workers demanded the reopening of the luxury casinos and the restoration of gambling. A wave of strikes spread in February and March, and Castro had to appeal to various labor groups not to strike or boycott the revolution.[34] Wealthy Cubans instituted an investment boycott. By the end of March private construction had generally stopped, and unemployment increased as a result. After the announcement of the Agrarian Reform Law, several landholding groups announced their opposition to Castro, and Antonio de Varona undertook to rally the conservatives to "roll back" the revolution. In June counter-revolutionary activities began. Bombs were exploded in a number of areas, and the president of the Tobacco Growers Association was arrested for attempting to smuggle Batista supporters out of the country.

The revolutionary government had inherited an economic recession, a depleted treasury, and a $50-million budget deficit from the last six months of 1958. The peso had been tumbling in value; by February it had depreciated from one dollar to thirty cents. The world price of sugar was declining; by June it had reached the lowest level since 1941. Cuba's balance of payments deficit, which had been running about $100 million per year, was expected to double. The United States government was demanding prompt and adequate compensation for any expropriated property belonging to Americans. Foreign capital investment declined about $25 million during the first half of 1959, and receipts from the tourist trade decreased by approximately the same

[34] Much of the specific information in this section is derived from the *Hispanic American Report* (Stanford University), and from MacGaffey and Barnett, *op. cit.*, Chaps. 14-17.

amount. Despite the increase in public projects, unemployment was rapidly rising and pressures were building up for additional government activity. The Cane Planters Association asked the government to take over forty-three sugar mills and also the function of supplying credit to the small mills.

In July 1959 the revolution came to a turning point. A writer for *Fortune* Magazine said at the time that Castro had only three choices open to him: reverse the revolution and return to "orthodox" economics; face a counterrevolution; or turn to Communism.[35] This dramatic statement was vastly oversimplified. But it echoed the sentiments of many upper-class Cubans, who, like their predecessors in earlier revolutions, declared in effect that there could be no basic social revolution within the framework of the free enterprise system. This either-or attitude also played directly into the hands of the most radical participants of the revolution, like Che Guevara, who had from the beginning been advocating and preparing for a sharp turn to the left. The revolution could go in only one of two directions—forward or backward. With its hard-core leadership committed to basic changes, the inevitable decision was to move to the left. As has so often happened in similar situations, the moderates had no place to go.

Castro had been cultivating a vague kind of mass movement up to this point, apparently without any definite plans or ideological framework outside the nebulous revolutionary "mystique." The old army had been disbanded, but otherwise the pre-1959 power structure of Cuba was generally intact. During the latter part of 1959, however, it seems that he made the decision to build a single-group society in Cuba, based on a general Marxist pattern; to establish a unified elite; to curtail social diversity; and to create a unified mass movement that would, through imposition of a national discipline, produce the cooperative effort needed for a socioeconomic development.[36] His own explanation was given in a well-known interview with Lisa Howard, in which he said: "What contributed most to my change was the revolution itself— the experience we gathered during the revolution itself." Castro had studied the abortive revolution of 1933, and there is reason to believe

[35] Freeman Lincoln, "What Has Happened to Cuban Business?," *Fortune*, LX, 3 (Sept. 1959), 110-12.
[36] Raymond Aron, "Social Structure and the Ruling Class," *British Journal of Sociology*, I, 1 (June 1950), 132-35.

that he thought *that* revolution was destroyed because it failed to do the things he was now planning. Mass support for Castro as the symbol of hope already existed. Prior to 1959 this support was generally concentrated in student groups and in *guajiros* in Oriente Province, but this base was rapidly broadened, especially among rural laborers, urban slum dwellers, and Negroes. All these groups were heavily represented in the Rebel Army and in the civilian militias organized during the latter part of 1959. Many Cubans in these groups had developed a religious loyalty to Castro as the messianic symbol of their hopes and expectations. As one woman living in the slums of Havana expressed it: "Fidel is my God, my soul, the light of my life. . . . But for Fidel we would still be living like pigs, without hope."[37] Such faith provided the motive power for the radicalization of the revolution.

In spite of the distinct move to the left during 1959, the future pattern of the revolution was still not definitely fixed. It was clear that it would be radical and authoritarian, but the ideological framework and the exact nature of the authoritarianism were still to be developed. The way they developed in 1960-62 was in part conditioned by internal and external pressures. As disaffected groups turned to counterrevolution and terrorism, repression and police state activities increased. The "reign of terror" phase began with the revival of the revolutionary tribunals in late October 1959 and continued until mid-1962. The Dominican Republic instigated an attack on Cuba in August 1959, including an attempt to kill Castro. Hypersensitive to criticism, the Cubans, steeped in the revolutionary "myth," were inclined to look for "devils." The anti-Americanism of these intense nationalists became more vocal —a development nurtured not only by attacks on the revolution in the American press and Congress but also by the "watch and wait" policy of the Eisenhower administration. Castro was not willing to ask for aid, which he believed would be tied to relatively "orthodox" economic policies, and his hypersensitive nationalism was offended by the lecture administered to him in April 1959 by two U.S. senators and by the fact that he as Prime Minister was interrogated by a congressional committee.[38] Mutual suspicion produced a pattern of spiraling reciprocal antagonism between Cuba and the United States. The power

[37] Franco, *op. cit.*, pp. 69-70.
[38] Javier Pazos, "Cuba: Was a Deal Possible in '59?," *The New Republic* (Jan. 12, 1963), pp. 10-11.

conflict of the cold war was drawn in as Castro began to look for out-side support. This led to more opposition from the United States, which in turn helped to put the Cuban revolution in closer relations with the Soviet Union during 1960. Like other revolutions, the Cuban revolution became increasingly involved in preexisting power conflicts, and this involvement, polarizing feelings on both sides, affected the future course of the revolution.

During 1960 Castro began to elevate the Communists to more pow-erful positions. The Cuban Communist party had played no part in aid to Castro in the beginning of his revolution; it had indeed dismissed him as a bourgeois reformer. But in late 1958 he had accepted their support, and in 1959 he had generally protected them on the grounds that loyalty to the revolution and unity were the two chief needs of Cuba. The Communists were forced to make a decision during 1959. Would they support Castro and accept a movement they did not con-trol, or would they push an independent policy? Those who were in favor of the latter were attacked by Castro on several occasions for act-ing as a divisive force. By mid-1959 the party leaders had decided to work with Castro, and they were subsequently rewarded for this sup-port.[39] Castro's obsession with unity and loyalty to the revolution and himself is a key to understanding not only why the Communists gained in influence but also why some in the revolution who denounced Com-munism were themselves denounced by Castro for creating dissensions in the revolution. The Communists in turn were reminded of this in 1961 and early 1962, after some party members had pushed for domi-nant power in the new Integrated Revolutionary Organization (ORI). In March 1962 Castro publicly flayed the party for these tactics, and he forced Aníbal Escalante, the most active offender, into exile.

The Communists contributed not only their support and organiza-tional structure but also a packaged ideology for the reorganization of society along the lines of a single class. This helped to fill a kind of ideological and structural vacuum in the revolutionary movement and to provide a philosophical grounding for Castro's own search for identi-ty. His pre-1959 thought seems to have been a muddled and compli-

[39] Max Frankel, "Cuba's Reds Are Confident Castro Is on Their Side," *New York Times*, Nov. 27, 1960. See also Popular Socialist Party of Cuba, *The Cuban Revo-lution* (New Century Publishers, 1961), pp. 26, 38-39; Fidel Castro's speech of Dec. 2, 1961.

cated mixture of Martí, Marx, Rousseau, and St. Thomas Aquinas. In spite of his later professed adherence to Marxism-Leninism, the influence of other philosophers and political thinkers is evident. Ideals of racial equality, the either-or moral choices imposed by a secular religion, and the messianic drive to "liberate" Latin America stem more from Martí than from any other source. This mixture has been well described by C. A. M. Hennessy:

> Revolutions are sustained by utopian visions; without these they are but rebellions. The visions may be those of nationalist mythologies or socialist ideologies. It is the unusual interweaving of such threads which has given Castro's Revolution its unique texture.[40]

By the end of 1960 most foreign property had been expropriated, and the process of reorganizing the economic system was under way. The years between 1961 and 1963 in Cuba were dominated, in the world's eye, by her involvement in foreign affairs—the Bay of Pigs invasion, Castro's efforts to export the revolution to Latin America and particularly to unseat the Betancourt government in Venezuela, and the worldwide nightmare of the missile crisis. On the domestic side, the Castro regime during those years was striving to establish a new social order in Cuba and to maintain national enthusiasm for the revolution in the face of numerous obstacles. The economic results were mixed, ranging from sharp declines in certain areas of production to marked increases in others and the development of new industries. Serious economic problems arose out of the interrelated combination of such factors as blundering planning, doctrinaire utopianism, administrative inexperience, insufficiency of trained manpower, several years of drought, the hurricanes of 1963 and 1964, the two-way embargo on trade imposed by the United States (including the closing of the U.S. market to Cuban sugar), and the almost complete disruption of traditional patterns of trade and investment. All these factors must also be viewed in the context of an extremely rapid transition from a private enterprise to a state-controlled economic system, with all the related problems of establishing different social incentives and a new set of economic values. Massive aid from the Soviet Union has enabled Cuba to avoid both economic collapse and extreme privation, but it is still an open question whether the morale of the Cuban people can be sustained for an

[40] Hennessy, *op. cit.*, p. 359

indefinite period of economic difficulty, social discipline, and political regimentation.

THE REVOLUTION APPEARED to have reached the leveling-off stage by 1963. It was still characterized by some fanaticism, but under pressure of economic realities the emphasis had begun to shift from complete change to a limited willingness to accept certain features of the pre-1959 social and economic order. The pattern of industrialization has been shifted from heavy industry toward production of consumer goods and toward the utilization of waste products of sugar. In line with this trend, the regime is again emphasizing the importance of Cuba's sugar production and stressing the need for more sugar to pay for imports. In August 1963, Castro announced that sugar and cattle would be the foundation for economic development during the next decade. The Cubans also began to try to strengthen their trade and other connections with non-Communist nations (except the United States). During 1963, some 700 Chilean technicians were at work in Cuba—many of them in positions of authority. Cuba has not completely broken with the past. She may even be trying to establish a broader base of relations with the world at large.[41]

Land expropriation has been halted, and restrictions on small farmers have been moderated. In 1963 private producers were still growing 60 percent of the island's sugar, and Castro told the small farmers' national convention that they could expect to produce between 30 and 40 percent in the future. The tradition of independent farming is still strong among these Cubans, and some have turned against the revolution because of its earlier policies. Those who had little or no land are more satisfied with the state farm arrangement, since this fits the older pattern of the *latifundio* except insofar as their economic status has been improved. In a real sense sugar production was highly collectivized prior to the revolution, and the government has preserved the *latifundios* rather than create *minifundios,* which have reduced agricultural production in other countries.

Other influences of the Cuban past can be seen in the trend back to   a regular army; in the great emphasis placed on cultural projects, such as

    [41] James O'Connor, "Cuba: Salvation through Sugar," *The Nation* (Oct. 12, 1963), pp. 212-14, 226-27; *Hispanic American Report,* XVI, 9 (Nov. 1963), 866; Claudio Veliz, "The New Cuban Industrial Policy," *The World Today,* 19 (Sept. 1963), 371-74.

the new fine arts center in Havana and ballet instruction for rural youth; and in the continuing spontaneity and organizational flexibility of Cuban society (a feature quite frustrating to Russian advisers). The historian's profession is not the prophet's. And yet one is tempted to try to guess about tomorrow on the basis of what is known of the past and present. If we were to assume that the Castro regime is not engulfed by some cataclysmic international development, and assume further that Castro himself is not brought down in some way that produces governmental chaos, what, if anything, can be descried on the horizon for the domestic life of the long-troubled island of Cuba?

Communism in Cuba has been modified from its models elsewhere. Within the framework of loyalty to the revolution, Castro has introduced minor democratizing elements, and some diversity of opinion is allowed. Leaders in the government attend church, catechism classes are held, and newspapers print sections of religious news and even criticize the government. Graham Greene reported in 1963 that "here in Cuba it is possible to conceive a first breach in Marxist philosophy (not in Marxist economics)," and he ventured the opinion, "This is a new voice in the Communist world."[42] Castro's emotional defense of José Martí and of the political testament of José Antonio Echeverría is indicative of his desire to maintain some diversity of thought. This was also illustrated by the press debate between Castro and the Communist leader Blas Roca over the showing of the Italian movie "La Dolce Vita." Blas Roca lost, and the Cubans have been able to see not only that movie but also a variety of other major European films. According to Castro, one does not have to be a Communist to be a good revolutionary—a heresy that the old-line Communists in Cuba have had to accept. Rigid Russian-style Communism, with its disregard for personal existence, is not at home in the Cuban culture, and it is unlikely that it ever will be.

Over time, revolutionary enthusiasm will subside, doctrines will be modified, and administrative practices will be changed. External opposition will probably impede these developments. But on the assumptions taken here, it is likely that many of the changes produced by the revolution will characterize the Cuba of the future. The large sugar

[42] Graham Greene, "Return to Cuba: The Revolution Is Still Alive," *The New Republic* (Nov. 2, 1963), pp. 16-18; Henri Cartier-Bresson, "An Island of Pleasure Gone Adrift," *Life* (March 15, 1963), p. 42; Donald Grant, "Cuba is Evolving Her Own Ideology," *New York Times,* Aug. 2, 1963.

68   ROBERT F. SMITH

plantations and cattle ranches will probably never be returned to purely private ownership. The era of the old sugar companies is over, and
some form of nationally controlled enterprise will continue to adminis-
ter their former holdings. Cooperatives of various kinds will also be utilized in other areas of agriculture. Diversified agricultural production,
especially aimed at making Cuba relatively self-sufficient in foodstuffs,
will continue to be stressed. If private foreign capital returns to the
country (as has happened in postrevolutionary Mexico), it will be in the
industrial sector.

In the future it would be difficult for any administration to restore
the former imbalance between town and country, and rural inhabitants
will demand their share of social services. Public education for all has
been firmly established in the minds of all as a right, and the populace
is sure to demand that the state have a role in health care, recreation,
and cultural affairs. It is reasonable to expect a greater degree of citizen participation in every area of Cuban society. The Cuba of the
future will probably have some kind of mass political party with a
political mystique and some form of ideological direction.[43]

The masses of Cuba have been irrevocably influenced by the revolution, and all future governments will have to deal with that historical
fact. As to this, we need no limiting assumptions. It will never again be
1959 in Cuba.

[43] One of the best sources for speculation concerning the future of Cuba is Seers
et al., op. cit.

TAD SZULC, from 1955 to 1965 Latin American correspondent of the *New York Times,* is the author of several books on inter-American themes, his most recent being *Dominican Diary* (1965) and *Latin America* (1966).

Exporting the
Cuban Revolution

TAD SZULC

The Cuban Revolution of 1959 has already won its place in Latin American history as one of the most memorable milestones and greatest turning points in the march of Western Hemisphere events. The advent of the revolution led by Fidel Castro, its initial survival against all imaginable odds, and its subsequent developments have produced an extraordinary impact on all the twenty Latin American republics, sometimes directly and sometimes indirectly, and this impact will inevitably go on being felt for years to come in still unpredictable ways.

The influence of the Cuban revolution, abrupt and violent in some instances and subtle and imperceptible in others, has affected to such a degree all Latin American political, economic, social, and psychological patterns that a possible material failure of the Castro experiment in Cuba or even the regime's sudden disappearance would not be likely to erase it altogether.

In objective and clearly defined historical terms, the obvious by-products of the Cuban revolution were the establishment of the first Marxist-Leninist (that is, Communist) system in the Western Hemisphere, the Soviet attempt at installing on the island its offensive-missiles launching pads, and the consequent world crisis of October 1962. It is likewise apparent that the Cuban missiles crisis has played a major

69

role in exacerbating the Soviet-Chinese feud, while at the same time leading to a détente of sorts between Moscow and the West.

But though all these events resulting indirectly from the Cuban revolution may, in time, be absorbed into the mainstream of world history and perhaps even diminished in the overall perspective of the cold war, it seems certain that the Cuban revolutionary influence will remain forever deeply embedded in the fabric of Latin American political life.

With nearly six years of perspective on Cuba's revolution and its reverberations from the Rio Grande to Tierra del Fuego, it may now be possible to begin assessing the nature of this revolutionary impact on every conceivable level in Latin America and, perhaps, to try to see it in its true interrelations.

A few very broad generalizations may be in order at this point. The first one is that the Cuban revolution has irrevocably altered the relationships between Latin America and the United States—both in terms of the new Latin American posture and attitudes toward the Colossus of the North and in terms of the United States response to them through such new philosophies as the Alliance for Progress.

This is so, essentially, because the Cuban revolution has either awakened or helped to articulate the long-latent sense of Latin American nationalism, in which a degree of defiance of the United States was always implicit, and because, even more importantly, it has given form to the Latin American aspirations for economic and social reform and improvement.

The second broad conclusion is that the impact of the Cuban revolution on Latin America is not measurable necessarily by Havana's ability to "export" its brand of revolution elsewhere in the hemisphere—an endeavor in which Premier Castro has been notably unsuccessful. It is, rather, measurable by the psychological and intellectual effects that have been and still are being generated everywhere.

Thus, despite manifold efforts by the Castro regime in that direction —most spectacularly so in Venezuela in 1962 and 1963—it has not been possible for Cuba to export her revolution anywhere or to force direct imitations of her experiment in any of the Latin American republics. It was the profound differences in the character and temperament of the Latin American countries and the varying nature of their problems and pressures that made these efforts fail. It might also be argued that, unfortunately for Cuba but fortunately for Latin America, no other revolutionary leader has emerged in the hemisphere to compare even in a small measure with Fidel Castro in respect of personality, drive, and charisma. Therefore no other Latin American country has followed Cuba's lead, and Castro's ambitious visions of a Cuban banner at the head of a continental revolution have gone unfulfilled.

In the space of less than one year, between late 1963 and September 1964, Castro suffered major defeats in Venezuela, Panama, Brazil, and Chile, which may well have marked the end of his direct influence in Latin America. The overwhelming defeat of Salvador Allende in the Chilean presidential elections, coming after the failure of the extreme leftist revolutionary effort in Venezuela, provided the convincing test that an important Latin American electorate was not prepared to choose freely the extreme leftist solutions for its basic problems, but preferred the more moderate "Democratic left" approach.

Broadly speaking, these defeats for the leftist revolutionary causes, as typified by Castro, seemed to stem from two sets of converging situations. One was that Castro could not export his revolution, through upheaval or election, because favorable conditions for it clearly did not exist in any of the Latin American countries. The other was that, notwithstanding all the economic and social pressures that in theory might have favored revolutions, the prophylactic effect of the measures undertaken under the general concept of the Alliance for Progress has acted as a major deterrent against the revolutionary trend. It might also be argued that the attachment to highly operative democratic political systems in countries like Venezuela and Chile played its part against the acceptance of extremisms. And, finally, the increasingly visible failure of the Havana regime to turn the Cuban revolution into an economic and social success, despite considerable Soviet-bloc assistance, loomed as an additional factor in this Latin American refusal to tolerate imitations of the Castro experimentation.

It would be an error, however, to assume that the reaction that has set in against the Cuban revolution in Latin America—through the good works of the Alliance for Progress, the resilience of democracy, and a string of military coups d'état carried out in the name of anti-Communism and anti-Fidelismo—has written finis to long-range revolutionary influences.

The Brazilian civilian-military revolution of April 1, 1964, has certainly prevented the sliding of Latin America's biggest country into the chaotic leftist-nationalist regime that the ousted President João Goulart had been striving to establish. The military coups in the Dominican Republic and Honduras in the latter part of 1963, and the earlier army interventions in Guatemala and Ecuador, were also designed to remove far-leftist and direct Fidelista influences. But in each case the new regimes must now take into account the fact that their drastic actions will provide no solution to their countries' underlying economic and social problems unless they promptly engage in meaningful reform and development programs.

While the revolutionary trends in Brazil and elsewhere had their real roots in purely local situations—with certain demographic, economic, and social pressures serving as their common denominator—it is unquestionable that the example of the Cuban social revolution promoted and discouraged these situations. Though quite obviously it was not the direct influence of Cuban agents, money, or arms that pushed Goulart and his associates to the brink of establishing a quasi-revolutionary state in Brazil, the psychological and intellectual influence of the Cuban revolution in this process was unmistakable, even though transmuted into purely Brazilian terms.

Regardless of present trends and the state of affairs in countries like Brazil and the Dominican Republic, the revolutionary—or the intellectual and inspirational—impact of the Cuban experiment is bound to continue. If the new rulers in these republics do not respond to this challenge, they may well be faced before too long with a new ferment, a neo-Fidelismo of some sort, which they may fight either with growing repression or with resort to a *Criollo* version of Nasserism, a military-directed experimentation with socialism. The first course would unavoidably threaten to create profound revolutionary situations that Communists might succeed in exploiting for their own ends, particularly in the light of the growing strength of pro-Peking factions in the Latin American Communist parties and among their Trotskyite and other allies. The second course, just as inevitably, would confirm Premier Castro's oft-repeated contention that real social and economic reform is impossible under democratic representative systems, and no greater ideological blow to the cause of Western democracy can presently be imagined.

Precisely for these reasons, the rebuff of the Castro-type extremisms in Venezuela and Chile carries a vast ideological significance in the context of larger hemispheric trends. At the same time, the burden of continuously proving the advantages of the democratic system now reposes on Venezuela's President Raúl Leoni, on Chile's President Eduardo Frei Montalva, and on other democratically elected Latin American leaders, like Peru's Fernando Belaúnde Terry. In historical terms, the credit of confidence given the democratic system by these nations may be withdrawn if the system fails to live up to it.

LATIN AMERICA'S DESIRE for economic and social reforms and its penchant for exaggerated nationalism have existed to a greater or lesser extent throughout its modern history. They assumed a recognizable shape with the Mexican revolution of 1910; the 1930 Brazilian revolution of Getúlio Vargas; the birth in the 1930's and 1940's of socially-oriented political parties like Peru's APRA (Alianza Popular Revolucionaria Americana) and Venezuela's Acción Democrática; the rambling *Justicialismo* of Juan D. Perón in Argentina in the 1940's and 1950's; the Bolivian revolution of 1952; and the Guatemalan revolution of 1953-54. All these events and efforts, however, were localized in their countries of origin, although the APRA once dreamed of spreading throughout Latin America, and General Perón made halfhearted and clumsy attempts to export his *Justicialismo*.

It took the scope, the radicalism, and the mystique of the Cuban revolution to act as a catalyst for the pent-up emotions, aspirations, and desires of the Latin American peoples. The Castro revolution has had a vast inspirational influence on Latin America because its seeds fell on fertile ground at the right psychological and historical moment. It was a case of history's own superb sense of timing. Where the Mexican and Bolivian revolutions—this century's only two full-fledged Latin American social revolutions before Cuba's—never left the confines of their mother countries, even inspirationally, the Cuban revolution instantly hit upon responsive chords throughout the breadth and length of the vast region. Its thrust went to the very core of Latin America's anxieties, confusions, and frustrations.

The reasons for this reaction were many, and they still lie at the heart of the Latin American problem. The reaction explains the ouster of Juan Bosch in the Dominican Republic and of João Goulart in Brazil—at best only transitional phases in the broad context of the mid-century Latin American revolution. It also explains the Chilean presidential election of September 1964, which was fought between two left-of-center candidates, one representing the Christian Democratic strategy of democratic evolutionary reform, and the other the Communist-Socialist Frente de Acción Popular (FRAP) coalition preaching advanced radicalism. The right and the right-center were simply eliminated from the picture.

The chief reason for this volatile Latin American reaction to the Cuban revolution lay in the economic and social situation in Latin America in the postwar years. The high rate of population growth, nearing a 3.5 percent annual average for the region, was not accompanied by a commensurate increase in farm and industrial production, in jobs, in social services, and, therefore, in living standards. With Latin America's farm production running at a lower per capita rate in 1959 (the year of Castro's victory in Cuba) than in 1938, fundamental distortion in the hemispheric economic structures was obvious. In the great majority of cases, postwar capital investments were concentrated in specialized sectors, such as steel and the automotive industry, or in inflation-hedging areas, such as real estate and urban building construction. The economies were thus being built, or hammered together, on dangerously narrow foundations, without allowing for an equitable distribution of national wealth and revenue to the population as a whole. In the absence of rational economic planning (it took the Alliance for Progress two years after the advent of the Cuban revolution to make the central planning concept acceptable), Latin America went on developing without a coherent sense of priorities, in the wildest and most incongruous way imaginable. Islands of urban prosperity, often based on inflationary speculation, emerged around the industrial centers of São Paulo, Mexico City, and Buenos Aires, but the sea around them was one of underdevelopment and misery.

Rural misery, stemming from the crowding by multiplying populations in dwarf farm holdings (minifundios) and their inability to produce adequately on the vast latifundios, pushed millions into migrating to the cities. There the new arrivals became slum dwellers, usually unemployed or, if they were lucky, just underemployed. The lack of jobs to absorb the migrants, the dire shortage of housing and related facilities, and the inflation which in most places destroyed the value of the meager income of these urban populations—all these factors created slum cultures and brought with them tremendous social pressures that inevitably became translated into leftist political trends. To be sure, the professional politicians wasted no time in turning this state of affairs to their own electoral benefit. They aroused hungry desires, made exciting promises, and rarely fulfilled them. This was the story of Perón in Argentina; of Vargas' second period in Brazil and later of Goulart; of Velasco Ibarra in Ecuador; and of others. It was the beginning of the modern Latin American wave of Populisms.

Superimposed on these real and desperately urgent needs of the populations was the nationalistic and intellectual ferment developing among the educated and articulate minorities. The nationalism, of course, was not new; its usual expression was found in efforts to eliminate foreign, and particularly United States, economic and political influences. The surging force of nationalism was evident in the Mexican oil expropriations in 1938, in Vargas' Brazilian "New State" in 1937, in the 1954 establishment of the Brazilian state oil monopoly, in Argentina's Peronismo in the late 1940's, in Bolivia's nationalization of her oil fields and tin mines in the 1950's, and in other examples around the hemisphere.

Reinforcing these political moves, there always loomed a sense of resentment in Latin America against United States economic power over societies that were primarily producers of raw materials. And the United States military interventions in Mexico, Central America, and the Caribbean in the 1910's and 1920's (sometimes curiously carried out in the name of the Wilsonian concept of democracy) had never quite vanished from Latin American memories. Cubans remembered the Platt Amendment to their constitution, vesting in the United States the right to intervene in their internal affairs. Nicaraguans and Dominicans remembered how the Marine occupations led to the emergence of the dictatorial Somoza and Trujillo dynasties in their respective countries. Colombians and Panamanians remembered the Washington-fomented revolution that artificially created Panama so that the interoceanic canal could be built and controlled by the United States. So, when the pro-Communist Arbenz regime in Guatemala was overthrown in 1954, with fairly visible United States aid, the cry of "intervention" again echoed across Latin America, and it was destined to plague the United States for years—before and after the explosion of the Cuban revolution.

As Latin America in the 1950's was thus going through the new phase

of economic and social protest accelerated by worsening situations everywhere, and as the nationalistic and intellectual ferment was mounting in a changing world, another dimension was added to the gathering
crisis by the spread of antidictatorial revolutions throughout South
America. Between 1955 and 1958 political dictatorships were forced out
in Argentina, Peru, Colombia, and Venezuela. And when Castro engaged the dictator Fulgencio Batista in Cuba, Latin America looked on
this event as the approaching climax of the liberating process.

When Fidel Castro finally triumphed on January 1, 1959, and proclaimed his social revolution on the ruins of the destroyed Batista dictatorship, every element was in place to make the Cuban experience an
immensely attractive phenomenon—if not an example to emulate—in
the eyes of millions of Latin Americans.

There was, above all, the intriguing and heroic figure of Fidel Castro
himself, the first authentic hero personality that Latin America had
known in generations. His bearded appearance, his flamboyance, his
fiery rhetoric, and the sense of excitement he generated, could not fail
to evoke a wave of admiring emotionalism throughout Latin America.
Castro's accent on nationalism à outrance, his growing defiance of the
United States, his proclamation of agrarian reform five months after
winning power, and the whole aura of mystique surrounding the
Cuban revolution, immediately and inevitably had an impact that still
reverberates around Latin America.

WITH ALL THE ATTENTION AND POPULARITY he suddenly com-
manded in Latin America, Castro wasted no time in turning toward
what subsequently became known in popular parlance as "exporting
the Cuban revolution." The term itself was a misnomer, as well as a
fundamental error in judgment on Castro's part. Events in Latin
America since 1959 have demonstrated that the revolution could not
be exported as such; its counterpart could occur only where and when
local conditions made it plausible and possible. It would therefore
be more accurate to say that Castro sought to *promote* revolutions
elsewhere in Latin America, first attempting to take advantage of
certain explosive situations already existing in several countries, and,
second, seeking to bring about advantageous revolutionary conditions.
These were the two main phases of Castro's efforts at exporting revo-

lutions. While they stemmed from distinct tactical motivations, they shared a common strategic denominator.

This common denominator was Castro's awareness from the very outset that his radical social revolution—and his deliberate defiance of the United States, which was an inherent part of the Cuban revolutionary dynamics—needed to become a *Latin American revolution* of the same brand if it were to survive, or at least not to become hemmed in and isolated. Castro evidently had enough foresight to realize that if revolutionary Cuba were to be surrounded by hostile powers ranging from the United States to the South American continent, his battle for survival would be at best a hectic uphill struggle—and more likely an ultimate failure.

Castro therefore aimed his efforts at creating or encouraging revolutions wherever possible in Latin America, while at the same time playing on deep initial sympathies for his own revolutionary experiment in securing political protection against mounting United States pressures.

Castro's first foreign foray was his visit to Caracas, Venezuela, a few weeks after capturing power in Cuba. Reliable accounts say that he immediately suggested to Venezuelan President Rómulo Betancourt, who had been inaugurated a short time before Castro's arrival, that they unite in a campaign against "Yankee Imperialism." The Cuban Premier's reasoning was simple: Venezuela, like Cuba, had recently been liberated from a dictatorship (General Pérez Jiménez had been ousted in the January, 1958, revolution); she had a social problem that was even worse than Cuba's; and, like Cuba, she presumably had reasons to resent the United States, among them United States dominance of much of the Venezuelan oil industry. Therefore, Castro reasoned, Venezuela might be persuaded to join Cuba in an anti-American revolutionary campaign. How important Venezuela's oil resources and her strategic position on the shoulder of South America were to Castro's broad, even global, aims, he was to demonstrate again four years later.

Despite his tumultuously joyful reception in Caracas, however, Castro was promptly given to understand that his rather naïve and overassuming approach was not acceptable to the Venezuelans. Betancourt, himself an old revolutionary, intended to solve his country's problems along the path of democratic social reform—"evolution and not revolution," he called it—and he made it clear to Castro that he had no intention of joining with him in any Havana-conceived adventures. But he did tell friends that if the Cuban leader had sought election in Venezuela at that time "he could beat any of us." As it was, Castro never forgave Betancourt for the rebuke, and as time went on the Venezuelan president—Castro's chief Latin American rival in the field of social improvement—became the favorite target for Havana's most outrageous vilifications.

Back in Havana, Castro embarked upon a series of different efforts to expand his influence in Latin America in this first phase of revolutionary export. In fact, these efforts came the closest to the notion of exporting revolutions, though in concept and execution they were as naïve as his political performance in Caracas.

This was the program for overthrowing the remaining right-wing dictatorships in the Caribbean and Central America and, apparently, for setting up new regimes that would be politically attuned to Havana's revolutionary thinking. If it had worked, Castro would have had under his control the entire and immensely strategic Caribbean region. In those days, the antidictatorial cause was vastly popular in Latin America. Castro's overthrow of Batista was the latest triumph in the string of political (and seemingly democratic) revolutions that had begun in 1955 with Perón's fall, and hemispheric public opinion was now awaiting the demise of the Trujillos in the Dominican Republic and of the Somozas in Nicaragua. Castro was still regarded as a champion of democratic and antidictatorial causes and of highly attractive social reform ideas (this was before he shut the doors on the promises for Cuban elections and long before it occurred to most people that Communism would penetrate his revolution). There was considerable enthusiasm for finishing off the dictators, once and for all.

Havana, in those starry-eyed days of early 1959, was full of exiles from the Dominican Republic, Nicaragua, Guatemala, and elsewhere—all of them willing and ready to do their bit for freedom at home—and Castro had no difficulties in recruiting manpower for his planned expeditions. Yet the first one he set on its way was *not* directed against a dictatorship, nor was it made up of bona fide political exiles. Instead, it was an assault on Panama, which may not have been suffering under a tyrant but which did possess the enormous strategic prize that is the

Panama Canal. Here Castro allied himself with Tito Arias, the Panamanian Ambassador to Britain, and a collection of bizarre characters, some of whom had backgrounds going back to the 1954 assassination of Panama's President Remón. Arias' interest was to seize power, and Castro's interest was to assist him in it, in order to create a political debt that he could later collect. In any event, the expedition was armed, equipped, and organized by the Castro regime and led by a Castro Army officer. It included more Cubans than Panamanians among the 100-odd men who landed or tried to land in Panama. The local authorities smashed the "invasion" within a few hours.

The Panama attack coincided with Castro's first and only visit to the United States after becoming Premier, which was followed by his trip to Buenos Aires to represent Cuba at the inter-American economic conference, where he blandly proposed that the United States give Latin America $30 billion in ten years for development. Not surprisingly, Castro won all the headlines at the conference. He went on to proselytize crowds in Uruguay after the Argentine authorities barred him from holding street rallies in Buenos Aires. These early assaults on Latin America were the political aspect of Castro's effort to build up his image—an image of the new emancipator of Latin American countries.

In June, shortly after Castro had gone home, he sent out an expedition to the Dominican Republic in an attempt to oust Trujillo. Here Castro could use legitimate Dominican exiles who had been trained in Cuba by his Rebel Army officers in guerrilla tactics. His idea had been to drop in the Dominican Republic a guerrilla force to establish itself in the mountains, as he had done in Sierra Maestra, while another group was to land on the northern coast. A planeload of rebels landed at Constanza, while two launches tried to disembark raiders near Puerto Plata. But the scheme failed because the population, terrorized by thirty years of the Trujillo dictatorship, did not rally to the invaders' aid. In fact, peasants helped the Trujillo troops flush out the would-be liberators, and the whole episode ended in a matter of days.

In the ensuing weeks and months, Castro attempted to land exiles in Nicaragua, Guatemala, and Haiti, but these tiny expeditions never produced results, not even a flurry of major excitement. In August 1959, the American Foreign Ministers met at Santiago, Chile, to discuss the problem of how democracy could be encouraged in Latin America. (The use of the military expeditions that Castro had been advocating

and supporting in the Caribbean was not on the agenda.) The outcome
was that the Pan American doctrine of nonintervention was reaffirmed.
In this instance, the dictatorships benefited, but it was not long before
Castro began claiming the protection of the doctrine for himself, while
at the same time engaging in acts of his own that neatly fitted into the
category of intervening in the affairs of others.

The Santiago conference marked, in a sense, the end of Castro's first
phase of exporting revolutions. It had become clear to him that these
rather blatant and amateurish attempts could not succeed; if anything,
they contributed to tarnishing the image of the Cuban revolution
among Latin Americans, so long and deeply committed to the doctrine
of nonintervention. A new approach had to be devised, and by 1960
Castro was able to set it in motion.

THE SECOND PHASE IN CASTRO'S POLICY of exporting, or encouraging, revolutions of the Cuban type was a much more sophisticated
operation, concentrating on political, propagandist, and psychological
techniques. It aimed at all of Latin America, not only at the Caribbean.
In the words of Major Ernesto (Che) Guevara, Cuba's leading guerrilla
ideologist, its objective was to turn the Andes "into Sierra Maestra's."
In its essential outlines, this phase is still continuing, despite grave
reverses for the Castro cause, such as the failure of the 1962-63 guerrilla
and terrorism campaigns in Venezuela, the overthrow of President
Goulart in Brazil in April 1964, and the Allende defeat in the Chilean
elections of September 4, 1964.

In developing the new approach, Castro operated on two main premises. One was the broad concept that economic and social underdevelopment are a breeding ground for armed insurgency. The other was his
belief that resentment against the United States and the local "oligar-
chies" was so strong in the Latin American republics that all the latent
nationalism and pressure for reform could be transmuted into revolutionary movements. A vital by-product of this effort was to be the creation of such a climate of sympathy for the Cuban cause among the
Latin American masses that few governments would dare to embark on
anti-Cuban actions without risking grievous internal troubles.

Castro's decision to move ahead with his propaganda-and-subversion
campaign coincided with his resolve sometime in the spring of 1960 to
lead his revolution toward Marxism-Leninism, to declare the United

States his official enemy, and to become aligned with the Communist world. If a specific time can be set down to signify the start in earnest of this campaign, it may well have been the Latin American tour in May by Cuban President Osvaldo Dorticós Torrado, during which the slogan "*Cuba sí, Yanqui no!*" was first heard. Simultaneously, the Castro regime began investing heavily in the mounting of a modern propaganda apparatus to support the campaign. Powerful short-wave radio transmitting equipment was purchased in Switzerland and elsewhere to make the voice of Havana heard throughout the world in a dozen languages, but mainly in Latin America in Spanish, Portuguese, French, Creole, and English. Subsequently, broadcasts in the Indian Quechua and Guarani dialects were added to Havana's radio output.

About the same time, Prensa Latina was organized as the regime's news agency, designed to distribute Cuban and other Latin American news everywhere in Latin America. Though virtually no Latin American newspaper ever used any of Prensa Latina's copy, the agency maintained large staffs of correspondents wherever they were permitted to operate and ran up immense cable tolls for the dispatch of thousands of words daily to Havana from the Latin American capitals. Almost automatically, Prensa Latina became a news- and intelligence-gathering organization for the Havana regime.

Cuban embassies and consulates in Latin America were turned into centers of revolutionary propaganda, if not of direct subversion. The involvement of Cuban diplomats, most of them young, inexperienced, and brash, in the domestic politics of the countries to which they were assigned became so great that government after government started to declare ambassadors, chargés d'affaires, and attachés to be *personae non gratae*. Even as friendly a government as Bolivia expelled the Cuban chargé in 1962 when it discovered that he was actively involved in an abortive plot to turn Bolivia into a "Socialist Republic." Brazil, likewise friendly to Cuba, regularly seized masses of Cuban propaganda arriving in diplomatic pouches. Mexico, which would not go along with any international moves to punish Cuba, was extremely severe with Cuban attempts to send propaganda or agents into its territory. In Panama, the young Cuban ambassador worked in depth to the extent of contributing his fine baritone voice to Sunday Masses at churches in the backwoods of the country and providing money to repaint churches. The embassies also busied themselves organizing local "Cuban

Friendship Associations" to act as political propaganda and proselytiz-
ing groups among students, workers, and intellectuals.

On July 26, 1960, the seventh anniversary of the foundation of Castro's revolutionary movement, the Havana regime launched the First
Latin American Youth Congress, to which hundreds of Latin American
students were invited, their expenses being paid by the Cuban government. After the Congress, large numbers of the visitors stayed behind
for several months in what was the beginning of the subversive training
program. The young Latin Americans were ostensibly taught farm and
other techniques fitting into the revolutionary program, but the instruction also gradually turned to Marxist-Leninist indoctrination and to
training in subversion and in underground and guerrilla techniques.
The idea was that these young people would return to their countries
to become the cadres of new revolutionary movements.

At the same time Castro began encouraging Latin American politicians to visit Havana, as if it were the mecca of a new faith. Many
came: some simply because they were invited, others because they
were curious about what was really happening in Cuba, and still others
because they thought it would do them good politically among the
leftist voters at home. In 1959 the Latin American visitors to Havana
included the outstanding names of the democratic left movements. By
1960 the roster of guests read like a compilation of professional extreme
leftists. There was Mexico's ex-president Lázaro Cárdenas and the pro-
Communist labor boss Lombardo Toledano, Chile's already once defeated (1958) presidential candidate Dr. Salvador Allende, Guatemala's
ousted president Jacobo Arbenz Guzmán, and British Guiana's Chief
Minister Cheddie Jagan and his wife Janet. Brazil's Jânio Quadros, who
then ran for the presidency on a centrist platform, came to Cuba early
in 1960, on his way back from Moscow, and brought along Francisco
Julião, the leader of the Brazilian Northeasts' Peasant Leagues, who was
to become Castro's chief apologist at home.

With the exception of Quadros, Allende, and the Jagans, the vast majority of these visitors to Cuba were small fry or passé figures as far as
serious Latin American politics were concerned. In fact, as it developed
later, one of Castro's greatest weaknesses was that he could not attract
politically any of the really important political figures from Latin
America. Quadros' election did result in a strongly pro-Cuban policy on
the part of Brazil, but it was much more for domestic Brazilian reasons

than because of any real sense of identification with Cuba, even though he did award a high decoration to Major Guevara. After Quadros' abrupt resignation within seven months of his inauguration, President Goulart continued and even strengthened these pro-Cuban policies, but again it was almost entirely in terms of local politics. Allende loomed for a time as an important figure in Chilean politics, and some observers gave him a chance to be elected president in September 1964 on his second try, but he scrupulously kept away from Cuba for several years, and the Cuban question was not one of his electoral themes.

If Castro failed during these years to export his revolution to any Latin American country, the impact of his example and pressures did buy him a considerable amount of political insurance: Many governments were discouraged from joining in anti-Cuban collective action sought by the United States as Cuba was being turned into an arsenal of Soviet arms.

It was not until January 1962 that Washington succeeded at the ministerial conference at Punta del Este in obtaining from the Organization of American States a decision to "exclude" Cuba from the inter-American system on the vague grounds that her Marxism-Leninism was incompatible with the hemisphere's dedication to representative democracy. But it was tough going, against the opposition of Brazil, Chile, Argentina, Bolivia, Mexico, and Uruguay, and it took an urgent arm-twisting operation to secure the vital vote of Haiti, without which the necessary two-thirds majority could not have been marshaled.

By that time, Cuban propaganda and subversive operations had already become severely curtailed. Thirteen Latin American governments had broken diplomatic relations with Havana, expelled the Cuban embassies and Prensa Latina correspondents, and, in general, applied severe vigilance to the activities of Castro agents. The only countries to maintain diplomatic relations with Cuba were those that had opposed the "exclusion" move at Punta del Este. Two months later the military ousted President Frondizi in Argentina, and the new regime promptly broke relations with the Castro government. Brazil broke relations in May 1964, after President Goulart's overthrow.

In July 1964, an emergency ministerial conference met in Washington to consider Venezuela's charges against Havana for interference in her internal affairs following the smuggling of weapons to the pro-Communist Venezuelan guerrillas. Acting upon the report of the OAS

Special Consultative Committee on Security, which corroborated and documented the Venezuelan accusations, the conference voted to condemn Cuba for aggression. It also ordered, as a mandatory step, the breaking of diplomatic relations between the American republics and Cuba, and recommended trade sanctions.

Of the four hemisphere governments that still maintained diplomatic ties with Cuba, three quickly complied with the conference order. They were Chile, Bolivia, and Uruguay. Only Mexico refused to abide by this decision, arguing that the World Court must first issue an opinion on this point. Interestingly, the widespread predictions that in breaking with Cuba on the eve of the Chilean elections President Alessandri would help Senator Allende's cause were proved wrong. The break with Cuba, less than a month before the voting, never became a serious issue and Allende went to his defeat at the hands of Senator Frei.

One of the most difficult elements in judging Castro's Latin American campaign is to assess the extent and intensity of his operations. The reports by the OAS Special Committee and the findings of United States intelligence agencies acknowledge that there has been only one verified case of Cuban-exported weapons appearing anywhere in Latin America—namely, the shipment of three tons of arms to Venezuela late in 1963, when Castro apparently thought that he was on the verge of overthrowing the Betancourt government.

There have been recurrent cases of small-scale, and invariably unsuccessful, guerrilla outbreaks in a half-dozen countries. While in several such instances, notably in Venezuela, Ecuador, the Dominican Republic, and a few Central American countries, it was possible to establish that some of these guerrilla leaders had been trained in Cuba, there is no evidence that they had received direct arms or supplies from Havana— again except for Venezuela—and in no case did they succeed in constituting a serious threat to the established government.

One of the unanswered questions, as far as both Havana and the United States intelligence community are concerned, is what has happened to the youths that Castro had trained with such care in Cuba. Except for a few instances, it has been virtually impossible to trace their personal histories after they returned home, largely because only a tiny number of them had become active in domestic politics or pro-Cuban activities. At the peak of the Cuban training program, in 1962, an estimated 1,500 Latin Americans had traveled to Cuba for varying periods during the year, but nobody professes to know how many of them actually received guerrilla or subversive instruction, how many just went for "the ride," or how many went for political indoctrination. The tightening of the travel restrictions to Cuba by most of the Latin American countries, and the highly efficient, discreet cooperation of Mexico, had cut down the number of these trips by about one-half in 1963, and the flow was even smaller in 1964. In most cases now, Cuban agents and visiting Latin Americans must take the long and expensive route through Madrid or Prague. Until the overthrow of the Goulart regime in Brazil, a Cuban airliner made periodic flights to Rio de Janeiro carrying visiting delegations back and forth, but under the new government this route, too, was closed. The Mexicans, who still allow Cubana de Aviación to operate occasional flights to Mexico from Havana, have become so tough on travelers that United States intelligence agencies occasionally run into interference with their own operations.

As far as the financing of revolutionary or extreme leftist movements is concerned, there is precious little evidence of Cuban money finding its way into Latin America, although it is assumed that some of it has flowed to different countries. There have been several reported instances of suspected Cuban agents being caught with large amounts of currency, and the Venezuelan government had one case of a traveler being intercepted at the airport with thousands of dollars in bills hidden on his person. But whatever financing is provided from Cuba is probably conducted in the main through hard-to-trace bank drafts to dummy corporations operating under false addresses. Some intelligence agents think, in fact, that Soviet and Chinese funds flowing into Latin America—now for reasons of the Moscow-Peking rivalry—by far exceed the money coming from Cuba.

Such direct Cuban-inspired subversive activities as have been discovered in Latin America—again with the exception of Venezuela—have often tended to the pathetic rather than the dangerous. Perhaps the classical story is that of a young Peruvian student, a promising poet, who returned from Cuba by way of Brazil, then sought to enter Peru over the jungle frontier, and got himself killed in an unnecessary fray with border guards. Incomplete and unverified claims have been made that subversive documents were found in the wreckage of a Bolivian airliner that crashed in Chile early in 1963 with several Cubans aboard, and that a high-ranking Cuban delegation returning from a conference in Brazil carried a compromising dossier when their jet airliner rammed a mountainside near Lima in mid-1963.

In sum, the *available* evidence suggests that Castro's direct efforts at exporting his revolution have met with a general failure.

But the indirect, or inspirational, influence of the Cuban revolution is another matter. It has played, and is playing, a significant role in Latin American developments, particularly in the countries where local conditions potentially favor revolutionary trends.

This influence operates on several levels. The most obvious level is that of local prerevolutionary movements, usually tied to land and hunger problems. In the Brazilian Northeast, Francisco Julião and his associates were able to construct a fairly important organization through their Peasant Leagues, gradually winning the support of students and such key politicians as Miguel Arraes, governor of the state of Pernambuco until the 1964 revolution threw him out of office. Julião, who declared himself a Communist within twenty-four hours of Castro's own confession in December 1961, worked against the background of huge portraits of the Cuban Premier that hung in his office and in the Leagues' assembly halls, and actively advocated a violent land reform on the model of Cuba and China. He had, incidentally, visited Peking and Moscow more often than Havana. The Leagues' organizers often directed armed seizures of land by poor squatters in a movement that subsequently spread from the Northeast to Central Brazil and the Rio de Janeiro area. But Julião was not blessed with gifts of real leadership, let alone of charisma, and he never succeeded in becoming anything beyond a second-rate regional figure. Subsequently, he was caught in the feud between the pro-Soviet and pro-Chinese factions of the Brazilian Communist party, and, according to rumors inside the party, even Castro turned away from him when Julião reportedly misused some funds that the Cubans had made available to him.

Julião and his organization (as well as the whole extreme leftist apparatus in Brazil) were ineffectual. This was underlined in April 1964 when nobody moved a finger to defend Goulart from the civilian-military revolution that ousted him in thirty-six hours. However, the revolutionary and protest potential in Brazil, indirectly drawing its inspiration from the Cuban nationalistic and reform movements, cannot be discounted even in the light of the seeming acceptance of the April revolution. Urgent structural problems, notably the problem of land, must be solved quickly if the leftist pressures are to remain under control, and thus it was encouraging that the regime of President Humberto Castelo Branco moved in the direction of arresting Brazil's runaway inflation while simultaneously rushing through land reform legislation.

The problem of peasant land seizures, inevitably exploited and led by extreme leftists, has also been a source of grave concern to the democratic government in Peru. The rate of these rural invasions rose alarmingly after mid-1963, coinciding with the take-over of Peru's official Communist party by the pro-Chinese faction. The alliance between Communists, Trotskyites, and pro-Cuban elements could further aggravate the situation, although the passage of agrarian reform legislation by the Peruvian Congress in May 1964, after six years of delays, was a step in the right direction.

The more sophisticated level on which Cuban influence operates is purely political. But it functions in terms of local situations and not as a direct result of Cuban subversive activities. The point is that the fact of the Cuban revolution has reinforced, through its historic example, powerful currents of nationalism and extreme-leftist trends. Put in other words, this influence and these pressures will not be halted even if Castro vanishes from the face of the earth, because they constitute part and parcel of the broader Latin American revolution. The trend toward authoritarian governments probably cannot control these forces indefinitely. And it can be argued that if it were not for the Cuban revolution the Alliance for Progress would not have been born, and the new military governments would not be dedicating as much effort and attention to economic and social improvement as they are now doing.

The strong leftist trends in Latin America, including anti-American nationalism, are by the same token attributable in part to Cuban inspiration. Brazilian quasi-neutralism in the Quadros-Goulart period grew out of this influence. Goulart probably would not have moved as far as he did in trying to build his worker-peasant leftist apparatus if it had not been for the Cuban example. He imitated Castro in trying to break up the monolith of the armed forces through his attempt to create leftist areas of power among the noncommissioned officers and young commissioned officers. But his scheme had not been blueprinted for him by Cuban agents in Rio or Brasília. It was a native Brazilian product.

The powerful leftist elements in Chile derive their influence not from any direct Cuban action but from internal Chilean causes, even though the Castro revolution evidently played a significant role in bringing to the surface many local demands and aspirations. On the eve of the 1964 elections, Chile did not bring to mind a prerevolutionary Cuba; much more, she resembled a France of the middle 1930's under Léon Blum's Front Populaire.

Perhaps the key to the whole Cuban failure to export the revolution lies in Castro's complete lack of understanding of Latin American conditions and psychologies beyond the narrow confines of his island. He may still be a hero to many Latin Americans, but they seem to prefer to keep him and his revolution at arm's length. He has been useful, to be sure, and Latin Americans are serious when they say "Gracias, Fidel" in speaking of the Alliance for Progress. In that sense, Castro has become a part of Latin American history. But he has found no imitators capable of carrying crowds with them. Africa has produced a Nasser, a Ben Bella, a Bourguiba, a Nkrumah, a Nyerere, and a whole generation of new leaders who, despite personal differences, by and large think and act much alike. In Latin America, Castro stands alone in his call for violent revolution, though the emerging new leaders do owe him an intellectual or emotional debt. It is a reflection on Castro's direct (as opposed to indirect) influence on Latin American politics that the politicians from various countries of the hemisphere who attended the fifth anniversary of the revolution in Havana in January 1964 were a collection of utterly obscure and meaningless personalities. Not even Cárdenas and Allende bothered to go to Havana this time.

But there is no better, or more important, example of Castro's failure to export his revolution than the case history of Venezuela.

THE VENEZUELAN STORY IS IMPORTANT because it was in a basic sense the turning point in the whole process of direct Fidelista impact on Latin America. It was a confirmation of the proposition set forth by Rómulo Betancourt and by the Kennedy concept of the Alliance for Progress that economic progress and social justice are possible in a working democracy.

The Castro failure in Venezuela (his first major political defeat since 1959) should, among other things, put to rest forever the notion mistakenly but fervently held by many observers in the United States that Latin America is caught between the opposing forces of Fidelism and right-wing oligarchy, with virtually nothing in between. In the Venezuelan case, which was the greatest test to date of Cuba's ability to impose a revolution from the outside, the real victory was precisely of the forces "in the middle," and it may well be the most significant political lesson to be derived from the Castro experience. Subsequent events in Panama, Brazil, and Chile bear a certain relation to the Venezuelan experience, in the sense of the assertion of the middle-ground forces against leftist and rightist extremism. These forces, too, were defeats for the Castro cause.

Castro's notion that Venezuela must inevitably succumb to the pressures of violent revolution dates back to his 1959 visit to Caracas. Rebuffed by Betancourt, he dedicated himself to the overthrow of the Venezuelan president with a persistent single-mindedness. His reasons, of course, were twofold. One was that Venezuela, with her deep problems and internal stresses, seemed like the ripest plum for his kind of revolution and, he hoped, the beginning of a hemispherewide revolutionary process. The other reason was that Betancourt's success in achieving economic and social progress in cooperation with the United States would offer a painful contrast to the continuous failures of the Cuban economy, notwithstanding the massive aid from the Communist bloc.

Castro's reasoning, which the Venezuelan Communist party and the even more extreme Revolutionary Movement of the Left (MIR) came to share, to their subsequent regret, was that Venezuelans would quickly become tired of Betancourt's gradualism in land reform and other economic developments, and that this impatience with the democratic process, along with the presumed hatred of the United States oil companies, would push them toward a national revolution. The fact that unemployment ran high in Caracas and the other cities, that the leftist groups had won Caracas in the 1958 elections, and that students were militantly in favor of a radical revolution, encouraged Castro and his allies in his analysis of the Venezuelan events.

The first step in the war against Betancourt was an attempt at direct insurgency to bring about his immediate overthrow. This took the form of the successive rebellions in 1962 in the ports of Carúpano and Puerto Cabello, which involved local Marine Corps garrisons, a handful of National Guardsmen, and contingents of armed civilians. These were the most serious insurrections since November 1960, when leftist students at the Caracas Central University barricaded themselves in their dormitories (one building was named "Stalingrado") to defy Betancourt by firing at the surrounding area. A group of leftist officers of the Marine Corps and some disgruntled rightist officers sparked the two coastal revolts, which from the first moment received the vociferous and enthusiastic support of the Havana Radio. But since the other units of the armed forces and the population at large failed to respond to these uprisings, the Betancourt regime had relatively little trouble in putting them down.

With the collapse of direct insurgency, Castro's tactics were changed. The new approach called for a campaign of urban terrorism combined with mountain guerrilla activity. The concept was that if enough havoc and destruction were caused, the Venezuelan military, which always distrusted Betancourt, would stage a coup d'état and establish a dictatorship to be able better to cope with the terrorists. It was assumed by both the Venezuelan revolutionaries and Castro that if a military dictatorship could be reestablished it would provide a rallying point for a national revolution in the same way in which the existence of the Batista dictatorship in Cuba several years earlier had supplied the necessary conditions for the Fidelist rebellion. What was standing in the way of the leftist revolution, it was reasoned, was Venezuela's democratic system and the painstaking but increasingly visible efforts of the Betancourt government to push ahead with his land reform and strengthening the national economy.

From the new strategy, there emerged the Armed Forces of National Liberation (known as FALN for its Spanish initials), which became the foremost terrorist-and-guerrilla organization in the country. Its leaders were Communist activists, such as Senator Pompeo Marques, and a number of extreme-leftist and extreme-rightist military officers. The latter made common cause with the Communists and the Fidelists because of their hatred for Betancourt. Among the guerrilla and terrorist commando chiefs there were numerous Cuban-trained youths and others who were instructed locally by the Castro cadres. The "troops" were made up in their majority from university students, motivated in equal parts by ideology, frustrations, romanticism, and a desire for adventure. They were recruited by their university colleagues, and in some instances by pro-Communist professors. According to the Venezuelan government, the recruiters were on the lookout for psychologically disturbed youths, who could be easily attracted to the FALN. Many were the children of families who had made fortunes through the corruption prevalent during the Pérez Jiménez regime, and some observers thought that the FALN had more activists from the so-called good families than from the underprivileged slum dwellers or peasants. It was not unusual, in fact, for FALN terrorists to use their expensive sports cars in their raids.

It is doubtful that the FALN ever had more than 1,000 or 1,500 active members, but it quickly developed into a highly proficient terrorist organization, operating boldly and imaginatively. While initially the FALN received virtually no arms or money from Cuba (the Guevara guerrilla theory was that insurgents must secure their own weapons), there was no question about Cuba's complete support for its operations. The Havana Radio continuously broadcast appeals to Venezuelans to revolt, recounted FALN's achievements, and sent operational instructions. It soon became obvious, and even overt, that Venezuela was Castro's chief target in Latin America.

FALN's well-planned and daringly executed operations succeeded to a degree in terrorizing Venezuela. National Guardsmen were murdered in the countryside, and even in Caracas, for their weapons. Banks were raided for money to finance the campaign. Installations of United States oil companies were blown up, and American-owned plants and buildings were set on fire. Small guerrilla bands established themselves in the mountains in several states of Venezuela, though they never became more than a nuisance. In February 1963, the FALN staged its most spectacular coup by capturing the freighter *Anzoategui* on the high seas and taking it to Brazil.

Yet the campaign failed to produce the expected results. There were two main reasons. One was that the Venezuelan military refused to step in to overthrow Betancourt, so transparent was the FALN scheme. The other reason, and a much more important one in the long run, was that the FALN terrorists and guerrillas found no support whatsoever in the Venezuelan population. In the cities, the sentiment ran high against the commandos (even in the "revolutionary" housing projects, where FALN snipers initially hid), because the population feared and resented what was becoming indiscriminate terrorism. It was a major psychological error to continue the terror. By persisting in it, FALN antagonized people and failed to win adherents. In the countryside, the peasants, on whom the FALN's hopes were centered, refused to support and aid the guerrillas. Instead, they often cooperated with the Venezuelan army in flushing out the *guerrilleros*. Inspired by Castro's experience in the Sierra Maestra, the FALN had assumed that the peasantry would become allied with the guerrillas. But the peasants in Venezuela (behaving quite differently from the peasants in Cuba under Batista) demonstrated considerable allegiance to the government. This was in part because of the traditional hold on them by Betancourt's Democratic Action party, which operated through the Peasant Confederation, but, above all, it was because the regime was actively pursuing land reform, offering the *campesinos* in deeds more than the guerrillas were promising in words. By early 1963, when the FALN guerrilla effort was approaching its peak, the Betancourt government had settled over 60,000 families (nearly 250,000 people) on their own land, under a broad concept of "integrated agrarian reform," which included rural credit, technical assistance, housing, electrification, and roads to markets. So the thunder had been stolen from the guerrillas.

In a broader way, the Betancourt government had also succeeded in improving the overall national economy to the point where the gross national product had risen by 6 per cent in 1962, despite the terrorism and the earlier flight of capital from the country. Blending the activities of the public sector with private enterprise, Venezuela succeeded in attracting back some of the capital, carrying out important public works, substantially increasing food production, encouraging industry, and making strides in housing and education. In short, the FALN and its sponsors were deprived of their *raison d'être*.

Cuban charges that Betancourt had established a dictatorship of his own with the military, through the stern measures employed against the terrorists, including the temporary suspension of some constitutional guarantees, made little impression in Venezuela. Most people, aware of what was happening, agreed with their president that a democracy had the right to defend itself.

Presidential elections for the five-year term beginning in February 1964 were scheduled for December 1 and the Betancourt regime staked its entire power and prestige on its ability to complete its own term in office and to assure a peaceful transition to the new presidency. If this could be done, it would be the first time in Venezuelan history that an elected president had completed his term and transferred his office to an elected successor. The whole concept of democratic evolution was made to hinge on this election. To FALN and to Castro, in turn, it became a matter of principle to prevent the holding of the elections.

The FALN turned to tactics of desperation designed to block the elections at all costs. By late 1963, terrorism reached unprecedented heights. All the stops were pulled out, and now the Cubans openly entered the campaign. In October, a FALN raiding party attacked a train carrying Caracas families to a weekend site, and numerous National Guardsmen were killed. The attack shocked Venezuelans more than any act of terrorism that the FALN had committed theretofore, and the already low stock of the "Liberation Army" sank to the bottom. Communist leaders in hiding telephoned government officials to claim that the train attack was an unauthorized incident and an error, and that the party had nothing to do with it.

Meanwhile Castro had set in motion what was designed to be a last desperate attempt at overthrowing the government and preventing the elections. A cache of arms weighing three tons was surreptitiously landed on the coast of Falcón state to equip the FALN for its planned do-or-die operation. This was going to be the "Plan Caracas," which called for more than 600 FALN commandos, organized in assault brigades, to capture the strategic spots in the capital, assassinate Betancourt and other government officials, and declare themselves as the new regime. But, as luck had it, Venezuelan fishermen discovered the cache and called in government troops to seize it. A few days later, the police raided several Caracas apartments and apprehended the detailed "Plan Caracas." That the Falcón arms actually came from Cuba and that the "Plan Caracas" was drawn up with Cuban complicity was subsequently established by an OAS investigating commission, which flatly charged Havana with aggression against Venezuela.

With its entire strategy smashed, the FALN had one final card to play. It issued a formal warning that any citizen coming to cast a ballot on election day would be killed by FALN snipers. The nation's response came on December 1. Promised military protection, more than 90 percent of the registered voters turned out at the polling stations in what became the quietest day in months.

No greater repudiation of the proposed revolution and no greater confidence in the democratic system could have been demonstrated by Venezuelans than their collective act of defying the FALN and trooping to the polls. And no greater proof could have been given in Latin America that revolutions cannot be exported from abroad if a nation does not want to rise in revolution.

THE VENEZUELAN EXPERIENCE was a fairly conclusive demonstration of the correctness of the Marxist-Leninists' own theory that "objective conditions" are required if a revolution is to succeed. Quite aside from the immediate Latin American problem, the failure of the FALN gave the Soviet Union an added argument in its dispute with Communist China—namely, that no "instant revolutions" should be attempted if the conditions are not ripe for them—even though Moscow had initially given its blessings to the anti-Betancourt operation.

If nothing else, the Venezuelan case is likely to deepen the divisions along the Soviet and Chinese lines within the Latin American parties, inasmuch as both Castro and the pro-Chinese Communist factions seem determined to go on with subversion and efforts at producing quick revolutions. In November 1963, when it should have been obvious to any rational observer that the FALN operation had failed, Castro was telling Herbert L. Matthews of the *New York Times:* "Of course we engage in subversion, the training of guerrillas, propaganda! Why not? This is exactly what you are doing to us."[1]

Castro did not say that his expeditionary guerrillas had already been operating in 1959, long before the United States or anybody else thought of subverting *his* revolution, and evidently his commitment to keep trying to spread his brand of insurrection is too great to be abandoned even in the face of a fiasco as great as that in Venezuela. But the events since the fall of 1963 seem to suggest that his blandishments will meet with even less success than in the past.

Although the Panama crisis that followed the Canal Zone riots in January 1964 seemed to offer Cuba a new opportunity for significant mischief, Castro was unable to take advantage of it, and the Johnson administration gave him undeserved credit for stirring up the trouble there. In the opening weeks of the long dispute between the United States and Panama, the Havana Radio plunged into it with all its resources, seeking to present the Venezuelan and Panamanian situations as identical "wars against imperialism." Castro had evidently

---

[1] Herbert L. Matthews, *Return to Cuba* (Bolivar House, Stanford University, 1964).

hoped that the Panamanian bitterness against the United States would lead before long to a popular revolt and the establishment of an extremist regime, handing him on a silver platter in 1964 that which he failed to win through his guerrilla expedition in 1959, but again his calculations proved wrong. The controversy was eventually worked out on terms that were reasonably acceptable to Panama. When presidential elections were held on May 10, a moderate candidate won, and Castro's most enthusiastic Panamanian follower, a woman deputy named Thelma King, was defeated in her bid to be returned to the Legislative Assembly.

The next blow to Castro's ambitions was the Brazilian revolution in April 1964. He had relied heavily on the Goulart regime as Cuba's chief protector in the hemisphere (Mexico had become downright cool, although she maintained formal diplomatic ties with Cuba) and as the instrument for leading Brazil toward a socialist system. Had the Goulart scheme succeeded, a revolutionary alliance between Cuba and Brazil would have completely altered the hemispheric picture in Castro's favor. But the reaction of the Brazilian moderates, supported by the armed forces, nipped this promising possibility in the bud. If anything, Brazil seemed to swing temporarily toward rightist excesses in the flush of the revolution. The Frei election in Chile five months later became the next in this long string of defeats for the Castro cause. Where did all this leave Castro in mid-1964, in the sixth year of his own revolution, which he had not been able to export anywhere? A victory by Salvador Allende in Chile with the votes of the FRAP, the Socialist-Communist coalition, would undoubtedly have given Castro a sympathetic regime in the southwestern corner of South America. But the world and Latin America had changed considerably since Allende's own visits to Havana three or four years earlier. After the September elections in Chile, Castro lost perhaps the last bastion he had any right to hope to conquer.

In Bolivia, which had already gone through a social revolution twelve years earlier, extreme-leftist elements pressed hard upon President Paz Estenssoro, and this was one country where Cubans were quite active and not altogether unsuccessful. But Paz's overthrow in November 1964 cannot be credited to Castro's efforts. In practical terms, a violent swing to the left in Bolivia—even the emergence of a Castro-type regime—would probably be of little direct use to Cuba, unless Bolivian agitation were to spread to the volatile population of the highlands of neighboring Peru.

In the Dominican Republic, leftist elements were picking up strength from the stagnation in which that unfortunate country again found itself after a brief fling at democracy following the three decades of the Trujillo dictatorship. A pathetic attempt at guerrilla warfare by the pro-Castro "14 of June Movement" followed the ouster by the military of President Bosch in 1963, but it was short-lived and ended in the massacre of the *guerrilleros* by the army. There was no evidence that Castro made any serious effort to aid the hapless mountain fighters.

If tentative conclusions can be reached at this stage of the Latin American development, it would seem that, by and large, the Cuban revolution has been taken in stride. It has been left behind, even if many of its deep influences not only persist but are actively present in the Latin American quest for new definitions and new destinies. But Latin America has also taken in stride the Alliance for Progress, in a sense a by-product of the Castro revolution. The present trend seems to be in the direction of absorbing some aspects of both phenomena into deeper social currents.

In terms of the Cuban problem, which has been lessened in the immediate sense but certainly not yet solved, most of the hemisphere is seeking to maintain and improve policies designed to discourage Premier Castro from further attempts to sow his revolutionary gospel. The United States policies of economic isolation of Cuba, the steady deterioration of the Cuban economy (due to the magnitude of the task undertaken by Castro and to his regime's continued mismanagement of Cuban affairs), and the state of virtual quarantine in which Cuba finds herself in the hemisphere have all contributed to make Fidelism less a continental danger than at any time since 1959.

In terms of the Alliance and of the general policies for which it stands, significant accomplishments have been chalked up, even if the millennium is still far away. In the majority of the republics, the statistical evidence suggests an improvement in economic performance and in living standards. Comprehensive development planning is becoming a fact, and the Inter-American Committee of the Alliance for Progress—the program's steering body created early in 1964—promises to play a crucial role in coordinating the whole effort. Unlike 1961, when the Alliance was born, it is Latin American thinking that increasingly prevails in the overall approach to development, even if the influence of the United States, tied to its function of financing the program, remains overwhelmingly important.

In Latin America's political course ahead, there can be no retreat from the objectives of land reform that the Cuban revolution did so much to dramatize or from other efforts to achieve new levels of economic development and social justice. There can be no return to the old relationships between the United States and Latin America, be it in the field of foreign policy or of economic relations. The Cuban revolution has helped to create a new vision of reality both in the United States and in Latin America, but this very vision—as demonstrated in Venezuela's and Chile's rejection of the exported revolution—has also proved the validity of the Kennedy concept that political democracy must march hand in hand with economic and social development if the hemisphere is to have a balanced and decent future. If either element in this equation is sacrificed, then Latin America must brace itself for new upheavals—or neo-Fidelismos.

J. WILNER SUNDELSON, Director of International Consulting and Licensing, Seaway Associates, Ann Arbor, was previously with the Ford Motor Company and the Conductron Corporation. He holds the Ph.D. in economics from Columbia University and has taught at Rutgers University.

A Business Perspective

J. WILNER SUNDELSON*

There exists no parallel to the unique political and economic relations between the United States and Cuba that prevailed from the termination of the Spanish-American War until the successful take-over by Fidel Castro. These relations reflected in part the particular geographic, economic, social, and political characteristics of Cuba. They also reflected early United States policies of various forms of intervention, including armed intervention, in the internal affairs of some of our smaller Latin American neighbors.

U.S. Business in Pre-Castro Cuba

Geographically, Cuba is the closest of the Caribbean nations to the United States. This nearness of Cuba could be, and was, translated into deep economic penetration and interdependence because of the resources and the potential productivity of the area. Cuba had a population largely, though not exclusively, of Latin origin and a very high per capita availability of level land of excellent fertility. Further, by the time the United States had become actively involved in Cuba, the island's economy had already moved in the direction of crops that lend

---

* The author is indebted to Armand A. Boucher of Ford International's Finance Staff for assistance in the preparation of this chapter. The conclusions are those of the author.

98

themselves to mechanization and other improved processes. Cuba was also not without inherent wealth in both metallic and nonmetallic mineral resources. The exploitation of these resources attracted United States investors, and the United States provided a ready market for the minerals, sugar, and tobacco produced in Cuba.

Beginning with the Platt Amendment of 1901, under which the United States made itself the legal guardian of Cuba, a whole series of special political and economic relations came into being; they augmented as well as tied down the close interdependence of the two economies. The United States, beginning in 1902, gave Cuba a sugar tariff reduction of 20 points. Compared with other off-shore suppliers, Cuba thus had a preferential status in the United States market. This was modified in 1930, and in 1944 a quota system was enacted in the Jones-Costigan Act. In 1948 the United States Sugar Act established revised quotas. The Act allocated to the Philippines, Cuba, and other countries the portion of United States needs not allocated to domestic sources. In addition, a basic preferential tariff arrangement applied to United States–Cuban trade in both directions; it continued until the disruption of relations in 1960. A preferential trade agreement is always of importance to a country, but in Cuba's case the United States sugar preference had a pervasive effect on the entire economy of the island, for sugar accounted for 70 to 90 percent of all its exports.

Given these favorable factors and the political climate that generally prevailed in Cuba during the half century prior to Castro, the United States business community responded as might be expected. The Cuban cane-sugar industry needed capital; and United States interests, given a protected though cyclically sensitive dollar market, moved into sugar production on the island. In 1950 the United States had forty-seven major sugar-producing facilities in Cuba, representing about 47 percent of total production. It is true that Cuban ownership of sugar production facilities increased in the 1950's, so that in the immediate pre-Castro period it had reached a high point of 121 mills, representing 62 percent of total sugar output. The Cubans, however, pointed out that for a long period the benefits of the United States sugar preferences and quotas to Cuba were enjoyed not only by Cuba and Cubans but by United States interests as well. And some Cubans claim that concentrated reliance on sugar worked against the economic diversification of Cuba,[1] for Cuba, under United States influence, traded sugar for most of the products it required, many of them from the United States.

The United States did not invest as widely in the production of Cuban products other than sugar but was still a large factor in the marketing of Cuban tobacco products, manganese, and, of course, nickel. Given the generally favorable Cuban balance of payments, the uninterrupted convertibility and parity of the peso and the dollar, and the absence of exchange controls, it is not surprising that Cuba and the United States were bound together by trade. Few markets in Latin America other than Cuba had dollars for United States products, and few granted preferential tariff treatment. Few foreign consumers, too, were as committed to our kinds of products. After 1950, Cuba increasingly found sugar markets outside North America, and new efforts were made by other suppliers to penetrate the Cuban market. But it was still true in 1957 that Cuba bought $618 million of United States exports (80 percent of Cuba's imports), while the United States share of Cuban exports, down from its early-century peak of 80 percent was still an overwhelming 69 percent. United States trade penetrated the Cuban market more than the market of any other country. The extent of United States domination of foreign investments in Cuba is well documented. The following statement appears to be a correct appraisal of the situation in pre-Castro Cuba:

> United States businessmen dominated the field of foreign investment although other foreign investors were represented. Before the Castro regime, over 90% of the telephone and electric services, one-half of the public service railways, one-fourth of all bank deposits, about 40% of sugar production and much of the mining, oil production and cattle ranching was in the hands of United States business. . . . American business naturally promoted ventures which promised dollar profits and American-controlled banks concentrated on the financing of the sugar industry and foreign trade.[2]

The close ties between the North American capital market and Cuba made it possible for Cuba to become by 1951 the most heavily capital-

---

[1] Grupo Cubano de Investigaciones Económicas, *Un Estudio Sobre Cuba* (University of Miami Press, 1963). Sugar was also the basis for a 1957 United States-financed $30-million raw paper and paperboard plant using bagasse.

[2] Wyatt MacGaffey and Clifford R. Barnett, *Cuba: Its People, Its Society, Its Culture* (prepared under the auspices of American University; HRAF Press, 1962), p. 177.

ized country (on a per capita basis) in Latin America and to have a relatively high living standard as well. Some particulars will confirm the generalization that United States business interests, and to a small extent the United States government, dominated the Cuban foreign investment field apart from their roles in sugar. United States interests in Cuba were in rubber, chemicals, pharmaceuticals, fertilizers, textiles, leather products, building materials, glass, furniture, petroleum and its derivatives, metal products, machinery, and matches. United States oil companies are reported to have spent $25 million prospecting for petroleum in 1945-59.[3] The United States government put a total of $90 million in the Nicaro Nickel complex. The names of the companies involved in Cuba read like a Who's Who of American business. Refineries were in the hands of Esso and Texas. (Shell of Britain was also present.) Tires were made by B. F. Goodrich, U. S. Rubber, Goodyear, and Firestone. The banks included Chase and First National City of New York. (Six of the fifteen principal banks were foreign-owned.) Ford Motor Company had its own credit company, and other United States automotive companies offered their dealers and customers similar facilities. Cubans bought most of their insurance from American and Canadian firms.

In 1960 United States investments in Cuba stood at approximately $1.5 billion.

Did U.S. Business Contribute to the Advent of Castro?

The special relations of American business and the United States government to the Cuban government and the Cuban economy are clear. Did these relations influence the emergence of Castro or affect his policies and practices when he assumed power?

After Cuba's liberation from Spain, the United States began its business activities in Cuba under a special extraterritorial relationship. This resulted in a whole series of actions to protect United States and other business properties and trade—actions that included the landing of Marines on several occasions. Such intervention, according to students of the period, was directly encouraged by many American businessmen in Cuba. The United States, under the Platt Amendment, had

[3] *Ibid.*, p. 78.

certain veto powers over acts of the Cuban government. As viewed by
the United States business community and affirmed by the Department
of State and successive administrations, the objectives of this special
relationship were the protection of Cuba and of Cuban as well as
United States investments; the expansion of Cuba–United States trade;
and the maintenance of the kind of stability that businessmen thought
they needed for the operation, profitable development, and survival of
their enterprises. While the United States and its business community
have always had, and continue to have, sympathy for certain basic revolutionary movements where the pursuit of democratic reforms is an
objective, United States attitudes toward such revolutionary forces in
Cuba cooled appreciably whenever the new social and economic goals
or the avowed policies of the revolutionaries and reformers threatened
the status quo of United States interests in Cuba. Though direct military intervention ceased in the early thirties, the magnitude of United
States economic interests in the island's economy and the strength of
American opinions and values were such that the United States could,
by simply failing to associate itself with internal forces seeking change,
continue to exert a powerful conservative influence.[4] By the time Castro was marching to Havana, some United States business interests in
Cuba offered him support, but such support was too late and too small
to have any favorable influence, assuming any such influence on Castro
was at that time possible.

It was inevitable that there should develop in Cuba a conflict between legitimate United States overseas economic interests and the
Cuban national ideal of self-determination. In the 1920's some anti-
American feeling became evident and brought to the forefront isolated
threats of a repudiation of debts and confiscation of property—the key
elements in the later Castro policies that, when carried out, alienated
the United States. It is obvious also that our foreign investments were
in large part of a character that militant nationalism usually condemns
most strongly: foreign investment in the extraction of subsoil assets, in
depletable resources, and in economic activities generating foreign exchange. Considering the relations between the two countries, one must
wonder that they lasted as long as they did and that the overthrow of
the special relations came as late as it did.

Seen in retrospect, a number of factors might have been read as

4 *Ibid.*, p. 313.

storm warnings against further United States economic involvement in Cuba. Certainly since the blossoming of Castro into a Soviet-oriented dictator, businessmen had reason to give more attention to such factors. The history of Cuba from the Platt Amendment through the Castro take-over is one of political turmoil, bureaucratic corruption, and inefficiency. The 1950 World Bank *Report on Cuba* stressed the inefficiency of domestic industry, the pervasive labor racketeering and featherbedding, the burdensome and complex taxation, the unreasonable government intervention, the inadequate marketing systems, and the abuse by government and pressure groups of tariffs and subsidy policies.[5] Labor-management relations were particularly bad, and as early as 1950 one might have foreseen a threat to stability from politically active labor unions. Public services were costly and inefficient. Railways were poorly built, equipped, and maintained. Corruption was widespread as a way of life; it reached new heights in the latter part of Batista's reign. There also might have been concern over the ultimate consequences of a monoculture and a monoexport economy—particularly an economy overwhelmingly based on an agricultural product subject to wide price fluctuations and without inherent protection against new or excessive production elsewhere. Cuban economists, refugees in the United States, writing of the country's economic history, speak of the fact that politically and morally Cuba developed little during the last forty years.[6] But the lack of needed changes in the economic, political, and social life of Cuba did not deter United States investment. Much United States investment occurred in the 1950 decade when Batista held power in Cuba (he was not the nominal head of the government in the first two years of the decade). Actually, the early Batista years were viewed as a welcome relief from the difficulties under the prior regime. Certain business interests, including some from the United States, sought to eliminate Batista and gave early support to Castro, but they were ineffective and inarticulate.

The Batista regime had suppressed revolutionary movements. This gave assurance to those businessmen who knew it was no longer possible to call out the United States Marines for the same purpose. Cuba was buying goods and services in large quantities from the United States, and United States investors were generally prospering and op-

[5] Economic and Technical Mission to Cuba, *Report on Cuba* (International Bank for Reconstruction and Development, 1951), pp. 170-90.
[6] Grupo Cubano de Investigaciones Económicas, *op. cit.*, p. 1275.

erating under what they thought were favorable circumstances. Yet Cuba's severe social and governmental problems were well documented by the World Bank's *Report on Cuba* as early as 1951. And in 1961 the State Department wrote:

> The character of the Batista regime in Cuba made a violent popular reaction almost inevitable. The rapacity of the leadership, the corruption of the government, the brutality of the police, the regime's indifference to the needs of the public for education, medical care, housing, for social justice and economic opportunity—all these in Cuba, as elsewhere, constituted an open invitation to revolution.[7]

It would appear that the failure of the business community to appreciate what was going on was shared by most members of the State Department. There were no appreciable or successful efforts to replace Batista with more liberal leadership. In the case of Guatemala such efforts have not been unknown or unsuccessful. The State Department did nothing to discourage United States businesses from investing in Cuba or operating there. In an exhaustive 200-page study of "Investment in Cuba," published by the Commerce Department in 1956, Cuba's potentialities and opportunities were stressed. Difficulties with Cuban labor were mentioned, but not a word of caution was given about the increasingly precarious political situation.[8] The period prior to 1958 was one in which a host country's pro-Western affiliation was apparently all that was required internationally, and the stability and nondiscrimination that United States business wanted were all the qualifications a foreign administration had to have in order to receive the support of the United States government.

The business community in the United States failed to appreciate the character and potential of the Castro movement. At the time Castro reached Havana and consolidated his power, no United States business group or public officials had established a mutually beneficial relationship with the movement, although some had tried. What was not understood was Castro's emotionally unstable and unpredictable character, which made him basically unapproachable. Apparently Castro's image of American business was one of opposition, since he detested

[7] U.S. Department of State, *Cuba*, Publication 7171, Inter-American Series (Government Printing Office, 1961), p. 2.

[8] U.S. Department of Commerce, *Investment in Cuba: Basic Information for U.S. Businessmen* (Government Printing Office, 1956).

private ownership—domestic and foreign—of Cuba's basic resources, trade, and industry. The United States business community, whatever it felt or thought, found that it could do very little to minimize losses from Castro's take-over. There are some indications that a very few resourceful businesses were able to reduce losses in the short period before the relations between the United States and Castro's Cuba deteriorated beyond the point of no return. Isolated instances are reported of heavy borrowing within Cuba, moving liquid capital resources in one form or another out of Cuba, and in a few cases disposal of assets by sale. It appears, however, that little of this could be done and little was accomplished. The business enterprises that cut their losses were those that had earlier begun, for one reason or another, to rely on local borrowing to the maximum extent possible, or had begun the process of liquidating their assets, or had refrained from shipping on credit. Moving deposits from Cuban banks to United States domestic institutions was another type of precaution. But not all businesses were in a position to do this. It is clear that, on the basis of the claims filed and other published data regarding losses, not many American business firms were able to salvage much.[9] None had the good fortune or foresight to liquidate in the last years of the Batista regime, as did some of the British interests. Very few, if any, appear to have liquidated portfolio holdings. It is particularly noteworthy that not a single United States investment in Cuba was covered by an investment guarantee, although guarantees were available.[10] Taken as a whole, the United States business community did not anticipate the disappearance of the favorable business climate. Judged by its actions, it did not seem to believe that Castro could take over, or stay on, or that the United States would be lacking in the leverage to prevent the worst.

A question that may never be answered is whether the United States government, as well as the business community in and outside Cuba,

[9] For a listing of firms that have filed expropriation claims with the United States government, see the *Congressional Record*, Vol. 108, Pt. 10, 87 Cong. 2 sess., July 11, 1962, pp. 13157-59. The exact value will never be known, but these estimates are confirmed to some extent by the claims that have been filed.

[10] Although the United States and Cuba had entered into an agreement in February 1957 to implement the Investment Guarantee Program, not one contract had been signed at the time the expropriation of U.S.-owned properties took place (two guarantee applications were being processed at the time but never reached the contract stage).

could have held Castro to the role of a successful domestic Cuban revolutionary leader with a platform of modest socialistic reforms. Some
still believe that the United States was shortsighted, if not at fault, in
failing to do what it could to win some rapport with Castro and to
learn to live with him. They contend that in 1959 and for the first half
of 1960 Castro would have responded to trade overtures, offers of assistance, or some other indication of understanding and tolerance.[11]

On the other hand, it may also never be known whether Castro, in
view of his complex personality and the closeness of his extreme left-
wing advisers, could ever have been diverted from his progressive so-
cialization of the island, from a total break of relations with the United
States, and from alignment with the Communist bloc. This view main-
tains that once the United States had failed to use whatever influence it
might have had in helping to dispose of Batista or in eliminating the
most objectionable features of his administration before the advent of
Castro, it could not then have solved the situation by finding a way to
cooperate with Castro. Could the business interests handling United
States–Cuban trade in Cuba and in the United States (the remaining
owners and managers of the sugar plantations and mills, mines,
refineries, and utilities; the manufacturers; the vendors of services;
those engaged in distribution, including retail trade) through cooperation and better understanding have diverted the early Castro revolutionaries from their goals? One is inclined to believe that the cause was
lost when no alternative to Castro emerged to the problem posed by
the latter period of the Batista dictatorship.

To put a slightly different question: Could a foreign business community that dominated trade in both directions, owned utilities, provided fuel, and owned and managed virtually every phase of Cuban
economic life—a community whose government determined the amount
of sugar it would buy but failed to insulate Cuba against world fluctuations in both price and demand—could such a foreign community and
its government have succeeded in establishing a *modus vivendi* with
the early Castro regime? Where Marxist or other extremist governments are concerned, we in the United States lack a tradition of putting trade and international politics on different planes. In any case,

[11] Press reports revealed that diplomatic intermediaries, acting on behalf of the
U.S. government, offered economic assistance to Castro early in 1960. The offer
was turned down, reportedly at the insistence of Che Guevara.

whether American business could have survived in Cuba is doubtful, for Castro's policies showed a definite anticapitalist bias even prior to his alignment with the Soviet bloc.

The new view strongly held in some private and governmental circles in the United States is that an American business policy of "enlightened capitalism" in Cuba—with emphasis on joint ventures, widespread ownership through local capital markets, use of local employees in skilled and managerial jobs, and a generally sympathetic attitude toward the less obnoxious forms of local nationalism—could have deferred Castro's take-over or headed off Cuba's transition to Communism. But this view is highly questionable, given the character of Castro and his followers. Xenophobia is a key element in modern revolutionary forces. There are few, if any, instances where extremist revolutionaries of whatever credo have allowed foreign-owned enterprises to continue to function, even in part. This is particularly true when the revolutionary regime is inimical to all concentrations of private capital —the wealth and power represented by large business enterprises. What has happened in Ceylon, in Burma, and to a large extent in Egypt and Indonesia, and what previously happened in Guinea, suggests that "enlightened capitalism," with cooperative ventures or locally-held ownership shares, would have been ineffective in altering the course of political history.

What leftist revolutionary government can permit utilities or the productive capacities for key export items to remain partly in foreign ownership? Few, if any, revolutionary governments permit the exploitation of their petroleum and mineral resources by foreigners. It is improbable that, given the leaning of Castro and his followers, much could have been salvaged by wiser, more tolerant understanding and by more cooperative behavior. Perhaps time might have been won by such policies, but the cause of foreign-owned enterprises was lost when Castro reached Havana.

Altogether, one is inclined to conclude that dedicating U.S. resources, public and private, to restoring or maintaining middle-of-the-road governments is worth while. We will be far less likely to achieve success if we try to avoid left-wing revolutionaries through supporting right-wing extremists, or if we try to live and do business with left-wing regimes after they take over. Another conclusion suggested by the Cuban experience is that foreign-owned business rarely has the incentive, or perhaps the ability, to put pressures on dictators to use moderation and to institute necessary reform and change.

Possible Future Commercial Transactions

If the time should come when a mellowed Castro permits a restoration of some kinds of economic relations with the United States, or if one assumes that Castro suffers the fate of the dictators of Venezuela or the Dominican Republic or the Communist head of Guatemala and disappears from the scene, there will be a changed climate in Cuba for United States business. Some idea of the kinds of beginnings under the first assumption can be seen in the developing relations between England and Cuba. British firms are currently supplying capital and other goods to Cuba on credits guaranteed by the British government. The newspapers report that since the British are taking the lead in destroying the effectiveness of the American embargo, Castro has offered, or is preparing to offer, compensation to the former owners of the expropriated Shell Refinery, as well as to other British claimants. This gives a clue as to what might happen if Cuba and the United States were to make a mutual effort to restore some relations via commercial transactions. By selling sugar in world markets for convertible currencies, Castro has acquired foreign exchange and can now make reasonable payments for purchases, or down payment on credit purchases, such as those he is making in Spain, Belgium, England, France, and elsewhere in Western Europe, as well as in Canada, Japan, and other countries. According to reports, the Soviet bloc took, in payment for its shipments, a color television transmitter, breweries, sugar refineries, distilleries, and other industrial assets valued at hundreds of millions of dollars.[12] Western nations generally sell for other kinds of payment. From isolated commercial transactions, business moves to the licensing of know-how and eventually to a provision for complete package plants. This process is taking place between Western Europe and the Communist blocs of Europe and Asia.

It appears that the United States embargo on Cuba will be ineffective if the United States observes it virtually alone. The embargo does not deprive the Communist-dominated Cuban economy, for there is very little in the way of manufactured goods, know-how, and plant-

[12] Grupo Cubano de Investigaciones Económicas, *op cit.*, p. 1595.

building capacity that Cuba cannot acquire from the Communist bloc, from Western Europe, and from Japan, or for which the United States has unique talents and resources. Of course, some parts and products were badly needed by Castro to maintain and operate equipment originally supplied by the United States or plants left behind by United States interests. But with time this need has declined greatly.

Now that new capital goods and equipment, plants, and technicians are pouring into Cuba, we are no longer urgently needed or wanted. One can wonder whether the 9,000 tractors that Soviet Russia claims it will have delivered by the end of 1964 will not dominate the island's tractor park.[13] The Nicaro Nickel plant is now run by Soviet technicians, who bring in their own equipment.

The business community is beginning to wonder whether our political goals are being best achieved by prohibiting American business from sharing in the benefits of the markets enjoyed by others. Some evidence suggests that a revision of American trade policies with respect to the Communist bloc of Europe may be under way. Cuba, if it reaches the point where commercial transactions with the United States might be initiated (together with some Cuban sweetening to be provided by the offer of compensation to selected claimants), will in time come up for review. It is also probable that in the transition from a Communist-bloc-dominated Cuba to one of a Tito status—or from a totalitarian economic system to a mixed economy, as in the case of Guinea in Africa—the first thaw in the ice will come with isolated commercial transactions. We are, however, not ready for such a development at this time. It took only twenty-four hours after the first press reports of Cuban interest in buying lard, the sale of which appeared permissible under the food and drug exception to the embargo, for the Department of Commerce to put lard sales under specific prior license. More recently all food and drugs, previously exportable without prior permission, have been subjected to license.

Even if we should optimistically assume a Cuba that has gone to a liberal democratic society or to some more probable nontotalitarian variation of such a democracy, and a United States eager to help assure the viability of the new state, we will still find that nothing like the previous business relations will be restored between the two countries. One must assume that when a democracy succeeds a Marxist, collectiv-

---

[13] *New York Times,* May 30, 1964.

110 J. WILNER SUNDELSON

ized society, the results will be different from those ensuing when democracy follows a right-wing or military dictatorship whose only virtues are "stability" and "order," as in Venezuela.

A changed political climate in Cuba would require United States business interests who resume trade with Cuba to make fundamental adjustments based on the following factors:

1. To begin with, the United States government and United States business do not have too good a record of cooperating to instill viability into newly installed, democratically inclined governments. The Dominican Republic is a case in point. In underdeveloped countries in general and in Latin America in particular, the survival capacity of liberal democratic regimes may be precarious. A government taking over from a Marxist regime will be even more vulnerable. This means that American business will be wary of taking risks in any new "democratic" Cuba—the risks of extending credit, making investments, sending technicians and managers to live there, and using Cuba in our year-round tourist search for the sun and sea.

2. We now realize that some kinds of investments are no longer profitable, or are extremely risky because of their sensitivity in a nationalistic climate. United States business interests owned some 90 percent of Cuban utilities and 50 percent of the railroads, and they owned the banks in which 25 percent of the country's deposits were held. It is extremely unlikely that United States private capital will go back into Cuban utilities or railroads. Regardless of a new political climate, some part of the business spectrum will most likely be outside the interest, or perhaps even the reach, of private investment, especially foreign investment. Utilities, the extraction of mineral resources, and the provision of mass-produced necessities, such as pharmaceuticals, are having troubles elsewhere with nationalistic regimes, even those untainted by Marxism.

3. Not only American business but also any future Cuban democratic leaders will have to cope with the powerful organized labor heritage of Castro and of the pre-Castro period as well. One need only look at the still tightly-knit, militant Peronist labor movement in Argentina and its political power to imagine what will happen in Cuba. This factor will certainly discourage investments involving large labor employment and make it difficult to envision the necessary political stability. In ad-

dition, the loss of a great part of the professional and middle classes will be a further deterrent to stability.

4. Business tends to follow preestablished trade patterns. Successive waves of United States exports and investments pushed the Cubans into United States consumption patterns, which they could not easily change. Some products will always come from the United States if they can be bought and imported. But for several years Castro has been acquiring products, material, know-how, technicians, and credits, as well as markets for his products, in the Communist bloc. The Communist countries are aggressively pursuing commercial transactions and providing services, such as shipping and airlines, and could well continue these if they saw political advantages in doing so. In 1962, 76 percent of Cuba's exports went to the Communist countries, and imports from these same countries exceeded Cuba's total 1958 imports in tonnage. More recently, with the breakdown of inhibitions and the ineffectiveness of United States pleadings as well as threats, England, France, and Spain have moved into Cuba with capital and consumer goods, with machinery, and with know-how. England and Spain are supplying trucks and buses, and France has agreed to supply locomotives. These trade relations are likely to continue. Spare parts for the trucks and buses now operating in Cuba will be bought from England, France, Spain, and the Communist bloc. In a hypothetical future of reopened relations between the United States and Cuba, we will in a sense be starting from scratch. United States business will have no distribution lines, its agents will have lost all their assets and connections, and credit from friendly American banks in Cuba may not be immediately available. According to press reports,[14] Cuba is shifting to consumer end products and away from capital goods. If this trend continues, a foreseeable consequence will be a reduction of traditional imports and protection of local Cuban industries.

Then there is the matter of a market for Cuba's sugar, once assured of 50 percent of the American market. The beneficiaries of Cuba's former place in that market are today our own beet- and cane-sugar growers and certain foreign sugar growers, including some in Latin America. Recent allocations for the supply of sugar to the United States were labeled "temporary" to signify the eventual necessity of restoring

[14] "Cuba to Cut Back Industrial Drive," *New York Times*, Feb. 26, 1964.

a quota to Cuba, but sugar experts doubt whether the allocations to other nations (the friendly nations) will ever be withdrawn. In turn, those who buy Cuba's sugar will most probably be the major suppliers of commodities to Cuba.

5. Claims of United States investors for property losses in Cuba have been filed for an amount estimated at $1.5 billion. This magnitude is about right, since just before Castro came to power direct investments and portfolio investments reached almost a billion dollars in value, and bank deposits, real estate holdings, commercial debts, personal assets, and the rest could bring the total to the estimated $1.5 billion. No Cuban economy can meet these payments, and it is doubtful whether the United States will intervene to pay off its own citizens. These claims will stand as a major deterrent to the resumption of anything like our earlier economic relations. The Soviet Union's repudiation of World War I debts and its failure to settle lend-lease accounts are still irritants limiting economic relations and providing a legal barrier against extending credits.

6. Finally, there is the intangible factor of how long "*Cuba sí, Yanqui no!*" will continue in the hearts and minds of the Cuban masses—those who must make up tomorrow's consumers, workers, traders, and bureaucrats. We must assume continued anti-American attitudes in labor circles in Cuba and possibly among university students as well. The longer Castro lasts, the stronger will these elements develop.

A post-Castro Cuba could well be a Burma, an Indonesia, or a Ceylon—countries in which the United States business community is either excluded or understandably unwilling to venture resources. But even if we assume the best—a post-Castro Cuba with a climate permitting private enterprise to function—the prospects for United States private enterprise in a "new Cuba" are not good.

All these factors give strong evidence that the Cuba we knew will never be recreated. Nor will the United States economic position in Cuba begin to approach its previous proportions. Not only is United States economic dominance not possible; it would not be accepted. At best Cuba will become an open Swiss-type market, in which we and the rest of the world would compete.

Lessons Learned from the Cuban Experience

One of the lessons to be learned by both our government and the business community is a need for an improved political intelligence and for improved government-to-business communications of a realistic nature on political prospects. In fact, there is today a much closer link than in the past between business and government in a two-way exchange of views. Toward this end, business channels for such dialogues are becoming more sophisticated. In 1961 the State Department described the inevitable collapse of the Batista regime, but prior to 1959 the Department raised no doubts whatever as a guide to the business community. Surely, we should be able to avoid repetitions of such situations. Further, business now knows more about the difficulties that occur whenever political leadership moves to the extreme right or to the extreme left. It can withhold its new capital, as many prospective investors do whenever an underdeveloped country veers toward political extremism. Business should consider whether it is willing to expose itself to losses under doubtful or marginal circumstances by taking whatever insurances and guarantees are available and by practicing the most prudent policies in the light of all the circumstances. We badly need protective devices such as investment guarantees, including a broadening of coverage of political risks.

Some losses will be incurred whenever a government steps in and takes over private investments without reasonable and timely compensation. But one may hope that business will try not to be as surprised as it was by the turn in Cuba, that businessmen will not be lulled into a sense of security while sitting on a dynamite keg, and that they will arm themselves with whatever weapons they can to minimize losses.

Compared with other Latin American countries, Cuba was not a major power or market. However, Cuba has had an overwhelming influence on Latin America and on the estimate of the United States business community as to what can happen in Latin America. The Cuban experience has reduced the flow of investments and credits in a twofold manner. First, Latin American regimes have seen the United States take what Castro has subjected us to. Leaders of both right and left have been encouraged to move toward expropriation, forced rene-

gotiation, and other practices inimical to United States business interests and relations. Secondly, the international investment and trading
community of the United States no longer cherishes a belief that "it
can't happen here." Instead, it has a whole set of deep new misgivings
and suspicions that were seldom expressed formerly and probably
never existed. Some few clairvoyant American businessmen in Cuba
saw someone like Castro inevitably coming, but they admit their timing
was wrong. Cuba not only showed what an extremist revolutionary
could do under our very noses, but also showed that, with some notable
exceptions, the Latin American governments are either not interested
or not able to invoke collective military or even economic sanctions
against a Castro. The states of the hemisphere voted economic sanctions against Castro only after Cuba's involvement in the Venezuelan
arms cache case had been persuasively demonstrated. The business
community, at least in this writer's opinion, does not generally believe
that it acted against its own interests or those of the United States in
pre-Castro Cuba. Nor does it believe that any different patterns of behavior in Cuba could have done very much to prevent an unpredictable
revolutionary such as Castro from coming into power.

Of course, leaders of the business community and some in the United
States government believe that there are situations and countries in
which enlightened business policies will strengthen democratic forces
and deter political leaders of the extreme left or right. But a distinction
must be made between the situations of developing countries and the
peculiar circumstances of the Cuban case. In some countries, aid programs can be effective. Programs may include laudable efforts to
strengthen the small group of indigenous entrepreneurs in the developing countries and to create and support institutions granting and
guaranteeing credit to small and middle-size business enterprises. But
in the case of isolated investments of foreign private capital and know-
how, their impact may be too small and too slow.

Cuba has taught the United States investor to look diligently for
signs of impending disappearance of a climate congenial to the successful pursuit of profits, and for portents of the accompanying disasters of
debt repudiation and expropriation. The recent drastic drop in United
States private capital flowing to Latin America suggests that sober
evaluations have resulted in some decisions not to make new investments. Brazil under Goulart frightened away investors who remem-

bered Cuba. Favorable decisions at this moment tend to cluster on projects in Mexico, Peru, and Venezuela. One characteristic of our time is that countries move in and out of a dangerous or a favorable category. The negative decisions appear whenever a judgment is made that the risks of new capital commitments outweigh the anticipated degree of safety and profitability. The countries are not difficult to recognize: one need only observe the changes in policies on export credit insurance of those extending such protection. At any given time there are countries this side of the Communist curtains that are barred for political reasons from eligibility for coverage. Those Americans who are investing abroad today are a much smaller segment of the investing community than those who held interests in Cuba. Public utilities and the extractive industries are absent from the list of new investors in all but isolated instances.

Judging from what the isolated investor seeks, and what students of the problem believe to be required, new protective "umbrellas" and incentive devices are needed if United States private investment is to participate more widely in developing countries. These are needed not only to provide insurance and guarantees but also to cover taxation, local currency availabilities, and changed antitrust attitudes. The Johnson administration has recognized this, as can be seen in the proposed tax credit against United States corporate taxation for new investments in less developed countries. There is also a need to develop more flexible policies, such as those Europeans have found successful, but United States business and Washington are reluctant to pursue them. These involve the blending of government capital and risk-taking with private management and limited entrepreneurial capital and commercial risks. The custom-made arrangements for the Volta River power and aluminum venture in Ghana offer an isolated example of this kind of cooperation. Other nations, notably Italy, are adept at blending governmental and private resources in a way that assures the ability of the participating private sector to cope with the limited risks it assumes.

Business involves the taking of risks. International business involves additional dimensions of risk. The shock of the Cuban experience has created some revisions in the prevailing attitudes of the American business community. It is now known that the United States and the rest of the Western World cannot be certain any longer of using intervention or other pressures to stem Castro-type extremists. The events in Cuba unquestionably had an adverse effect on the flow of investments to the rest of Latin America. (Events in other countries also contributed to this effect.) As a result of Castro's revolution, the green pastures of the increased population and the rising gross national product in Europe have appeared even greener, in spite of the competition and other difficulties in entering European markets.

Will United States private capital play the role it once played in meeting a large share of the capital and know-how needs of the under-developed countries? We think it will, in spite of Cuba. However, United States business will not soon again misassess the risks of strong nationalism bringing in its wake extremists of the Castro variety.

KALMAN H. SILVERT is Professor of Government at Dartmouth College and Director of Studies of the American Universities Field Staff. *The Conflict Society: Reaction and Revolution in Latin America* (1961) and *Chile Yesterday and Today* (1965) are among his numerous Latin American studies.

A Hemispheric Perspective

KALMAN H. SILVERT

The emergence of Cuba as a revolutionary Marxist socialist country brought to conscious and critical levels the full range of international political concerns. The missile crisis raised profound questions of security for the United States, Cuba, the Soviet Union, and indeed the world. The Cuban ideology as revealed by confiscations and by Messianic revolutionism and its accompanying subversion of neighbors' polities has put under enormous strain all programmatic designs for hemispheric organization abuilding since 1889.

Selective perception of the Cuban phenomenon beclouded interpretations everywhere. The American business community joined with conservative Latin American elements to see Fidelism as a total threat, leading many of its spokesmen to an early advocacy of force to destroy the Castro revolution in its home. The American intellectual community shifted from broad sympathy to antagonism as time revealed ever more of the design of the new Cuban government. Behind these reactions was a mass amorphous welling of enthusiasm for Castro. Though part of this enthusiasm was certainly faddish, it extended even to some banking circles—an asset squandered by Castro, the victim of his own deterministic views of a United States ineluctably dominated by Wall Street.

Latin American nationalists passed from an early period of infatuation into a polarization of points of view as the march of events carried

117

Cuba all the way to military, economic, and political alliance with the Soviet bloc and to involvements with China. These differing perceptions were predictable. The United States by and large interpreted a communized Cuba above all else as a threat to national security, then as an economic and ideological defeat, and lastly as a nuisance in the conduct of foreign policy. In the early phases of the Castro regime the Latin American nations saw Cuba as an ideological and legal problem leading to troublesome international negotiations; only very late did Cuba become a basic security matter for them. It was the missile crisis, perhaps more than any other factor, that forced the issue of national integrity on Latin American policy planners, creating a primary community of interest between North and Latin America, which has as yet to be fully exploited .

The special relationship between the United States and Latin America had as its traditional basis the role of the former as the "protector nation" of the hemisphere.[1] The exercise of this security function has not been appreciated by many Latin Americans. For geographical if for no other reasons, appreciation weakens with distance from the United States. For a short time after World War II, this special relationship was at its peak, supported by the economic strength of the United States, which was almost monopolistic before Europe recuperated. However, the atomic stalemate, the economic resurgence of Europe, and the growth of modern nationalistic ideologies in Latin America, reinforced by the worldwide abolition of colonialism, have changed the meaning of U.S. power in the hemisphere. But the missile crisis revealed that the bedrock layer of interest in U.S. protection was still there, and perhaps more solid than ever.

The Latin American nations followed different paths on the measures appropriate to their defense, according to their estimates of their own domestic strength and their historical position with respect to the United States. The troubled Caribbean nations, even before the missile crisis, favored decisive military action against Cuba, and some extended warm hospitality to Cuban rebel forces. But the stronger and

---

[1] For an excellent debate on the issue of the special position of the United States in Latin America see Ypsilon, "A Note on Inter-American Relations," Albert O. Hirschman, "Abrazo vs. Coexistence: Comments on Ypsilon's Paper," and Lincoln Gordon's rejoinder, "Abrazo vs. Coexistence: Further Comments," in Albert O. Hirschman, ed., *Latin American Issues: Essays and Comments* (Twentieth Century Fund, 1961), pp. 53-68.

more distant nations did not share these sentiments. The more freedom of political maneuver a given country enjoyed in internal affairs, the more difficult it was to persuade it to support joint hemispheric security measures, as distinguished from the internal precautions against Fidelist movements each might exercise. The government of Mexico, for example, took a strong international position against any measures implying interventionism,[2] but domestically it adopted stringent laws against "social dissolution," in order to contain domestic Fidelist subversion. Chile, Bolivia, and Brazil reacted in accordance with their traditional foreign policy and their own internal political arrangements, resisting U.S. "adventurism" in Cuba and striving to maintain normal relations. Temporarily weakened Argentina vacillated and finally reacted in foreign affairs consistent with her internal disarray and her need to find external support—first opposing Cuban expulsion from the Organization of American States, and then favoring it after pressure was applied to President Frondizi by his own military.

The positive result of this belated understanding of the breadth of the Cuban problem was to make a wide spectrum of Latin Americans potentially receptive to the North American point of view. The clear meaning of the missile crisis forced many romantic believers away from emotional support of Castro and into independent or neutral attitudes, causing a renewal of interest in what might possibly be forthcoming from the United States in the way of ideological as well as material assistance toward modernization. Although the extensive Latin sympathy for President Kennedy provided a ready means for the expression of such American support, this opportunity for political discourse was never seized. The United States saw the Alliance for Progress in a grand political sense, but Latin Americans gutted this approach by treating it as simply another unilateral assistance program.

[2] Francisco Cuevas Cancino, "The Foreign Policy of Mexico," in Joseph E. Black and Kenneth W. Thompson, *Foreign Policies in a World of Change* (Harper & Row, 1963), p. 658, states: "Intimate geographical and strategic ties make it impossible for Mexico to maintain a position of onlooker with regard to what happens in Cuba. Toward the revolutionary government, she seeks refuge in her traditional policy of non-intervention. She believes that this government constitutes one more stage in the self-determination of the Cuban people. With this policy, she is trying to face the situation which changes assumptions which have existed since the Clayton-Bulwer Treaty (1850) which established Anglo-Saxon superiority in the American Mediterranean. Leaning on her conscience of law and on the free determination of peoples, Mexico acts on the assumption that the Cuban Revolution will unfold without affecting her own development."

An aspect of the Cuban experience that has been little understood in the United States is that socially and politically the little island is the Iberian cultural world's first almost-modern state. Of course, there are many significant pockets of political modernism in other Latin American countries, but the Cuban government seems to have been the first to evoke as well as impose forcefully a kind of national coherence throughout its society. Latin American interest in Cuba thus goes far beyond an understandable pride in "one of our boys making it" in standing up to the United States and surviving. It probably goes even deeper than the question of whether Cuba is attempting to demonstrate a Soviet (as opposed to Western) path to modernization, for in social and political, if not economic, organization the island may well be already modern or almost so.[3] (There is, unfortunately, little hard information concerning attitudes, values, and social structure on which to make a firm judgment.) It is taken for granted in Latin America, however, that Cuba has broken out of traditional Latin American molds and into the early stages of modern nationhood.

Modern social organization, as the phrase is used here, refers to a social system sufficiently open to permit broad interclass mobility—a system possessing communications and attitudes that transcend class lines. In its related political sense, modernization then implies the growth of the national community as the claimant of the citizen's primary loyalty. An open class structure, training and formal education to promote mobility, status rewards as well as economic rewards, and the containment and channeling of class differences by the building of super-class, community-wide loyalties—these are necessary elements of modernism. They permit citizens' armies, industrialization and urbanization, and the devices of social control, which, when unfettered, produce despotism, and when dispersed and controlled and rooted in an enlightened citizenry create the conditions for democratic processes.

Many bits of evidence suggest that Castro's Cuba is functioning in certain respects like a modern nation-state. The destruction of major parts of the middle groups by death, emigration, escape, and exile created a social vacuum that must perforce promote mobility for at least a limited time. The power of the government to withstand adversities—

---

[3] Throughout I have used political modernity to mean the existence of the secular nation-state and the correlative attitudes and ideologies required for its legitimation. For a fuller statement, see my "Introduction" in K. H. Silvert, ed., *Expectant Peoples: Nationalism and Development* (Random House, 1963).

blockade, cultural and political isolation, the work of exiles in sabotage and attempted invasion, drought, hurricane, and massive technical inefficacy coupled with uninformed political experimentation—implies a strength that can only be based on a high degree of consensus from certain groups and a special kind of opposition from others. Although there can be no demonstration of this analysis,[4] it is probable that the anti-Castro opposition within Cuba is split between those willing to re- volt with assistance from abroad and those who reject such measures because they are treasonous. Indeed, this schism affects even the Cuban exiles. Perhaps the most important piece of evidence is the to- talitarian nature of government in today's Cuba. The government's power seems to be the product not only of extensive policing techniques and saturation propaganda, but also of the active participation of large groups of Cubans. Distasteful as these methods are to those of us com- mitted to the democratic process, we know that totalitarianism is not incompatible with high levels of educational achievement, mass com- munications, and industrial urbanization. (How viable such politics are for long-term dynamic development is another matter.)[5]

Whether in fact Cuba has or has not crossed the frontier from the last century to this one, most policymakers in the hemisphere act as though it has. The island is being dealt with, willy-nilly, as a national society, and not as a banana republic—even though the latter treatment, too, was tried at the Bay of Pigs. The internal changes in Cuba, whatever

---

[4] Current sources on domestic affairs in Cuba are contradictory not only factually and interpretatively, but in the very essence of the understanding each author brings to his subject. For example, Jean Daniel in his "Boycotting Cuba: Whose Interest Does It Serve?," *The New Republic* (Dec. 28, 1963), pp. 19-22, and in his well-known interviews of Castro at the time of President Kennedy's assassination, is directly opposed to the feel of Theodore Draper's article, "Five Years of Castro's Cuba," *Commentary*, XXXVII, 1 (Jan. 1964), 25-37. The reader may also be inter- ested in comparing Tad Szulc's *The Winds of Revolution: Latin America Today— And Tomorrow* (Praeger, 1963), with Leslie Dewart's *Christianity and Revolution: The Lesson of Cuba* (Herder & Herder, 1963). In these two cases, we have a difference of focus. The only empirical data available can be found in Maurice Zeitlin, "Working Class Politics in Cuba: A Study in Political Sociology" (unpub- lished doctoral dissertation, University of California at Berkeley, 1964). This in- vestigation, based on interviews of 210 workers in 21 plants in 1961 and 1962, cannot be definitive, but it is inferentially supportive of the national identification thesis.

[5] For a discussion of this question see George F. Kennan, "America and the Russian Future," *Foreign Affairs*, XXIX, 3 (April 1951), 351-70. Also, K. H. Silvert, "Peace, Freedom and Stability," in William Manger, ed., *The Alliance for Progress: A Critical Appraisal* (Public Affairs Press, 1963).

their defects, seem to have been sufficiently effective to support these implicitly held external views.

The present situation of Cuba in the hemisphere may be summarized as follows:

1. Time has worked its usual wonders. Gone is the always unfounded fear that Cuba could be turned into a showcase of Communism in a matter of months. The appeal of Fidelism has not disappeared, but with respect to the problems of development Castroism has become highly distasteful to most Latin Americans. The nationalistic component of the ideology has been weakened by Cuba's cold war involvement, but it seems still to be strong. Time has also afforded reflection to the other nations of the hemisphere.

Almost all Latin American governments now agree with the United States that all levels of international affairs are involved in this dispute, and that problems of fundamental sovereignty, long-range policy reformulation, and ad hoc difficulties are sure to go on. Tactical divergence still continues, however. The United States has eschewed unilateral armed action against Cuba unless cold war military-security matters again arise, but it would like effective multilateral isolation of Cuba on all fronts and with enthusiastic Latin American cooperation. Some of the weaker states would now like to see an inter-American invasion of the island, but, because of the opposition of the major Latin American powers, are following the containment lead of the United States. Argentina, in a probable realignment with Brazil, Mexico, and Chile, as supported by Bolivia for special reasons, opposes any invasions of Cuban sovereignty and has only reluctantly conceded to some aspects of isolation. Although aware of Cuba's subversive intentions, these countries remain faithful to traditional forms of safeguarding sovereignty; they presume that they have enough internal strength to avoid falling into Fidelism. The policies are pursued at the governmental level, of course, but dissident groups in every Latin American country, from the right as well as the left, oppose them.

The various perceptions of the significance of Castro Cuba have grown more alike but still remain significantly apart. The fundamental reason is a divergence of interest. Development remains Latin America's major problem, whereas security in a world of rapidly shifting power blocs, as well as increasingly pressing domestic questions, claims the primary political attention of North America. In an immediate sense, this need for security can only be met by the United States with policies designed to halt Cuba's insistent attempts to subvert other Latin American political systems. Because political publics vary widely among the nations of the hemisphere, perception also varies—not only on the basis of ideology but also on the basis of social class and, in some Latin American countries, caste.

2. A broader spectrum of communications and policy has become available in the hemisphere. American political leaders have publicly stated that all forms of social and economic organization are acceptable in the hemisphere so long as affiliation with the Communist bloc is not implied. Military coups in Argentina, Peru, Ecuador, the Dominican Republic, Guatemala, and Honduras have put North American political intentions to a severe test. Though intentions and deeds have not been in full harmony in these cases, enough of the new liberality has remained as a point of attention. The appeal of Fidelism has sharply decreased; this has made possible some understanding response from broad segments of the Latin American national publics.

3. New policies have begun to evolve, both in the United States and in Latin America. These are discussed in the following sections.

The Alliance and Social Change as Arms of International Relations

A policy of containment has been the consistent element in American action against Cuba. Critics have complained that containment is mere negativism, but the policy had its very positive side and its ethical justification when applied earlier in the cold war to the Sino-Soviet bloc and later in its extension to Cuba. The "X Paper" of George Kennan argued that drawing firm international lines could assist in creating the conditions of security and gaining the time necessary for the internal dynamics of the Soviet Union to push that country into a more responsible internal and international posture. Kennan's theoretical argument was that self-sustaining development must create patterns of responsibility, if not of democracy. He also argued that the justification for saying nay to others must be the conviction that the Western system, although imperfect, is in greater harmony with the nature and dignity of man than totalitarianism. The only conclusion for a reasonable man, as he saw it, was that the Western democracies must strive for greater

human freedom and dignity, not only because of their intrinsic human-
istic value but also because such striving would serve as an example
and would justify containment morally. Kennan wrote:

Any message we may try to bring to others will be effective only if it is
in accord with what we are to ourselves, and if this is something sufficiently
impressive to compel the respect and confidence of a world which, despite
all its material difficulties, is still more ready to recognize and respect
spiritual distinction than material opulence.[6]

American aims in Cuba were at times mixed, of course. The initial
economic sanctions and the Bay of Pigs invasion were attempts to destroy the Castro government. Short of that, however, the recurrent policy has been one of isolating Cuba from the hemisphere in negative as
well as positive senses. That is, American economic sanctions to harass
the island, military and intelligence efforts to seal off the export of
weapons and of trained revolutionaries, and political measures to coun-
teract ideological affronts were all combined with affirmative
justifications—the commitment to change those conditions in other
countries that encouraged Fidelist sympathies, the promise that the
United States would exert itself in favor of all brands of non-Communist modernization, and even perhaps a hint (whether real or fancied is
not publicly known) to Castro after the missile crisis that he would be
free of external invasion threat to work out his path toward political
decency as best he might within the surrounding set of other political
imperatives.[7]

The Alliance for Progress is the major instrument of these
justifications for sealing off a neighboring state. Despite the bitterness
of many of the criticisms of the Alliance, much can be said in its defense. Certainly the Alliance program is not merely more of the same.
Old and persistent Latin American requests for their own Marshall

---

[6] George F. Kennan, *American Diplomacy: 1900-1950* (University of Chicago
Press, 1951), p. 154.
[7] This matter has occasioned much debate. Some persons have purported to see
in President Kennedy's television address to the nation during the missile crisis an
implicit guarantee against U.S. invasion of Cuba if the island ceased to pose a cold
war military threat. The sentences are: "These new weapons are not in your interest. They contribute nothing to your peace and well being. They can only under-
mine it. *But this country has no wish to cause you to suffer or to impose any system upon you.* We know that your lives and land are being used as pawns by
those who deny you freedom." [Italics added.] The President continued with an
exhortation to the Cubans to throw off foreign domination, at which time they
would be welcomed back "to the associations of this hemisphere."

Plan were manifestly unrealistic; to offer economic assistance to already developed states is different from aid to underdeveloped areas. The examples of Argentina, Uruguay, and Chile—Latin America's old economic leaders—have finally been seen in Washington as demonstrating that economic development in itself is either not enough or not quick enough to provide the social and political bases necessary to ensure American security in the hemisphere and to promise self-sustaining development to the Latin American states. The Alliance undertook a combined program of social and economic development, with the overt political aspects once again underplayed in the largely unexamined hope that desirable politics follow in the wake of industrialization, literacy, decent housing, and so forth.

The social development objectives of the Alliance are designed to chip away at the barriers separating lower middle from upper lower groups in Latin America. The impermeability of this relationship impedes the automatic operation of the "trickle system" relied on by the economically orthodox to keep the capital investment cycle going; the "trickle" is simply not permitted to go all the way down, thus limiting effective demand, inhibiting labor availability and mobility, and creating resentments among mass groups that make such groups accessible to the appeals of political extremism. The agrarian, tax, and other reforms proposed under the Alliance also have for their purpose a change in social structure and in the distribution of political power. Insofar as participation, mobility, and identification are necessary concomitants of development, the Alliance has not been pursuing illogical or irrational ends. On the contrary, these measures are imperative, no matter what may be the ideology of the modernizing groups.[8]

To pass judgment on the success or failure of the Alliance at this time is unjustified. Three years are not enough for the program to take effect. The problems that have arisen to harry the future development of the Alliance include the recalcitrance of some (by no means all and by no means most of the influential) Latin American political leaders. More important, many Latin American leaders do not know how to go

[8] "No real economic development consistent with the goals we have set ourselves is possible without a social structure which permits the great mass of people to share in the benefits of progress, and affords each man a fair expectation of social justice. This often means basic, even revolutionary, changes in the structure of society."—Dean Rusk, "The Alliance in the Context of World Affairs," in John C. Dreier, ed., *The Alliance for Progress: Problems and Perspectives* (Johns Hopkins Press, 1962), p. 112.

about promoting and channeling the social change they desire, even when they have the power sufficient for some substantial reform, as they may well have in Chile and Uruguay, for example. Other problems stem from the fact that social development funds call for offshore purchases, inevitably implying a drain on dollar reserves in a time of exchange concern in the United States. Difficulties that the U.S. Congress faces in foreign assistance matters are notorious, and all too often aid planning has been confounded by the exigencies of immediate political crisis. Another major problem is that massive amounts of money for economic and social purposes are not being made available. Latin American capitalists have not flocked to stimulate their national economies; Congress has given the Alliance less money for nineteen countries than the Soviet Union has extended to Cuba; and the American business community lacks confidence in Latin America and has alternative investment channels of greater attractiveness. A comment on U.S. investments in Latin America follows:

> Latin American politicians sometimes say—and others probably think—that the United States "cannot" withdraw her interest from Latin America. This is not the fact. She should not, if it can be maintained. But she "can." The United States does not need Latin America as a field of investment for her capital. There is, and increasingly will be, more than enough work for American capital at home. . . . Everything taken into account, American capital does not yearn to go abroad at all and does not go abroad easily. In recent years it has been difficult to induce it to go to Latin America. Nearly 80 percent of the capital actually exported to the area has been expended for discovery and development of oil.[9]

If the criteria for granting Agency for International Development funds are to be related more directly to immediate political considerations, the amounts will have to be increased to bolster the power they are supposed to supply. Further, if the Alliance is to carry out its objectives, the social development aspects of its program cannot be neglected. In addition, if the hemisphere is to proceed with all deliberate speed toward democratic as well as modern organization, strong political persuasion, together with an operationally adequate knowledge of the essentials of total development, is indispensable.

Observers have said that the Alliance offers no magic in Latin Ameri-

⁹ Adolf A. Berle, *Latin America: Diplomacy and Reality* (Harper & Row for the Council on Foreign Relations, 1962), p. 8.

ca. The blame is usually attached to the submergence of the myth factor—the absence of an appealing ideology in the program. Tad Szulc writes, "Even as late as 1963, it was not fully understood in Washington that the success—even the acceptance—of the Alliance for Progress as a workable cooperative scheme hinged to an immense extent on its political impact on the Latin Americans." He continues: "Among the many elusive and often contradictory feelings now rising in the Hemisphere is an undefinable malaise that can only be described as a 'weariness of the West.' "[10]

A basic weakness of the Alliance is that it has commonly been seen as everything, when in reality it is only a highly necessary part. At large, the hope has been that machinery and houses can manufacture developed people. The Cuban idea has been the opposite—namely, that participants, or those who can be fooled into thinking of themselves as participants, are the first cause of national power. This idea, illusory or not, can be useful, as the present Cuban regime's experience shows. A Latin American sociologist has put the matter clearly:

If it is of course true that in some countries of longer democratic tradition—such as Argentina, Chile, Uruguay, and others—the only way of obtaining legitimacy is through a proper election; in the majority of the less developed nations, *especially outside of the cities*, the vote lacks symbolic value or has it negatively. When Castro asserts that the Cubans have something more than the vote, for they have been given a rifle, he certainly does not express a conception of democracy acceptable to the urban workers or the middle classes of the more developed countries of Latin America, but indeed he does probably reflect an attitude which can be extended to a large part of a recently mobilized population or one in a rapid process of mobilization. [Italics added.][11]

The Alliance's inability to generate political sex appeal stems in important part from Washington's discomfort with and suspicion of Latin America's nationalist movements. From the Mexican Revolution to the present, every Latin nationalist movement has caused policy vacillation in the United States, even though stable and fruitful accommodations are eventually made. In nationalism lies warm, human, earthy magic, and not the cold rationality of "sensible" moderation. The political ap-

[10] Szulc, *op. cit.* The first quotation is from p. 185, the second from p. 186.
[11] Gino Germani, *Política y sociedad en una época de transición* (Buenos Aires: Ed. Paidós, 1962), p. 161

peal of Castroism remains strong in Latin America to the extent to which the Cuban revolution continues to be seen as a success for nationalism. Fidelism, of course, is not Latin America's only example of nationalism. Between the right-wing, neo-fascist nationalism of Argentina, the Christian Democratic nationalism of Chile, the Social Democratic nationalism of Venezuela, the pragmatic nationalism of Brazil, and the Marxist-Leninist nationalism of Cuba lie broad ideological gulfs. Because nations aspiring to develop share some nationalistic foreign policy commitments, there is a community of interests and even of subtle understanding among the more advanced Latin American governments (Uruguay, Argentina, Chile, Brazil, Bolivia, and Mexico). Implicit identifications with Cuba have stayed the hands of these nations against Castro and led them into other international actions that overlap many of the less extreme measures of the Castro administration. The only exception among the more developed nations is Venezuela, which was made a special target of Fidelist Messianism and thus has a survival interest in the destruction of the Castro government.

Brazil's policy of "neutralism benevolent to the West"—the best-known example in foreign policy of the new nationalism—is certain to be a potent factor in the hemisphere. Underestimation of the aspirations of some Latin American political leaders and ideologists is all too common in a world accustomed to thinking of that region as permanently benighted. The outlook for Brazil was recounted by Frank Bonilla in 1963:

> In the rather blood-chilling exercise in *Realpolitik* which closes [a nationalistic treatise by the Brazilian intellectual, Helio Jaguaribe] . . . the author outlines a policy in which, by judiciously playing all the actual or potential major power blocs off against each other, Brazil will eventually emerge as a major power in itself, completely equipped with a store of advanced ballistic missiles and atomic weapons. There is no reason to doubt that this kind of hardheaded analysis of future possibilities is going on wherever such decisions are being made in Brazil. The new outlook has recently been quite succinctly stated by a former Minister of Finance in a newspaper defense of his dealings with the International Monetary Fund: "Let us not create anew in Brazil the impression that to deal with the Monetary Fund and other credit agencies of friendly countries is an act of submission or *entreguismo*. *We are already too big and too powerful to feel shy about contending with other nations*." [Italics added.][12]

[12] Frank Bonilla, "A National Ideology for Development: Brazil," in Silvert, ed., *op. cit.*, p. 253.

Brazil is not the only ambitious state of Latin America. Argentina (its dreams of having an A-bomb were not simply the maunderings of Perón) is now in the Chinese wheat trade. Uruguay has been quietly trading extensively with the Soviet Union, including massive petroleum imports, for the past several years. Chile has long threatened to expand contacts with Iron Curtain lands and has from the beginning been an independent voice of noninterventionist conscience on Cuban affairs. Mexico has demonstrated political independence on the international scene many times during the past three decades. Cuba has certain policy components that are similar, although the Cuban departure from hemispheric comity is in its extreme character of a qualitatively different order from neutralism.

To take perhaps the most important example, Brazilian neutralism is different from the neutrality of India. Recognizing their intellectual and cultural attachment to the West, as well as the economic facts of international life, Brazilian nationalists aspire to an independent foreign policy line which they often compare with that of Britain. In pursuit of this objective they seek diplomatic and commercial ties with all countries of the world, insist on complete freedom to determine their domestic political arrangements, and do not hesitate to disagree with the spokesmen of friendly nations. Such an objective must carry with it disappointments and failures. The long-standing disagreement between Brazil and the International Monetary Fund, for example, is rooted in the contradiction between the attitudes of Brazil's leaders and the capacities of the country's economy on the one hand, and a certain unreality in the IMF's recommendations on the other. Paradoxically, the Fund wants Brazil to engage in stabilization measures akin to those that were successful in highly developed Germany and Great Britain. The Brazilian answer is that such a recommendation is a violation of Brazilian sovereignty and is in any event impossible to the Brazilian polity. The success of Brazil in withstanding external economic pressure is testimony to her growingly effective political power.

Even though many official and semiofficial spokesmen in the United States have begun to insist that economic and social orthodoxy are not required for good standing in this hemisphere, neutralism in foreign affairs and such internal measures as the nationalization of industries strain the fabric of U.S. policy. Latin American foreign policy independence inevitably means a weakening of the Organization of American

States and, in turn, a strengthening of the United Nations and its sub-ordinate agencies. But the United States is deeply committed to hemi-spheric agencies and to a certain bilateralism in its dealings with Latin America. Neutralism also implies closer economic relations between Latin America and the Soviet bloc. The United States has doubts about the Latin American states being sufficiently strong to resist the politics that accompany trade. Expropriations are often symbolically necessary to new nationalists, and sometimes also have implications for the heavi-ly *étatiste* development planning characteristic of emergent lands ev-erywhere. Such action is embarrassing to the U.S. government when it faces its domestic business constituency, and it hinders the develop-ment of the private capital aspects of the Alliance. Independent foreign policies not only bring Latin American states closer to the United Na-tions but also lead them into identification with Afro-Asian nations. The expansion of the United Nations with the recent birth of so many new states has caused Great Power problems.

The United States will have to become accustomed to such tensions, for they are the price of the political nationalism which seemingly is a natural accompaniment of economic and social development. The Cuban experience impelled the United States toward greater toleration of nationalistic stirrings than it had before. Attempts by the United States to interest allied European nations more deeply in Latin Ameri-can economic development, as well as in certain aspects of hemispheric security, indicate that the logic of multilateralism is slowly permeating hemispheric relations. The threat of the French style of international relations, however, is a cause of worry in the United States, for its con-sequence is an intensification of neutralism and its corollaries. The de-bate as to whether the United States should have a special role in Latin America will continue, as will the slow emergence of Latin America into a less isolated and subordinate role—into participant membership in the Western World, instead of simply into the Western Hemisphere.[13]

In this scene of a generalized international response to the domestic processes of modernization, the role of Cuba has been extraordinarily instructive. Cuba has demonstrated a clear difference between neutral-ism and overt commitment to the Soviet bloc, between pragmatic stat-ism and totalitarian *dirigisme*, between the self-willed inferiority

[13] See Hirschman, *op. cit.*, especially pp. 59-63.

which Latin America has for long endured and the real possibilities for emergence into the modern community of nations. Never again will we be able to say that Catholic Latin America is immune to Communism; but never again shall we be able to say, either, that Catholic Latin America is immune to modernism.

The Modernization Process and Receptivity to Castroism

The central issue is how to find a modernization process containing a minimum risk of totalitarian development. To be receptive to modernization does not mean an automatic receptivity to Castroism, which is by no means Latin America's only authoritarian alternative. Some of the highly developed parts of Latin America are not very receptive to Fidelist ideology, although they may be most hospitable to falangist authoritarianism. Other areas are so backward socially as to provide only meager promise of followership publics. The distinction drawn here between generic modernization and specifically Fidelist totalitarian development is important if the Alliance on the U.S. side and the varying approaches on the Latin American side are to create techniques for international assistance fitting the particular circumstances of each Latin American country.

Specialists in comparative politics make use of typology in order to arrive at an understanding of the sociopolitical relations of nations. Typologies set up categories linked by common theoretical assumptions. There are typologies of Latin American countries by such criteria as their political systems, economic and social levels, and degree of national integration. There are even categorizations according to what some scholars think those republics are. Such constructions are useful because they prevent us from thinking either that all Latin American countries are alike or that they are all dissimilar. Typologies may guide predictions realistically and for certain purposes. In regard to Latin America, they may help to indicate where Fidelist sentiment is most likely to occur, where drives toward development exist, and how attitudes penetrate the social structure. Rational policy for specific groups of countries may then be developed.

Some conceptual dangers attend the making of typologies. For example, the figures ordinarily used are simple averages by country. But the fallacy of averages is particularly to be guarded against in dealing with Latin America, where not only inter-country differences but also intra-societal variation can be so large as to make meaningless even a per capita income figure—as in Brazil. What can be the meaning of an average that squashes into a single number the incomes of Amazonian Indian tribes, of disaster-ridden farmers and villagers in the Northeast, and of modern city residents such as those of São Paulo? Unhappily no typology of Latin American societies yet devised effectively takes account of differences among states and degrees of difference within each state. The result is that the classifications always afford a higher predictive value to the cases at each end of the scale. The countries at one end of the scale have such small upper groups and such massive lower ones that the averages are little affected by the few on top. In their turn, the advanced lands at the other end have relatively homogeneous populations (like "white" Argentina, Uruguay, Costa Rica, and Chile), and therefore their averages do not obscure the comparative aspects of the division into types. However, the countries in the middle, undergoing rapid change and with enormous social distances separating ethnic as well as class sectors, are the ones the statistics can handle least well. Obviously, they are also the ones that are most unstable politically.

This warning is not meant to discourage the use of typologies, but rather to encourage its use with caution and to suggest that more adequate categorizations are needed in order to produce better statistics and better theory. Germani has perhaps devised the best typology by social stratification characteristics.[14] Some of the criteria for establishing types are literacy and higher-education rates, the number of persons engaged in farming and mining and other primary activities, the percentage of persons in middle and upper social strata, the annual rate of urbanization, and so forth. These measures are very appropriate to finding those situations in which populations are ready for admission to the modern sectors of society, but in which the channels for full participation in national life are lacking or insufficient. Such frustrated groups are presumably those most likely to seek extraordinary solutions to their aspirations and to be most receptive to the promises of demagoguery.

[14] Germani, op. cit., p. 168. For a related discussion of stages and an early version in English, see Gino Germani and K. H. Silvert, "Politics, Social Structure and Military Intervention in Latin America," Archives Européenes de Sociologie, Vol. I, No. 2 (1961).

The Latin American republics can be divided into the following groups by social stratification, in order of modernity (according to figures of circa 1950, the last year for which relatively complete data are available):

GROUP I.   Argentina, Uruguay, Chile, Costa Rica

GROUP II.   Mexico, Brazil

GROUP III. Cuba, Venezuela, Colombia

GROUP IV.   Panama, Paraguay, Peru, Ecuador, El Salvador, Bolivia, Guatemala, Nicaragua, Dominican Republic, Honduras, Haiti

This distribution is realistic in certain important ways. For instance, Costa Rica appears in Group I despite its unindustrial and generally rural nature, which in other typologies usually condemns this advanced little state to a low position. The large rural populations of Mexico and Brazil do not so override their enormous modern sectors as to push them into statistical equivalence with much less developed states of more even economic characteristics.

The governments of Cuba, Venezuela, and Colombia—as late as 1958—were dedicated to the mutually untenable propositions of (1) maintaining unchanged social structures; (2) continuing industrialization; and (3) retaining military authoritarian rule. Since then Cuba has broken out into Fidelismo, Venezuela has been making the hemisphere's most valiant and earnest attempt at institutional change toward the consciously chosen end of expanded democratic values, and Colombia has experienced only relatively superficial political shifts on top of an essentially unchanged social situation (the death toll from civil violence since 1948 exceeds 200,000).

The striking political changes in Cuba and Venezuela underscore another element difficult to capture: velocity of social change. Dazzling is the only word for the rapidity with which Cuba moved into Communism, and Venezuela passed rapidly from a horridly repressive military tyranny into Social Democratic developmental endeavors. These rapid changes are, of course, rooted in long preparatory periods.

The following typological classification of Latin American republics is based on the degree of national integration:

GROUP I.   Highest degree of homogeneity in social structure and policy: Cuba, Argentina, Uruguay, Costa Rica.

GROUP II.   Strongly demarcated and homogeneous national sectors in coexistence with large groups alienated for class or ethnic reasons: Chile, Venezuela, Brazil, Mexico. (The national sectors of these countries may exhibit a higher level of national integration than some of the lands in Group I, but their attaining full, integrated nationhood is impeded by social differences.)

GROUP III. Superordinate groups split by value disagreement concerning the desirability of national values and integration, again in coexistence with large groups alienated for class or ethnic reasons: Bolivia, Colombia, Peru, Panama, Dominican Republic.

GROUP IV.   Little or no consensual acceptance of national integration among superordinate groups, with large subordinate groups, alienated for class or ethnic reasons: Guatemala, Ecuador, El Salvador, Paraguay, Nicaragua, Honduras, Haiti.

This typology is open to much disagreement. For example, whether Bolivia fits comfortably into Group III is a matter for some debate, with any definitive settlement rendered difficult by the lack of information about attitudes and values among Bolivians. This typology is informed guesswork, presented here as a sample of what is needed for articulated policymaking. It suggests that Chile, even though it has few Indians, might well be in the same functional category as Mexico because both countries possess strongly integrated sectors and functionally alienated ones, signifying that the former cannot count on consensus or the other attributes of national participation from the latter. Thus in both cases law will be less universally effective than, say, in Uruguay, where the polity has broader coverage. Whether or not this particular typology is accurate, this kind of approach is necessary to an ordered knowledge of Latin America's various political systems, and thus, more pointedly, to a knowledge of the likelihood of manifestations of significance in hemispheric relations.

This organization of materials permits the supposition that Argentina, Uruguay, Chile, and Costa Rica will remain relatively calm despite the activities of their internal Fidelists. They all have more or less powerful nationalistic movements of their own, which have drawn otherwise potential recruits to Castroism. Except for Venezuela, which has ascended rapidly in degree of national integration, the appeal of Fidelist solutions is probably strongest among middle and upper social elements in whichever countries of Group III the channels of national identification are not clearly marked by domestic political ideologies.

Violence can be expected in the smallest and poorest countries, as Panama, Haiti, the Dominican Republic, Guatemala, and Honduras have demonstrated. If Fidelism is to affect these republics, it can only be through leaders sufficiently cosmopolitan to understand and accept the idea system involved. Indian villagers and the alienated and suppressed peasantry of most of these countries are little susceptible to this kind of appeal in any depth, although they are often immediately available for short-term peasant revolts. If these traditional manifestations of violence among the peasantry are to be consciously exploited in a program of continuing revolutionary activity, it can only be through the efforts of leaders from higher in the social order acting in the name of an ideology having nothing whatever to do with peasant thought. This pattern was followed in Cuba, where the revolution of the peasantry was not at all that of their middle- and upper-class coordinators.

Conclusion

The United States is most fortunate that it was Cuba (and not Venezuela or Colombia) that chose to march into the Soviet bloc. The smallness and relative weakness of the defector has given the remainder of the hemisphere time to examine the case and to inquire into the strange power ratio of the United States to Cuba which has allowed the latter to survive. Rational democratic discourse has not been our lot, however. There have been laments about the erosion of United States power in the hemisphere as newspapers report revolution in Cuba, then in Argentina, Peru, Ecuador, the Dominican Republic, Haiti, Guatemala, Honduras, Panama.

Perhaps United States power is not being lessened. It may be that what is changing is the *nature* of the relationship between U.S. power and the power of other countries, and that what is required is simply recognition of what it now takes to achieve desired goals. Hans J. Morgenthau has described the situation:

The United States has at its disposal the greatest concentration of material power existing in the world today . . . it is the most powerful nation on earth. Yet the government of that most powerful nation is incapable of making the actions of even the weakest of foreign governments conform to its desires. . . . Some of these peoples [of the weak nations] have become active participants in the process of emancipation, and they now have governments that govern in their name and with their support. Thus, a strong nation intervening with military force may not accomplish its task by removing the government or even conquering the country. It may also have to subdue the population at large, which may take up arms against it. While these possibilities do not rule out the use of force, they make a powerful nation think twice before resorting to it.[15]

The United States does not wish to use unilaterally applied armed force against Cuba. A contained uprising of Cuban rebels with some limited United States support is obviously one thing, a quasi-national war a very different thing. Castro's running defense against invasion rests in the charismatic loyalty he can command; his *ultimate* defense against invasion, however, is that the United States does not *choose* to destroy him under these conditions. Is this impasse the result of a lack of United States power? If we are speaking of power quantitatively, the answer must be No. If we speak qualitatively, the answer must be Yes, for the United States apparently lacks a diversity of *types* of power. To use a military analogy, the United States has been unable to fight an immediately successful diplomatic bush war in Cuba. It is not that power is lost, but rather that no new appropriate ways of employing power have been found. To cite Morgenthau:

Our impotence in the fullness of our power is, then, in some measure the result of objective conditions over which we have no control and which restrict the power of other powerful nations as well. In good measure, however, the source of that impotence is in ourselves. We are paralyzed because our moral, intellectual, and political judgment has gone astray. Our judgment must be reformed before we can expect to recover the use of our power, and upon that recovery the improvement of our foreign policies must wait.[16]

The effect of Cuba on the hemisphere has been like the salt in a stew: little has really been added, but all the tastes have been accented. The meat-and-potato problems remain the same. They are all the old ones:

[15] Hans J. Morgenthau, "The Impotence of American Power," *Commentary*, XXXVI, 5 (Nov. 1963), 384-85.
[16] *Ibid.*, p. 386.

(1) how to promote responsible nationalism; (2) how to encourage social development; (3) how to push economic development; (4) how to secure political dispensations in Latin America acceptable to domestic politics in the United States and the several Latin American republics; (5) how to keep the cold war out of the hemisphere; and (6) how to develop administrative mechanisms that will make it possible to solve the foregoing problems in ways appropriate to each Latin American republic.

It may be said that the United States has so far succeeded in depressing Communist influence in the nineteen republics, in keeping atomic weapons and long-range missiles out of Cuba, and in making a realistic innovation in linking social to economic development in the Alliance. In all other respects the United States has suffered a flat failure by default—a failure because it did not even try. Only vague words have been occasionally sounded to assist the growth of Western ideologies of national identification in Latin America. Social development has been translated only into the materialistic terms of housing, literacy, and land reform but not into terms of status and identification. Economic development has been toyed with as a simple apolitical matter of marketplaces and capital allocations—an exercise in dehumanized gamesmanship.

Aside from the loss of Cuba to the Western World (it is hoped that the loss is only temporary), Castroism has worked no fundamental change in hemispheric relations, though the fall of the island to Communism has exacerbated preexisting problems and cast them in a new light. Democratic groups still have time to find proper solutions, however, and there is little reason to think that the ration of time is not fairly generous in most of the republics. If a relaxation in East-West tensions leads to a relaxed attitude in the United States toward the developmental problems of Latin America, neutralism may undergo changes. If the United States is successful in infusing the hemisphere with political excitement and public hope, the reward may well be an enlargement of the effective Western community—providing increased basic security for all, a commonality of long-range policy, and the friendly converse of brothers in the dealings of the day.

Most recommendations for the improvement of United States foreign policy have been of "Ugly American" persuasion. That is, they have concerned themselves with the administration of day-to-day problems, with the instrumental part of the task alone, and even that in a narrow sense. Thus we are told that all will be well if our representatives in Latin America speak Spanish and Portuguese, if their personalities are warm, and if they get out and talk to the people. This portion of the problem is one for adequate administrative management. It is by no means an unimportant consideration, for the tone and style of daily affairs depend in good measure on the routine activities of United States representatives abroad and their counterparts at home. Inefficiencies here can cause small incidents to become serious ones, or they can cause bad reporting and information evaluation, which would impede rational direction from Washington. There has been improvement at this level, and the quality of United States representation abroad has risen sharply. It might be added that greater interagency coordination seems patently desirable—a matter not only for administrative housekeeping experts but also for the draftsmen of guidelines in Washington.

At the opposite extreme from day-to-day problems lie the profound policy interests. To make any recommendations for action here seems pointless, since everyone agrees that man should be good and free and decent. It is this core of values that publicists like to project as an image. An explicit awareness of implicit attitudes can be helpful: for example, Franklin D. Roosevelt was beloved of the Latin Americans although his administrations did little of material benefit for them, and the great sadness of the assassination of President Kennedy called forth a profound sense of identification from all peoples of the hemisphere. The United States, to take another example, has often been singled out as the most revolutionary factor in Latin America because of the stimuli for change, emulation, and aspiration with which it bombards other countries merely by existing. Many public opinion polls taken in Latin America reflect this fundamental identification with what the United States symbolizes,[17] although the same persons who express this primary sympathy may also attack specific United States foreign policy with great bitterness.

[17] See, for example, Alain Girard and Raúl Samuel, *Situación y perspectivas de Chile en septiembre de 1957* (Santiago de Chile: Ed. Universitaria, 1958), in which we find the United States the most favorably seen non-Latin American country by a third of the Chileans interviewed; West Germany is next with 20 percent, and only 4 percent chose the Soviet Union. About 85 percent named democratic Western states.

The filling of the psychological and ideological gap in the hemisphere depends on some definition and projection of basic values. The accomplishment of this task is not in the hands of bureaucrats, except in its relatively secondary technical aspects. The crystallization of "image" depends from the topmost levels of government, where style, conviction, and decision flow together. If the executive establishment itself does not choose to reflect attitudes appealing to the deepest convictions of Latin America's modernizing nationalists, hemispheric relations will have to struggle along without much emotional warmth.

The Latin American modernizing nationalist seeks sovereignty, international respect, economic advance, an end to personalism in administration and politics, and a full measure of the consensus and political legitimacy patterns of the nation-state. He is something of a populist, for his views demand that all persons in his society should be included within the polity and the economy. Unless he establishes a functioning national community, he cannot have the markets needed for industrialization, the voters needed for his support, the initial popular enthusiasm required for him to brush away the vestiges of Iberian feudalism. He wants the United States to be a colleague in his endeavors. When he speaks of freedom and dignity, he is not thinking in the structural and administrative and procedural terms of the United States. What he fears is that he is not speaking in our basic value terms, either. Once he is reassured in this respect, United States policy will have gained freedom at the applied policy level, and gaffes in day-to-day relations will not disturb the deeper identification.

The United States should have a deep interest in the cultural integrity and security of Latin America as a growingly active and contributing power in Western life. Adolf Berle is correct in saying that economically the United States can live without Latin America. But is there here also an implication that we can live as well culturally if a potentially major group of Western nations chooses developmental paths that may isolate the democracies of European orientation conceptually and ideologically more than they need to be? Latin America is the largest readily available reservoir of recruits to Western modernism in the world.

The most difficult intellectual task of the statesman is to recognize his country's basic values and to transmute them into long-term policy statements. Even when such policy seems firm, its formulation and its application in specific situations is open to attack. Whatever the political difficulties, effective policy need not always be consistent or entirely predictable, but it must at least be coherent and fit the conditions for which it has been designed. The incoherence in our hemispheric actions may arise because we sometimes immediately and directly address a problem, successfully solve it, and pass on; or we may become alarmed and try to stop the tides. There are many cases of skillfully applied power and policy that do not become well known, for it is failure that makes news. Some very difficult problems of diplomacy vis-à-vis Brazil have been handled with exemplary skill. But we have often beat the air in our fear that all Latin Americans were being restrained from rushing into the embrace of Castro only through our own efforts. We have tried to stop such tides as the Mexican Revolution and the growth of national politics in Venezuela, only to find that in both cases stable, complex, and mutually beneficial accommodations could indeed be reached.

The Latin American course is in the direction of modernization—toward industrialization, nationalism, effective social organization, and economic progress. An affirmative support of Latin America's modernizers, with the insights gained from our own history of democratic development, is the only effective bulwark against totalitarianism.

RAYMOND ARON, Professor at the University of Paris, is a member of the French Academy of Political and Moral Sciences and the author of many books and articles on international political themes. ALFRED GROSSER is Professor at the Institute of Political Studies in Paris.

A European Perspective

RAYMOND ARON & ALFRED GROSSER

For the United States, Castro and "Fidelism" have constituted a major and at times obsessing problem. For Europe, the problem has so far been engrossing on only two occasions: in April 1961, when the fiasco of the Bay of Pigs jeopardized the international authority of an ally whose power had been the Old Continent's guarantee of security; and in October 1962, when the direct confrontation of two super-Powers, each possessing thermonuclear capability, could have triggered a worldwide catastrophe.

The rest of the time Europeans have been inclined to watch the vis-à-vis of the United States and Cuba—Goliath and David—with the rather ironic detachment of onlookers, as if the matter was neither of personal concern nor of much intrinsic interest. What little curiosity there was about the affair varied according to a given group's area of interest. Here and there, it was seized on as an opportunity to manifest the resentment that is inevitably felt toward an ally who is experienced as a dominant power and as a protector. And for once it was not necessary to call on history and culture to establish one's equality with the Big Fellow; one could identify, more or less subconsciously, with the Little Fellow who was defying the big one and getting away with it.

Certain other attitudes were no doubt related to the comparisons that could be drawn between the Castro problem and the French and English decolonization experience in Asia and Africa. Our American friends had been generous with good advice when we were at grips

141

with Habib Bourgiba and the King of Morocco, with the Viet Minh, and with the Algerian National Liberation Federation (FLN). Nationalism should not be resisted, our friends told us, for at the same time that it rejects external domination it expresses aspirations for social progress—the revolution of "rising expectations." Why shouldn't we have been inclined to repeat to our advisers of yesterday the thesis they had recently and so rightly propounded to us?

We are aware that the American definition of colonialism presumes some infringement of sovereignty. Thus, since the abrogation in 1934 of the Platt Amendment (which, incorporated into the 1903 treaty between Cuba and the United States, gave the latter a quasi-protectorate over the island), Cuba's sovereignty has—on paper—been unrestricted. But Europeans, whether Marxist or non-Marxist, do not acknowledge so readily that colonialism begins with the assumption of sovereignty by the colonial power and ends on the day a colonized country becomes sovereign in a legal sense. When a country's mineral resources are exploited largely by foreign companies, when its external trade is practically monopolized by a powerful state that is both customer and supplier and is at the same time represented by an inevitably influential ambassador, the Marxists are likely to talk of "colonialism," and the masses are likely to feel resentfully that the differences between dependence and independence are imperceptible. While the objective observer does perceive the differences, he is also obliged to admit that the distinction is often hazy, especially when he notes the reactions of the masses.

However, whether the comparison of the United States–Cuba relationship to the France–North Africa relationship is or is not an accurate one need not concern us further here. Suffice it to say that the comparison *was* made in some European spheres, and that it was inevitable. The challenge of Castro has been interpreted in the light of the precedent created when the African and Asian colonies presented a challenge to their former colonizers. Perhaps the French would have commented more leniently or—if you prefer—have shown less malicious pleasure (*Schadenfreude*) if the Americans had earlier judged the colonialism of others with less severity and self-righteousness. In any event, the Bay of Pigs landing in 1961 evoked memories of the Suez expedition in 1956. The so-called Machiavellism of the French and the British ("we want to separate Egyptians and Israelis") was no more cynical or maladroit than the American formula ("the political exiles are conducting the operation"). In both cases, the weakness, the use of force, and the quick failure of the undertaking were a combination that in the end strengthened the man and the regime whose downfall had been sought.

In European leftist circles, a psycho-political phenomenon of another sort can be seen. Fidel Castro had become the hero of a numerically negligible but intellectually important segment of European opinion. Many of those who find themselves somewhere midway between the Communists and the Social Democrats (Nennists in Italy, *heimatlose Linke*[1] in Germany, "intellectuals of the left" in France) have a nostalgia for the old revolutionary upheavals that Europe's prosperity now makes less and less likely, but for which they refuse to abandon hope. When the hope is not realized at home, these revolutionary romantics of the left wander from one country to another, from one continent to another. Tito and Yugoslavia, when exposed to the fury of the Stalinists, gave their hopes a temporary haven. When Tito was reconciled with the Soviet Union and was also receiving American aid, he lost his martyr's halo and his appeal; once again, in the rebels' eyes, his role was merely the prosaic one of the successful reformer. Later on, the nationalist movements in Africa and Asia attracted the would-be revolutionaries. And then it was Fidel Castro, an ideal hero for them—anti-American and anticapitalist, with "bread and freedom" as his slogan. In 1959 when Jean-Paul Sartre was welcomed to Cuba, Castro was the prophet whom the intellectuals of the extreme left, rejected by Stalinism and disgusted by reformism, had been seeking in every corner of the world. Nor were many of the youth and the intelligentsia of the United States, during the first year of Fidelism, indifferent to the charm of the "bearded one."

By the beginning of 1964, however, Fidelism had lost a great deal of its freshness and prestige. In 1961, by declaring himself a Marxist-Leninist, Castro left the narrow path he had been treading between Sovietism and Western democracy. In October 1962, he laid himself open to the accusation, if not of deliberate war-mongering, at least of sharing responsibility for a crisis in which world peace seemed to be at stake. At that moment Fidel Castro and his partisans throughout the

[1] Translator's note. The term has no brief English equivalent; it signifies "leftists who find no existing institutional framework that satisfies them."

world were able to measure the cost of a clear adherence to the Soviet camp. The dialogue between the two K's took place over the head of the self-styled *líder máximo*. Nikita Khrushchev agreed to withdraw the ballistic missiles from Cuba without consulting Castro's desires. President Kennedy proclaimed the quarantine of the island and addressed himself to the man in the Kremlin, not to the man in Havana. The Cuban regime and Castro's personality seemed to account for very little when world peace was clearly at stake.

And the positions that the European nations took at that time were dictated not by sympathy for or aversion to either the Cuban revolution or American "colonialism" but by various interpretations of the situation's meaning to themselves. In the Federal Republic of Germany, American firmness was approved without reservation. If the United States, when its security was directly threatened, yielded to Cuba, located about 90 miles from the coast of Florida, how could the U.S. government expect to convince the rulers of the U.S.S.R. that Soviet encroachment on West Berlin would not be tolerated? In a way, the Germans felt that the fate of Berlin was at stake in Cuba; thus a Soviet withdrawal, with no compromise, seemed necessary to the future security of the former capital of the Reich.

In Great Britain, up to the moment when the success of the operation was assured by the Soviet agreement to withdraw the rockets, most of the press was hostile to the "quarantine" and to the American demands. Here also, it was not Cuba but the international significance of the crisis—specifically, the risk of war—that determined the comments of newsmen and politicians, if not the acts of the government.

In France, President de Gaulle approved the action of the United States explicitly. His affirmation of solidarity with an ally at a moment of danger was in line with his traditional concept of alliances-compacts among equals, but without integration. In the Caribbean, it was of course the responsibility of the United States to take the initiative and make the decisions. In a similar situation in Europe, should it not be the Europeans—the nearest to the danger and the most directly affected —who assumed this role, at least to a certain extent? In a subsequent press conference (January 14, 1963) General de Gaulle made three remarks related to the Cuban crisis. The United States, he said, acted without the prior agreement of its allies. He also brought up this point: Would the United States demonstrate to the same degree that determination of which it gave proof when its own vital interests were at stake in a case where Europe was concerned? And he added that, in any case, the means mobilized in the Cuban case would not be available in Europe, and that in general the U.S.S.R. is now able to deter the United States just as the United States is deterring the U.S.S.R. Whatever the merit (or lack of it) in these points, it is clear that for de Gaulle they added up to his stated conclusion: France must equip itself with a deterrent force of its own.

As 1964 began, Cuba was no longer making front-page news, although feature articles and books continued to be published on the picturesque, economic, or ideological aspects of the regime. And once again the romanticists of the revolutionary left had been disappointed by a prophet—by the regime's failure to build an industrial structure, by Castro's proclaiming himself a Marxist-Leninist, by his inability to keep Cuba non-aligned (although Castro today is not embroiled in the Sino-Soviet rift). On the other hand, despite the few thousand Soviet soldiers still on the island, it is doubtful that the Kremlin contemplates either another anti-American operation there or the construction of a military base for use against the United States.

Consequently, certain questions can be asked. What *is* the objective of American policy concerning Cuba? What is the United States seeking? Overthrow of the Castro regime? Breaking the ties between the Castro regime and the main countries of the socialist camp—Soviet Russia and China? And, if this break were achieved, reintegration of the Cuban Republic into the Organization of American States? To put it another way, Is the United States fighting a socialist regime as such, or a regime tied to the Soviet Union or China, or a socialist regime that is attempting to export revolution to other parts of Latin America?

These questions are being asked by all the emerging nations of the world. And they are being put to the United States with particular emphasis throughout Latin America, for the policy adopted toward Fidelism will affect the entire American policy toward Latin America.

THE UNITED STATES HAS TRADITIONALLY considered Latin America its private "hunting ground," and has exercised a predominant influence there. The Latin American governments in their turn have in general seen to it that conditions would be favorable to the business activities of American corporations. They were thus firmly anti-Communist, and declared themselves to be an integral part of the free world. As long as these two conditions existed—governments favorable to capitalistic enterprise and adhering to a policy of anti-Communism—the only problem that Washington frequently had to face was the lack of conformity of this or that Latin American regime to the ideals of liberal democracy. The problem was complicated by a certain contradiction. How might the United States reconcile its principle of nonintervention in the domestic affairs of states with a refusal to recognize or do business with despotic regimes? On the other hand, the *de facto* support given to the despotic regimes, through supplying armaments or sending military missions, was considered by opponents as a form of intervention.

From 1934 on, following the repeal of the Platt Amendment and the initiation of the Roosevelt Good Neighbor policy, the United States on principle denied itself the "right" of military intervention (which it had exercised many times with respect to Cuba) solely to protect the investments of private individuals or companies. In cases of nationalization, it claimed that an equitable indemnity was due the owners of expropriated property, but it no longer sent the Marines. When Mexico nationalized its oil, the result was a diplomatic conflict with the Roosevelt administration, but no military retaliation.

Since the end of World War II and the beginning of the cold war, concern about American investments has gradually given way to concern about a regime's relations with "international Communism." From the point of view of the White House, protecting private capital invested in Latin America was in theory less important than keeping Soviet influence out of the area. (We have heard a highly placed official of independent wealth say that the best solution would be the purchase of all private American investments in Latin America by the United States government to permit their nationalization.) At the same time, any move toward nationalization could well be denounced either by capitalists or by some anti-Communists (more prejudiced than clear-minded) as a first step on the road to Communism.

There has been a plethora of discussion in Europe, as well as on the American continent, of the degree to which American policy may have been responsible for the turn that the Cuban revolution took toward Marxism-Leninism. We have no intention here of reviving this much-iterated discussion but will simply note a few facts and theories that need to be taken into account in any future consideration of the Cuban matter.[2]

In 1958 and 1959, United States policy toward Cuba was faltering and weak. By announcing, for example, on March 14, 1958, that arms shipments to Fulgencio Batista were being suspended, the United States undoubtedly contributed to the collapse of the Batista regime. Yet it did not thereby declare itself an ally of the revolutionaries. At the same time it maintained its military mission in Havana, and the State Department was probably hoping to the last that a successor to Batista other than Fidel Castro could be found.

The Eisenhower administration, during the year and a half between the new regime's assumption of power in January 1959 and the quasi-rupture of relations in July 1960, seemed incapable of adopting a firm policy line and sticking to it. In part this vacillation may have reflected the favorable view of Castro that had been created for Americans by a substantial segment of the American press during his Sierra Maestra days. New York Times correspondent Herbert Matthews had especially contributed to the glamour of the "bearded one" and his fellows. In the spring of 1959 Castro was welcomed in Washington cordially and even with some pomp and circumstance, and he was acclaimed later at Harvard University. But even in this period of "good feeling" the administration failed to pursue vigorously one of the theoretically possible alternatives: a decision to sacrifice private American investments in Cuba and accept Castro's socialism, on the single condition that he remain nonaligned, if not pro-American. Neither did it pursue the other alternative of influencing the course of events by an immediate and resolute opposition to Fidelism.

In retrospect, the majority of observers agree that the first alternative would have been preferable, but the proposition still remains in the realm of theory. The fact is that, even had both the problem and its possible solutions been clearly conceived, President Eisenhower would have encountered great opposition to a policy of "appeasement"—a policy that implied not only sympathy with the new regime but also tolerance of nationalization of American investments without equitable compensation. At that date the American government and its citizens had still not abandoned the longtime habit of considering the nearby

[2] One of the present authors spent several weeks in Cuba in 1961 and thus has some direct knowledge of the problem.

island as solely within the sphere of United States influence. Thus, public opinion would probably have been adamant against the idea of a socialist republic pledged to a so-called neutralism more or less favorable to the Soviet Union. In short, what might possibly be accepted in the United States today or tomorrow, given the experience of the years 1961-1962, was probably unthinkable in 1960.

The United States, in this regard, is undergoing an apprenticeship that reminds the French observer of a recent event at home—Algerian independence. The inevitability of the event could have been foreseen from the start, yet in 1956 French public opinion simply could not have accepted it. Democracies have one common feature in their foreign policies: each state is clairvoyant about the affairs of others. On that basis, we would be inclined to support the following thesis: Although Fidel Castro's evolution toward Marxism-Leninism may have been accelerated by the policy (or lack of it) in Washington, that evolution was probably inevitable. Certainly Washington could have been more resolute in supporting one or the other course open to it, yet the outcome would probably have been little different than it was in fact. No American administration could have reacted dispassionately at that time to the liquidation both of investments and of United States political and moral positions in this close-by island, which for so many decades had welcomed tourists and capital from its all-powerful neighbor.

Even if the dialectic of hostility—Cuban nationalism and Fidel Castro's suspicions on the one hand, American disappointments and retaliation on the other—had not been set in motion or had been stopped before the final breach, Castroism, it seems to us, was bound to shift from a revolution with a democratic keynote to an authoritarian socialism. We do not, however, subscribe to the theory of a "Communist plot" or to the hypothesis of a Castro pledged to Marxism-Leninism from the start and concealing his faith in order to deceive his fellow revolutionaries and the people of Cuba. We are convinced that a leftist Latin American intellectual who achieves power in a country like Cuba is obliged, for psycho-political rather than economic reasons, to prefer an authoritarian socialism—more or less shaded with Marxism-Leninism—to a constitutional restoration and a so-called bourgeois democracy.

Economically, Cuba is known to be among the most fortunate of Latin American countries in its natural resources. Its economic development presented the fewest difficulties. The "takeoff," to use W. W.

Rostow's phrase, was within the reach of even a moderately efficient government. During the late 1940's and much of the 1950's sugar exports supplied around $600 million a year for a population of 6.5 to 7 million. The middle class, which contributed many of the most active fighters against Batista and which is to a large extent now in exile, was increasing in the towns. Cuban capital had repurchased part of the land and many of the factories formerly owned by American capital. Small manufacturing enterprises were emerging. Though from 40 to 50 percent of the peasant masses were still illiterate and suffered seasonal unemployment and a consequent low standard of living, the necessary reforms (diversification of agricultural production, improvement of the condition of the farmers, acceleration of the industrial effort) did not exceed the capabilities of a pluralistic and liberal regime.

It was against a brutal and sterile despotism that the educated classes of the nation fought in the mid-1950's. Under a democratic regime, Cuba could have achieved, in only a few years, even more rapid progress than Puerto Rico had achieved. An emigration of manpower would not have been necessary, since the potential resources are so plentiful compared to the size of population. The democratic revolution that the many who helped to overthrow Batista were fervently calling for might have been only one episode in Latin America's history, and would have aroused world concern only slightly. The United States might finally have found that regime which it sought: a regime entirely in conformance with U.S. democratic ideals and policy interests. That matters have turned out otherwise is deplorable but not surprising.

Even if Fidel Castro, who was an intellectual of the extreme left, had not been surrounded by "true" Communists such as Raúl Castro and "Che" Guevara, he would have been anti-American (the United States supported Batista and "colonized our country") and anticapitalist ("American capital has seized the national resources and exploits the popular masses"). He would have been suspicious of electoral procedures and representative institutions, which he had often seen manipulated by an oligarchy in this or that country where the peasants were illiterate. Under these conditions, what virtue (in the ancient sense of strength and moral courage) would Fidel Castro have needed to lead him to surrender his power to the hazards of universal suffrage! How overwhelming the temptation must have been to set himself on the path, bristling with obstacles it is true, at the end of which he, the *líder máximo*, might become a figure in world history: the first to build a socialist republic in the Western Hemisphere, the first to imitate Nasser and the "positive neutralists," and the first to establish ties with the Soviet Union and China. Victorious or beaten, the man who had tried to do all this would be a "great man" in the vocabulary of the historians, since he would have disproved the widespread belief that no regime within the American sphere of influence could survive without the consent of Washington.

Ironically enough, that is the belief of an earlier age. The diplomacy of gunboats is out of date, and the new fashion is that the Soviet Union is always ready to grant aid and support to countries that shake off the "imperialist yoke" (and the United States is ready to do the same for the defectors from the socialist camp). By proclaiming that the use of force to solve international disputes is condemned, the United States has itself pointed up one of the characteristics of the present situation: the inability of the Big Fellows, whatever their military potential, to impose their will on the Little Fellows.

Military force aside, it is true that recourse can be had to subversive practices, including assistance to political refugees and guerrillas. In Guatemala such a technique of subversion (with the help of the CIA) succeeded in getting rid of a regime that Washington suspected of leaning toward Communism. But anyone who believed that the same technique, without overt intervention of American military forces, would have sufficed to get rid of a team as determined as Castro's, supported by a large proportion of the popular masses even after an important part of the opposition had gone into exile, would have been entirely ignoring the dynamism of the Fidelist revolution.

Some ten years ago, D. W. Brogan wrote an article on the myth of the "all-powerful" United States. According to the myth, when the Communists prevailed in China the blame fell on the men or the party in power in Washington. A Communist victory in any part of the world was equivalent to the "loss of a country," even if the country had never belonged to the United States. That the power of the United States has not been able to prevent the installation of a hostile regime only 90 miles from the coast of Florida is a fact that has not yet been acknowledged—still less accepted—by American public opinion, but it is nonetheless indisputable.

It will never be known with certainty whether American policy, by taking a clear position for or against the Fidelist revolution from the middle of 1959 on, would have been able to overthrow or to convert Fidel Castro. But once he was solidly established, with an apparatus of power installed and police at his call, what weapons against him were available to any nation? However near and powerful a nation might be, in the final analysis the weapons were three in number, and only three: *landing; subversion supported from abroad; economic pressure.* What use was made of these three weapons? What use could be made of them tomorrow? Given the available means, what could be, what should be, the objectives of American policy?

IT IS UNIMPORTANT TO ASK if the United States should or should not have dealt with the "Cuban revolution" as the Soviet Union dealt with the "Hungarian counterrevolution." By now, an answer to the question would in any case be purely academic hindsight. Even if one disregards the moral aspect, the political or military implications were not, in Cuba, what they were in Hungary. Obviously, American armed forces *could* have occupied a major part of the island and have set up a "friendly" government there. But even in April 1961 the undertaking would not have succeeded without a fight, and in all probability defensive guerrilla and underground activities would have gone on for months or even years. By 1964, Castro had available numerous relatively well-equipped troops, so that occupation of the island would have required a large-scale military operation, even without taking into account possible Soviet intervention or retaliation.

Since the conditions on which the late President Kennedy made the unilateral commitment of the United States not to attack Cuba in case the Soviet rockets were withdrawn have not been completely met (particulary international inspection), the commitment itself could be said not to be binding. But whether or not one considers the commitment valid is not of great importance. On the day of the Bay of Pigs landing, when President Kennedy denied even an air-cover to the political exiles, he excluded the possibility of military action to overthrow the Fidelist regime—*barring an act by the latter that would be considered aggressive.*

The installation of Soviet missiles constituted such an act. One of the possible answers at that time would have been a decision to secure not only the withdrawal of Soviet rockets but also the downfall of Fidel Castro. Such a decision would have involved a risk much greater than the risk actually taken. Khrushchev would have had to accept both the elimination of the troops he had sent into the area and the overthrow of the government whose protection was the official justification for the far-flung expedition. Not only would the risk for the United States have been increased beyond measure; the moral significance of the crisis would also have been altered. By limiting the demand to the reestablishment of the *status quo ante*, President Kennedy maintained both the merit of being moderate in victory and the prestige of making his rival pull back.

The use of military force by the United States against Cuba had been excluded as a solution in April 1961. The crisis of 1962 provided an opportunity to renew and reaffirm the decision that force would not be used to overthrow a regime located in the Caribbean very near American shores (and thus in the area covered by the Monroe Doctrine), even though it claimed to be Marxist-Leninist and confessed solidarity with the Soviet Union.

Up to now the United States government seems not to have arrived at what many people consider to be the logical consequence of its refusal to resort to military force—to wit, since Castroism exists, the best course is to accept it. President Kennedy chose a course that seemed to Europeans fairly typical of American policy: a double refusal—denial of diplomatic recognition to Cuba and at the same time abstention from armed intervention. What remains uncertain to the observer is the purpose of the double refusal and the possibilities of achieving that purpose, whatever it may be.

It seems fairly obvious, however, that the maximum goal of the present policy is to bring about the downfall of Fidel Castro. The severing of all trade relations between the United States and Cuba and the steps taken both to discourage shipping companies from placing their ships at the disposal of the Soviet Union and to make transportation of goods to the island as costly as possible have the intent, it seems, of weakening the Castro regime by making it more difficult for Moscow to supply aid to Cuba—aid that has become indispensable to the latter. Simultaneously, the economic blockade tends to dissuade other Latin American countries from following Castro's path. If Fidelism were officially tolerated, if Cuba were reintegrated into the Organization of American

States, if Marxism-Leninism appeared compatible with membership in the Western Hemisphere family and with receiving United States aid, Fidel Castro would no doubt enlist new admirers and new followers. Therefore anti-Yankeeism must be made unprofitable.

The Latin American leftists, however anti-Yankee thay may be, have no desire to break with the United States, the more so since such a break, as the Cuban example demonstrated, may result in exchanging dependence on the United States, which they can resist to some degree, for a still closer dependence on the Soviet Union. Theoretically, the existing American policy serves to warn the Latin American revolutionaries that if they go beyond a certain point they will have to assume the responsibility of their extremism: they will not receive Soviet and Western aid simultaneously.

But there is a counterpart to the advantages of current U.S. policy. The blockade has increased the economic difficulties of Fidel Castro, and has probably increased the cost to the Soviet Union of aiding Cuba,[3] but it also provides the leaders of the Cuban Socialist Republic with an excuse for their folly.

As Theodore Draper has demonstrated, the mistakes made by Castro and his fellows are beyond belief. First they decided to cut back sugar production; now they have had to renege on this decision, and they are discovering that Cuba is an agricultural country after all. They had cherished the idea that the Soviet Union would supply them with complete factories, but they forgot to take into account the cost of the raw materials to be processed by these factories. Unloaded in Cuba, raw materials cost more than the finished products that the factories would have produced. After five years, the Fidelists started again almost from scratch. They renounced their industrialization program, attempted to restore agricultural production without thereby renouncing collectivization, and expropriated medium-sized farms. The percentage of collective farms (people's farms) will be raised to 70 percent. But as long as Castro can counter popular discontent by putting the blame for economic difficulty on the blockade and Yankee imperialism, his government may not have to suffer the consequences of its colossal errors.

Another objection, probably more serious, is the unlikely feasibility

---

[3] On the other hand, the increase in the price of sugar on the world market in 1963 helped Fidel Castro and (probably to a considerable extent) decreased the cost to the Soviet Union of its aid to Cuba.

of maintaining the blockade. The shipping companies concerned are protesting the black list established by the United States, because it entails a practice contrary to the traditional law of the sea. Freedom of maritime traffic in peacetime has, for centuries, been a principle generally respected by trading nations. Although the United States at present is not maintaining a naval blockade, it is violating the spirit of international law by denying access to American ports to any ship that has called at Cuba or carried Soviet goods to the island. Beyond that, the semiblockade has not been very effective and will be less effective as time passes. The British, French, Italians, and Germans, in fact, are refusing to accede to the American policy and are now treating trade with Cuba as they have treated trade with the Soviet Union: they will refrain from selling Cuba goods that are included on the list of prohibited exports, but they will sell goods without military value or so-called strategic importance. How can Washington convince the signatory states of the Atlantic Treaty that Cuba is more of a peril than the Soviet Union? When the United States is selling millions of tons of grain to the Soviet Union, why should Great Britain refuse to sell a few thousand buses to Cuba?

We are not underestimating the strength of the arguments that the American government could put forth in rebuttal. The Cuban Republic is close to the United States; it is a center of subversive activities and provides ideological and specialized training to professional revolutionaries and guerrilla leaders who are to be sent to other Latin American countries. Is it not in the common interest of the Atlantic countries not to frustrate the United States by aiding the spread of Fidelism in Central or South America? And is not economic quarantine the best method of preventing this spread?

To this the European observer who is most favorable to the American government's present thesis would reply: "Perhaps. If all Western countries were capable of such discipline in trade matters, the blockade as practiced at present would in the long run become effective. It might not hasten the downfall of the regime; but it could make the survival of Fidelism very costly for the Soviet Union and the economic success of the Cuban Republic impossible. What in our view condemns the present American policy is that it is obviously being weakened, and will be further weakened, by the noncompliance of the allies of the United States. We have seen how other countries of the Atlantic Alliance are carrying on trade with mainland China, which is prevented from trading with the United States. The story is much the same for the Cuban Republic."

This analysis, then, arrives at the conclusion that the economic quarantine of Cuba cannot and should not be considered by the United States as a long-term policy. However, the United States certainly cannot go abruptly from one extreme to the other and resume relations with Cuba as if that country were any other Latin American republic. By disavowing its stand, the United States would lose face and discourage its friends and encourage its enemies. But when one considers that military intervention is excluded, that subversion, reluctantly applied, has been ineffective, and that the quarantine is clearly inefficient, one must therefore consider that Castroism, in one form or another, will persist for some time. Thus the determination of the long-term objectives of American policy again becomes of current and vital interest.

In the abstract, compromise is easy to conceive. Fidel Castro, while still remaining a socialist (or even a Marxist-Leninist), could recover some autonomy in his relations with the Soviet Union and China, and could come nearer to a neutralism, or a nonalignment, of the Yugoslav type (the departure of *all* Russian troops, perhaps desired by Moscow, would be the symbol of this half-retreat). Simultaneously, the Cuban leaders might renounce, in fact if not officially, their intentions of exporting their revolution and supporting those groups in Venezuela and elsewhere who attempt to overthrow established regimes by violence.

The compromise would require acceptance by the United States of socialist regimes in Latin America—regimes that might liquidate American investments but would not become adherents of the Soviet bloc. American public opinion may not be ready for such acceptance, but this is not the only obstacle in the way of such a compromise. Would Fidel Castro be ready to cooperate sincerely? Particularly, could he resign himself to "Fidelism in only one country"?

Let us make ourselves quite clear. The revolutionary movements and the anti-Yankee feelings that have been boiling up in many Latin American countries are not created or even manipulated solely by Castro agents. By pointing out Fidel Castro as the inspiring leader responsible for all Latin American disturbances, United States propaganda has managed to confer on him an exaggerated prestige. On the other hand, the Cuban obsession with the United States has contributed to

the image of potency of the "bearded one," just as the Yugoslav obsession with Stalin assisted the fortunes of Tito. Nevertheless, Castro re-
sembles Tito not at all. He is essentially a romantic, and he has not yet
been submitted to the harsh Communist party discipline. He makes use
of the Cuban Communists, but he has so far not been used by them.
Nothing proves, nothing even suggests, that he considers renouncing
his revolutionary enterprise outside the country's borders and resigning
himself to concentrating on building the socialist structure at home.
Even if he does not repeat the mad mistakes of 1960-62, it seems clear
that Cuban socialism will never satisfy his personal and ideological ambitions. Had he been concerned only about sugar cane and living standards, his course since 1959 would have been entirely different.

In other words, the compromise that at first sight appears to be reasonable—the acceptance by the United States of a nonaligned socialism, more or less close to that of Tito or Ben Bella—may well be
rejected by American public opinion and by Castro himself. And if
Castroism lends its aid to all those who fight pro-American regimes,
how can the United States deny support to those who fight Castroism?

The foregoing paragraph suggests that the conclusions of this brief
survey are negative. Certainly in the immediate future one would expect a continuation of the dialectic of hostility: economic quarantine on
the one side, export of revolution on the other. But the possibility cannot be excluded that on both sides a transformation could start—first of
minds, then of actions.

On the American side, this major premise will perhaps be acknowledged: Since the use of force to overthrow a hostile regime is excluded,
the consequences of the new situation must be faced. Henceforth,
Latin America is not a private hunting ground for the United States, no
more than Africa or Asia is. Europeans have learned how to make a distinction between socialist regimes (which do not respect private investments), authoritarian regimes (which do not respect individual and political liberties), Marxist-Leninist regimes (which claim kinship with the
1917 Russian Revolution), and, finally, regimes that give allegiance to
the Soviet Union and China. In like manner, the United States, and
above all its organs of public opinion, must learn to resist the temptation to lump together all regimes whose political mores differ from its
own. Learning to make such distinctions will be especially difficult for
Americans, since the first regime to avow itself as socialist went all the

way to Moscow (and probably would have done so whatever course American policy had taken). But it would be extremely unfortunate if the conclusion were drawn that anti-Yankeeism in Latin America would inevitably lead socialists or revolutionaries on the road to Marxism-Leninism. The danger exists, to be sure, but one needs to resist increasing the danger by borrowing from the Marxists the idea that the glide from anticapitalism to Communism is automatic.

The Castroists, despite their braggadocio, have discovered in one fell swoop that planning cannot be improvised, that they were themselves ignorant, that not every country is adapted to an accelerated industrialization, and that administrative management of collectivized agriculture is not automatically productive. Moreover, the experience of October 1962 (when Cuba appeared as a pawn in the game that was going on between the two super-Powers) and the subsequent breaking off of economic relations between the Cuban Republic and the United States have carried a lesson to the progressive parties throughout Latin America that has not gone unheeded.

Thus it is not impossible that conditions may be in the making whereby coexistence between the United States and various socialist regimes in Latin America could come about, although the immediate fulfillment of such conditions seems unlikely. Meanwhile, no one can say whether Fidel Castro will ever resign himself to being only what he is and to be content to tend his own garden in Cuba rather than pushing on to become the *líder máximo* of all Latin America.

RAYMOND CARR, Director of the Latin American Centre at Oxford University, has visited Cuba at intervals since Castro's accession. His articles about the Cuban revolution have appeared in *The Cold War*, edited by Evan Luard, in *The Observer*, and in *The World Today*.

The Cold War in Latin America

RAYMOND CARR

The Caribbean made the cold war a reality in Latin America. Until 1960 the conflict between Russia and the United States had little meaning for the Latin American nations; they could not believe in the reality of an external military threat to the hemisphere. Geography and inclination made them natural neutralists. Many Latin American politicians sought to find a third course between what Perón termed the "materialist collectivism" of the U.S.S.R. and the "materialist individualism" of the United States.[1] With Guatemala in 1954 and, more dramatically, with Cuba, the cold war was imported into the hemisphere because the issue of nonintervention against a Communist Cuba raised a principle that was at the core of hemispheric relations as the Latin American nations conceived them. This core was defined at the Buenos Aires Conference of 1936. Intervention was inadmissible "directly or indirectly, and for whatever reason in the external or internal affairs of any other of the parties."

It is not surprising that the Caribbean acted as a catalyst. The security (in the sense of the exclusion of any foreign power) and stability of the Caribbean area was traditionally a main objective of U.S. policy. The classic exposition of this interest is perhaps that of Henry L. Stimson, made in 1927:

---

[1] Of course Perón's "third position" had respectable antecedents in Argentina's repeated assertions of its independence of U.S. diplomatic tutelage. See A. P. Whitaker, *The United States and Argentina* (Harvard University Press, 1954), pp. 98 ff.

158

There are certain geographical considerations which impose upon us a very special interest as to how certain Latin American nations fulfil the responsibilities which go with sovereignty and independence. I refer to those nations whose territory lies adjacent to and in a naval sense commands the great sea route from our eastern to our western states via the Caribbean sea and the Panama canal. This situation does not arise out of the Monroe Doctrine but from certain broad principles of self defense which govern the policy of all nations which are in any way dependent upon the sea.

The direct interest of the United States in "*certain* Latin American nations" cast its shadow over the *whole* Latin American policy of the United States. Intervention in Chile or in Argentina was unlikely, but the defense of nonintervention in the Caribbean affected the dignity of all Latin American nations.

The strategic sensitivity of the United States to events in the Caribbean area is not always understood by its allies. To Europeans, unaware of the historic roots of U.S. concern in Cuba, the U.S. position appeared to be derived either from reaction to what was called "spitting in our face" by Cubans after 1959 or was seen as part of an obsessive concern with "Communism," by which was meant both the Communist party and any movement of the extreme left that might open the door to direct Communist influence. On the basis of this analysis, the North Americans were presumed to feel insecure, not in any strategic sense but in the inner citadel of values. The presupposition that all Latin American nations really wanted to fashion their destinies on the model of democracy, as the United States understood the term, had been challenged by the existence of the Cuban revolution.

The Cuban issue engaged the U.S.S.R. in Latin America as it had never been engaged before. What was striking about the U.S.S.R.'s concern with Latin America was its almost formal nature until the mid-1950's.[2] Of course, the Latin American nations had long been presented as groaning under the economic imperialism of the United States. But Stalin in the 1930's was more concerned with British imperialism in India, where something might be accomplished, than in Latin America, where little could be hoped for; it was a "reactionary" area with no revolutionary possibilities. The Communist parties were weak in most countries of Latin America, even after the gains that had followed their "democratic" line in World War II. They were often discredited by

[2] See the graph in "Latin America in Soviet Writings," *Hispanic Foundation Bibliographical Series* (Library of Congress, 1959).

deals with dictators—a process that Communists attempted to ensure against by the device of double parties, one legal which collaborated and a clandestine party which resisted. They were confronted with Populist parties, like the Peruvian Alianza Popular Revolucionaria Americana (APRA), or confused by challenges like Peronism in Argentina.[3] Chile and Brazil were the only major countries with strong Communist parties. Nor did it seem that Russia sought to fight a cold war seriously in the hemisphere. It scarcely attempted to evolve a propaganda line for Latin America: Bolívar was an aristocratic separatist; not until the 1950's was he made into the symbol of leader of a National Liberation movement for the Indian masses.

Nevertheless, the U.S.S.R. possessed advantages which it would capitalize once Latin America became a potential battlefield in the cold war.

First, the end terms of the Marxist analysis of the historical evolution of Latin America corresponded almost exactly with the natural assumptions of many Latin Americans. The successor of Great Britain as the exploiter of a primary-product "colonial" economy was the United States. The North Americans regard their economic power in Latin America as a natural result of free enterprise and often risky investment—as did the British in the nineteenth century. It was not their *fault*, they argued, that the prosperity of Latin America depends on the price paid for its products by U.S. importers or that its development demands U.S. capital. Anti-Americans argue that this dependence denies the Latin American nations independence and control of their own natural resources. These nations are victims of "monopoly capitalism," denied the power to decide their own destinies. Hence, expropriation is a *sine qua non* of extreme nationalism. This imperils the emergence of sensible solutions certainly envisaged by Washington and favored by moderate politicians in Latin America.[4] Communist propaganda can thus be presented as a defense of national independence, to be

[3] For interesting criticisms of Communist policies in Argentina, see Rodolfo Puiggros, *Historia crítica de los partidos políticos argentinos* (Buenos Aires: Editorial Argumentos, 1956), which covers the thirties; and for the later period see Juan José Real, *Treinta años de historia argentina* (Buenos Aires, 1962). Some of the Communist political blunders were truly astonishing.

[4] Consider the conflict in Brazil over the buying out of American interests. Leonel Brizola challenged a "moderate" solution by a doctrine of expropriation based on the right of the "people" to any industry aided by government conces-

achieved by the elimination of the monopoly capitalism of the United States. The appeal of this simple solution is enormous and provides a powerful escape mechanism. In the nineteenth century Latin Americans explained their political and economic "backwardness" in terms of national or racial vices, which would be cured by imitating France, England, or the United States. In the twentieth century this passionate self-criticism was replaced by an equally violent criticism of the Yankee who exploits Latin America as a colony and obstructs both its economic growth and political progress.[5] All that the Communist propaganda does is to put long accepted "truths" of the Latin American left into an international framework: Latin America, like the Afro-Asian countries, must seek freedom by alliance with the socialist camp.[6] The answer to monopoly capitalism and the road to freedom are to be found in trade with the Soviet bloc. *Ex hypothesi,* the Alliance for Progress is a dead end.

Secondly, nationalism is, perhaps, the most powerful single force in Latin America. It is anti-Yankee and is therefore available for exploitation by Soviet propaganda. "Nationalism," wrote one anti-Communist in the 1950's, "has converted itself into the best auxiliary of the Kremlin."[7] It is not to defend U.S. policy to say that the inbuilt prejudices of nationalism have resulted in frequent exaggeration of the shortcomings of U.S. policy.

The reasons for this exaggeration are clear. Nationalism is most easily defined in terms of an enemy; especially if that enemy can be seen as the main obstacle to economic development. This factor is particularly acute in those nations with little cultural foundation for nationalism. What was Cuban nationalism other than the struggle first against Spain, and after 1898 against its successor, the United States? Anti-Americanism is a psychological necessity for many Latin Americans, even for those who, via the demonstration effects of a "superior" culture, have adopted, in their behavior as consumers, an "American way of

sions—e.g., the automobile industry and the press because both enjoyed tariff advantages. (*Hispanic American Report,* XVI, 6 [Aug. 1963], 627.)

[5] See the brilliant remarks of A. O. Hirschman, ed., *Latin American Issues: Essays and Comments* (Twentieth Century Fund, 1961), pp. 3 ff.

[6] For the standard Communist line in Latin America see "Gegenwarts Probleme Latein Amerikas," in *Deutsche Aussen Politik,* Sonderheft 11 (Berlin, 1961).

[7] Eudocio Ravines, "La estrategia comunista en América Latina," in *Estudios sobre el comunismo* (Santiago de Chile, 1954).

life."[8] Perhaps the deepest conflict in many countries is between the adopted American way of life and a formal, psychological anti-Americanism, which, for obvious reasons, cannot translate itself into open economic or diplomatic warfare.

The third advantage of the U.S.S.R. is that interventions (on twenty occasions between 1898 and 1920 U.S. forces entered Caribbean states) cast doubts over the whole place of the United States in any inter-American system. Although the U.S. primary concern was with the stability and security of the Caribbean, its methods of fulfilling these aims were inconstant. They varied from Theodore Roosevelt's "I took Panama" to Franklin D. Roosevelt's Good Neighbor policy. Since an important crisis of policy concerned Cuba, these lurches and reappraisals must be examined.

Intervention by military force was abandoned, not because its morality was questioned but because it was ineffective. It did not produce stability and ordered government unless we may take the Somoza government in Nicaragua as the type of government the United States regarded as stable and desirable—an unlikely hypothesis. Yet the abandonment of intervention created a difficult situation. What was the United States to do with the influence that intervention had created and which still persisted? The Cuban crisis of 1933 exposed the paradoxes inherent in the use of influence and the difficulty that has always dogged U.S. policy. To intervene against Machado, by 1933 an intolerable dictator, was a breach of the principle of nonintervention; not to use the enormous influence the United States exercised in Cuba was to run the risk of a charge of supporting a tyranny. Sumner Welles, as Roosevelt's envoy, sought to solve the problem by easing Machado's departure; he then sought a "stable" government acceptable to the nation. His own interpretation of this aim led him to refuse recognition to Grau San Martín's government. He dismissed it as "a group of the most extreme radicals . . . whose theories are frankly communistic . . . the initiators of a social revolution" supported by the "ignorant masses." The refusal to recognize Grau San Martín was a "negative interference" which meant the defeat of radical revolution in Cuba. Thus to

[8] The prophet of anti-Americanism in the fifties was Juan José Arévalo of Guatemala. It is of some interest to note how many of the arguments of *El anticomunismo en América Latina* (Buenos Aires: Editorial Patestra, 1959) are now outdated even as propaganda.

Cubans Washington was responsible for the "frustration" of a radical revolution that would have made Castro unnecessary.

The Good Neighbor policy after 1933 did much to alter the image of "big stick" diplomacy.[9] By and large, it was successful. Its apparent contradictions—for example, the tolerance by a great democracy of tyrants like Somoza and Trujillo—were emphasized by an increasing concentration on hemispheric defense. Thus, the need for cooperation in World War II tended to favor incumbent regimes, and the war itself tended to freeze existing political situations. The good will accumulated by good-neighborliness turned into a liability for the process of postwar adjustment. This liability was emphasized by the military concept of hemispheric defense, which helped existing regimes to maintain themselves: thus Batista was equipped with U.S. arms.

IT WAS THE CARIBBEAN that made the cold war a reality in Latin America. Events in two small nations—Guatemala and Cuba—altered the terms of battle in the hemisphere. In both, a non-Communist revolution was taken over by the Communists or, as Cuban Marxists would argue, was driven by the "objective conditions" (i.e., the contradiction between imperialism and national freedom and social justice) into socialism. In both nations, the United States sought to overthrow the resultant regime. In Guatemala the effort was a success; in Cuba it was a resounding failure.

In Guatemala, the alarming factor was the ease with which Communists succeeded in permeating a non-Communist government. In 1944 President Ubico, a military dictator, was overthrown by students waving the Atlantic Charter. O tempora, o mores! Ten years later, Communists were a stronger factor in the labor movement and political life of Guatemala than in any other country outside the Iron Curtain.

How is the rapid success of a party that scarcely existed in 1944 to be explained? In part its success was a function of the political vagueness, the lack of hard doctrine, under the rule of Juan José Arévalo (1944-50). His "spiritual socialism" degenerated into the rule of opportunists. To young politicians and students, Marxism appeared both systematic and "pure."

[9] For a splendid account of the prospects and paradoxes of good-neighborliness see Bryce Wood, The Making of the Good Neighbor Policy (Columbia University Press, 1961).

Arévalo's successor, Jacobo Arbenz Guzmán, trusted Communists *faute de mieux.* The Communists gave him trustworthy support when moderate politicians wavered, and they brought the labor unions behind the government. They pushed agrarian reform and began to bring the *campesinos* into political life. They drew Guatemala—via extreme nationalism—into alliance with the socialist powers.

Certainly many Guatemalans disliked the alliance with Communism. It was of crucial importance that the majority of army officers increasingly disliked the policies of Arbenz and were unwilling to shed blood (either their own or others') in his defense. They were particularly alarmed by the purchase of arms from Eastern Europe—not merely for its diplomatic repercussions, but because the arms might be used to equip a popular militia as a force against an "unreliable" army. The masses were still loyal though unenthusiastic; they could not be organized by the Communists against the invasion of Castillo Armas and his Liberation Army from Honduras. Arbenz was ousted without a real struggle.[10]

In the end the Communists were defeated by those very conditions that underpinned their success. A disciplined party could easily dominate formless political groupings and an unsophisticated labor movement. The Communist party then used these advantages to draw Guatemala hard and fast toward the socialist camp and into violent conflict with the United States. Those who objected to this process could overthrow the regime for the simple reason that, although the Communists could control hitherto amorphous labor movements and popular parties, they could not make them fight for a Communist-controlled state. With greater moderation the Communists could have hoped for a longer stretch of power. And in 1954 no effective gesture of support could be made by the U.S.S.R.

The Guatemalan experience is essential for the understanding of the Cuban experience. The United States seems to have deduced that intransigent opposition in the international field and the activities of the Central Intelligence Agency could end an undesirable regime, and that this success might be worth the great unpopularity that the "tough" line in Guatemala brought the United States throughout Latin America. The Cuban Communists deduced that they must organize the masses more effectively into the party, and see to it that the national bourgeoi-

[10] For an account of the Arbenz regime see R. M. Schneider, *Communism in Guatemala, 1944-1954* (Praeger, 1958).

sie, opposed by its own interests to the "conciliatory" bourgeoisie dependent on foreign capital, was effectively reinforced in its anti-imperialism by pressure from beneath. Otherwise, as in Guatemala, imperialists would play on the "double character" (half nationalist, half drawn toward international capitalism) of the bourgeoisie and tempt it to desert the democratic revolution: "The working class and not the national bourgeoisie must be the directing force in national liberation."[11]

Cuba was in some respects, but only in some, an analogue of Guatemala. As in Guatemala, nationalism was by definition anti-American, and anti-American sentiment was stimulated by the existence of powerful U.S. economic interests. The presence of the United States was psychologically oppressive in Cuba as in no other country, except possibly Panama. No one who has talked to a Cuban can escape the myth of a prostitute economy maintained by, and for, the American tourist and American trade.

With nationalism and anti-Americanism, the similarities end. Cuba was an island with no hostile Honduras on its borders offering shelter to a "Liberation Army." With 200,000 exiles waiting to return, it is difficult to exaggerate the advantages Cuba has derived from being an island. Whatever Castro is, he is no Arbenz, who was devoid of charisma. Russia's commitment to Cuba was decisive, and by the end of 1960 the hold of Communists in Cuba was more secure than it had ever been in Guatemala. Finally, the Cuban revolution had captured the imagination of the Latin American left as the "October Revolution" of 1944 in Guatemala had not. Thus the Cuban situation was a more difficult and intolerable problem to the United States, and, by the same token, offered incontestably greater advantage to Russia. It made the cold war a reality to Latin Americans, because the alternatives were no longer Russia *or* the United States but the Cuban revolution *plus* Russia *versus* the United States. The defense of Cuba against "intervention" *was* meaningful. It involved the sacred principles of self-determination and nonintervention. To Mexico or Brazil, the United States drive against Cuba in the Organization of American States seemed to threaten the inter-American system as they understood it. It was to "import the cold war into the OAS," which had no concern with the extra-American disputes of the United States.

[11] C. del Campo, "La Revolución Guatemalteca," in A. Rumianstev, ed., *El movimiento contemporánea de liberación nacional y la burguesía nacional* (Prague, 1961).

HOW DID CUBA BECOME AN HONORARY MEMBER of the socialist camp, the first nonaligned state to do so? The Castro revolution was not, in its inception, Communist. The ideology of the revolution derived from José Martí, the prophet of the Cuban independence movement against Spain, and from the programs of left-wing Cuban radicals rather than from Marx. The doctrine of the "frustrated revolution" was the key to Castro's early thought. Cuba was not a democratic sovereign state. Since the War of Independence (1895-98) the independent Republic had been "captured" by the United States, just as the radicalism of the 1930's and the program of the Ortodoxo reformism of the early 1950's had been cut short by Batista. Given that Castro saw his task as the revindication of Cuba's sovereignty in every sphere, the logic of his position entailed the end of Cuba's special economic relations with the United States.

This meant an attack on United States interests in Cuba. Emotionally the revolution had to feed on hostility to the United States—on the sensation of a revolution besieged by foes—and Castro's excessive sensitivity to criticism in the U.S. press reinforced this tendency. It is difficult to detect in 1959 a determination by the Eisenhower administration to isolate and "punish" Cuba. Even though the administration took a narrowly legalistic view of the expropriation of American property, it did not want to oust Castro. But the 1960 breach—that is, Cuba's drift toward Communism and toward the Soviet block—changed the U.S. administration's attitude.

Though few Cubans were as politically naïve as most Guatemalans in 1953-54, the failure of the Cuban revolution to evolve a doctrine and a party and the lack of trained politicans left a political vacuum that could be filled by experienced Communists. That this process should be resisted was natural. The Cuban Communists, like the Communists in other Latin American countries, had a long history of cooperation with dictatorships when such a course suited their immediate aims. Blas Roca, the toughest of the Communist leaders, had argued that Castro's guerrilla resistance was misconceived, and the party had only patched up an alliance with Castro late in the day.[12] Of course, one of the supreme tactical advantages of Communism is that its *ultimate* revolu-

[12] Blas Roca's evolution from his position in the fifties can be traced in the later editions of his "Fundamentals of Socialism" and his views on the recent course of the revolution in "El desarrollo histórico de la revolución cubana," in *Cuba Socialista*, Vol. IV, No. 29 (1964).

tionary credentials are impeccable, whatever tactical contrivances may
seem, at any given moment, to discredit its struggle against imperialism. Nevertheless, sometimes this argument does not convince. It did
not convince some of Castro's originial supporters: these protesters
were disciplined by the trial of Huber Matos (December 1959).

By spring 1961 Communist influence had achieved singular triumphs,
such as the capture, with the aid of the government, of the Trades
Union movement.[13] But at the very time when the process of political
disillusionment with Communist control and the discontent at short-
ages of consumer goods were gathering strength, the United States permitted the folly of the April "invasion." It is pointless to debate whether
the evolution toward socialism was inevitable or whether it was fostered by the supposed follies of U.S. policy in 1954-60. Cuban Socialists
would argue that the reaction of the United States to the economic and
social legislation of 1959-60 shows that the clash between national revolution and imperialism was inevitable and that only the timing was dependent on the actual course of U.S. policy. They are good historicists:
the United States is what it is and acts as it must. However, the point at
issue here is that Playa Girón (the invasion beach) convinced most Cubans that what Castro was telling them was true: the United States was
in league with the counterrevolutionaries and "bourgeois" elements in
an attempt to crush the revolution.

THE CATASTROPHIC FAILURE OF THE INVASION restored immediately both Castro's domestic position and his prestige throughout
Latin America.[14] Playa Girón is the Tenth of August of the Cuban
revolution, the watershed of blood, the point of no return once patriot
blood called for revenge. No one could accept the argument that the
invasion was an exile affair, for which no blame attached to the agencies
of the U.S. government. Castro immediately appeared as a symbol
of the independence of the Latin American nations. Although he had
defeated an ill-conceived invasion by an ill-supplied group of exiles,
he could present himself as the David who had defeated Goliath in
all his might. More significantly, Russia was henceforth clearly committed to the defense of Cuban independence.

[13] For a polemical examination of these trends see Leo Sauvage, *Autopsie du
Castrisme* (Paris: Flammarion, 1962), p. 206-7.
[14] For a remarkable examination of the invasion, see Tad Szulc and Karl E.
Meyer, *The Cuban Invasion* (Praeger, 1962).

The miscalculation of April was particularly disastrous in that U.S. policy under the new Kennedy administration was making a determined effort to counter the spread of Castro-type revolutions in the continent by accelerating a revision of hemispheric policy that had begun under the Eisenhower administration. This revision was overdue: a negative version of the good-neighborliness could no longer be a successful policy. Even before the threat of Castro, the U.S. government was turning toward a more active policy. Beginning as part of a general concern for Latin America, this revision now became concentrated on the problems created by the existence of Castro.

Castro posed as the hero of a pan-American revolution against American imperialism, supported by and supporting the Soviet bloc. It was an axiom of some intelligent policymakers in Washington that Communism and extreme revolutionary movements, of which Fidelism was an example, were transition phenomena. Latin America was experiencing rapid economic and social change, which created violent situations. These were exploitable by Communism only for the limited period before self-sustaining growth brought all-round prosperity. Walt Rostow presented the following view:

> Communists know that their time to seize power in the underdeveloped area is limited. They know that, as momentum takes hold in an underdeveloped area—and the fundamental social problems inherited from the traditional society are solved—their chances to seize power decline. It is on the weakest nations—facing their most difficult moments—that the Communists concentrate their attention. They are the scavengers of the modernization process.[15]

Ergo, the optimist conclusion runs, by easing and guiding the modernization process the threat of Communism can be exorcised and Latin America gained for the free world.

American policy in Latin America since 1945 had been conceived largely in strategic terms and resulted in military missions, equipment standardization, and the Mutual Defense Agreements made from 1952 on.[16] Since in purely military terms the pacts were useless, it remained open to question whether such military aid was the best instrument to secure general political support. Was the best way to "fight commu-

[15] W. W. Rostow, in F. M. Osanka, ed., *Modern Guerrilla Warfare: Fighting Guerrilla Movements, 1941-1961* (Free Press, 1962).
[16] For these agreements and their consequences see E. Lieuwen, *Arms and Politics in Latin America* (Praeger for the Council on Foreign Relations, 1960), Chaps. 8 and 9.

nism" internally the formation of military alliances with incumbent regimes, whatever their political complexion? The political atmosphere of Latin America was undergoing changes that made the U.S. award of the Legion of Merit to Pérez Jiménez (Venezuelan President ousted in 1958) look dangerously like what Castro came to call backing the wrong side in the process of historical development.

Thus on the eve of the Cuban invasion the postulates of U.S. policy were these:

1. Economic aid to the modernization process is preferable to Mutual Defense Agreements as a means of combatting Communism and gaining general political support in a cold war.[17]

2. The United States must appear as a free society supporting free societies ready to help themselves; only thus can it appear as the champion of a better way of life than that modeled on the Soviet bloc or Cuba. It must therefore see to it that aid goes to progressive democracies.

These were the premises of President Kennedy's Alliance for Progress.

However, the more negative conception of hemispheric defense (e.g., the use of the OAS to put sanctions on Castro and Communism) was not abandoned. It was tested diplomatically at the Punta del Este meeting, where the United States attempted to retrieve some of the losses sustained in April 1961. This conception was based on an interpretation of its fundamental instrument (the Inter-American Treaty of Reciprocal Assistance, signed at Rio de Janiero in 1947). That interpretation was unacceptable to neutralist Latin American states such as Brazil and Mexico.

It was only the support of the smaller states that allowed the United States a limited success at Punta del Este. Castro and the Eastern bloc immediately pointed out that only the shameless manipulation of votes of "imperialist puppets" had allowed the United States to escape a major humiliation. The "peoples" of Latin American had defended Cuba, self-determination, and nonintervention.

ONCE THE DUST OF PUNTA DEL ESTE had settled, the cold war seemed to resolve itself into the Alliance for Progress, backed by the United States, versus the revolution of national liberation. What were the terms of the battle?

---

[17] Military cooperation did not cease; it changed its emphasis as the danger of guerrilla movements intensified.

The Alliance for Progress implied support of economic moderniza-tion within democratic states. What were the prospects of economic prosperity and of finding respectable democratic states that Washing-ton could support?

Many Latin American observers are pessimistic, the blackest pessi-mists being those who imply that democratic forms are incompatible with rapid growth when rapid growth is what economic nationalism demands. The "structuralist" school (which explains inflation in Brazil, Chile, and elsewhere in terms of supply inelasticities and deep societal hindrances) sees growth as possible only after fundamental—particular-ly agrarian—reform. This, it is argued, the Alliance for Progress, in spite of good intentions, will not force on recalcitrant governments. Those who explain current difficulties in terms of a deep-seated "asymmetry," which must result in adverse terms of trade for "peripheral" primary producers as against the industrial "center," see the Alliance for Pro-gress as a guilt payment by an "advanced" country—a country that fills in with charity the gap it creates by not paying "fair" prices for imports from Latin America. Combined with an excess of bureaucratic controls, these pessimistic views allow some Latin Americans to label the Al-liance for Progress "already a failure."[18]

This view, tenable in 1963, is perhaps less tenable today. Its persis-tence is, perhaps, one more example of the Latin American predilection for external scapegoats, and reflects an attitude that neglects the self-help principles on which the Alliance is founded. Nevertheless, there is a case for saying that the West generally must take an attitude toward developing countries more dynamic than the mere provision of loans. If it is too much to ask for some mechanism to stabilize the prices on which the economic well-being of the Latin American "periphery" de-pends, there is a case for tariff reductions that would favor Latin American products. Together with free trade in Latin America itself, this might create a healthier economy that would not stagnate when import substitution had reached the limits of the internal market. Eco-nomically the prospects for the Alliance for Progress are still uncertain. Yet it is on its efficiency as a promoter of growth that its utility as a po-litical weapon depends.

It has been argued that the political presuppositions of the Alliance

[18] For a characteristic view of the pessimist left, see R. Ramírez Gómez, "El Informe Prebisch," in Cuadernos Americanos, CXXXI, 6 (Mexico, 1963), 7 ff.

are utopian and self-contradictory. Latin American progressive parties are anti-American by definition, and yet it is these parties that the Alliance must favor if it is to appear democratic. It has also been argued that the "middle classes"—reformists in the 1930's—have turned into respectable social climbers aping the aristocratic establishment. The intellectuals have become alienated from this middle class and may take the leadership of some form of Populist revolution.[19] Curiously enough, the Communists do not think that the role of the "national bourgeoisie" is exhausted. "It is true that in certain periods the bourgeoisie has betrayed the workers and may betray them again. But this does not mean to say that nothing can be done with the bourgeoisie."[20] The national bourgeoisie can cooperate—indeed *must* cooperate—in the anti-imperialist revolution of national liberation. Hence the zeal Soviet analysts display in the identification of a national bourgeoisie and its distinction from a "conciliatory" bourgeoisie, which will always side with the imperialists. It may be that both the United States and the U.S.S.R. base their policies on a class that does not exist, and that therefore Popular Fronts and Western-type democracies are alike nonviable. Clearly, the answer to this problem will differ from country to country. Perhaps there has been a tendency to speculate too much about the absence of a "normal" middle sector or of an entrepreneurial class.[21] The rigidity of political structures or parties (for instance, the declining but still numerically important parties like APRA) is probably a far more serious immediate problem than the existence or nonexistence of a "satisfactory" middle sector.

If there are limitations on the successful deployment of the Alliance for Progress, there are also limitations on Russian interest in Latin America. To exchange students on a large scale is one thing (though even this was often a disillusioning process), but it would be another to load the Soviet Union with the task of underpinning a series of bankrupt revolutionary regimes. Just as U.S. aid had become vital to Bolivia's continued existence, so the aid of the Soviet Union has become

[19] Claudio Veliz, "Obstacles to Reform in Latin America," *The World Today*, Vol. 19, No. 1 (Jan. 1963).

[20] Galo González in the Tenth Congress of the Chilean Communist Party.

[21] Much of the debate is semantic. For example, what is meant by "native" entrepreneurs in Peru? Criticism comes from a civilization with a high achievement motivation. Much of the criticism, by U.S. investigators and businessmen, of the Argentinian business world appears strange to British minds. We appear more like Argentinians than like North Americans.

necessary to keep a shopwindow of revolution in Cuba. Moreover, the spectacle of bearded revolutionaries was not altogether sympathetic to party bureaucrats who had not seen a revolution in years. A continental revolution, with Castro as its prophet, might involve Russia in the maintenance of expensive revolutions that could not be controlled by reliable local Communists. In Cuba itself, the old-style Communists had been edged aside by a new party "built from below." This process was initiated by Castro's attack on the old-style Communist leader Aníbal Escalante, who was denounced in March 1962 for "sectarianism"—that is, for an attempt by Old Guard Communists to plant their followers in key posts to the exclusion of devoted followers of Castro himself. People who had been "under their beds" in the revolution were not to be permitted to dominate the party organization of revolutionary Cuba or threaten the ascendancy of Castro himself. There were frictions with Russian technicians: Cubans felt that the Eastern bloc was not always giving of its best to Cuba, and the Russian technicians felt that Cuban economics were a little too Bohemian. Given these limitations, how far would Khrushchev go in the defense of Cuban independence? How far would he go in backing Castro-type revolutions throughout Latin America?

The missile crisis was the test of the first issue. The result was undoubtedly more favorable to Kennedy than to Khrushchev. The actual presence of Soviet missiles alarmed Latin American states; this was proved by the reaction of the OAS. Moreover, the settlement over the head of Castro brought Latin America into the area of the Sino-Soviet dispute.

There had always been the seeds of discord in Latin American issues. The Chinese model of revolution, the Chinese view that national liberation had priority over peace, the Chinese advocacy of "averaging out" aid to national liberation movements rather than concentrating on the demonstration effects of a prosperous Soviet model—all had attractions for the Latin American left. The whole Castro thesis of the viability of guerrilla tactics ran against the 1961 reaffirmation by the Communist Party of the Soviet Union (CPSU) Central Committee that a "premature" rising was a bourgeois trap: "Under all circumstances let the revolutionary forces grow until the seed is fully ripe." This concern with what Communists were once in the habit of calling the "objective conditions" of revolution was clean contrary to the Cuban thesis as expounded by Che Guevara: a guerrilla movement in a peasant country would "induce" its own revolution.

From 1956 the Chinese themselves began to emphasize their sympathy for Latin America, and in 1960 Peking launched a campaign of friendship toward Latin America. By this date, invitations to China and the other customary cultural exchanges appeared less as cooperation in a common struggle than as a competitive bid. Nevertheless, the Communist parties of Latin America, though troubled, remained loyal to Moscow. The Chilean party (November 1961) went even further in denouncing "polycentrism" than the CPSU. The Brazilian party was in one of its divisive crises; it nevertheless endorsed the party line after the CPSU XXII Congress.

The missile crisis allowed the Chinese to expose Khrushchev as a man frightened of paper tigers. Given his premise that invasion had been prevented and that the United States had formally guaranteed Cuban independence, Khrushchev's defense of his policy was convincing.[22] Given the premises of the Chinese, his conduct was taken as "cowardice."

The principle of peaceful co-existence can apply only to nations with different social systems, not to relations between oppressed and oppressing classes. . . . Those attacking China extend their idea of "peaceful co-existence" to cover relations between the colonial and semi-colonial people on the one hand and the imperialists and colonialists on the other. . . . Doesn't this kind of talk mean that the Chinese people, the Korean people, and the people of other countries who rose in revolution have all violated the principle of "peaceful co-existence" and done wrong?[23]

The Chinese Communist Party (CCP) consistently referred to a "second Munich" over Cuba, and the weeks after the Cuban crisis saw the most serious bid by the CCP for Latin America. Even Castro himself might be prised away. The U.S.S.R. behavior as a Great Power rather than as a leader of the National Liberation Movement threatened Castro's position as the leader of a continental rebellion against imperialism. Thus to secure the allegiance of Castro by flattery and generous economic aid became a necessity for Khrushchev in the battle against Peking.

[22] Khrushchev's Report to the Supreme Soviet of the U.S.S.R., Dec. 12, 1962, in A. Dallin, ed., *Diversity of International Communism: A Documentary Record, 1961-1963* (Columbia University Press, 1963), pp. 670 ff. Paper tigers, Khrushchev insisted, now had atomic teeth.

[23] "The Differences between Comrade Togliatti and Us," editorial in *Jenmin jih-pao*, Dec. 31, 1962.

Since the October 1962 crisis it has been clear that the Chinese have attracted *some* support in Latin America against the old-style Communist leaders. This support comes from the general pool of leftish-revolutionary sentiment, whose unifying ideology is a derivate of Fidelism. Clearly, the Chinese view of the primacy of revolution periodically attracts sections of the Venezuelan party. But we can get a different view of the situation in Chile: those who sympathize with China include a miscellaneous collection of revolutionary Communists, Trotskyites, and Fidelistas. In Ecuador and Peru, the old-style "Moscow" leadership has been violently criticized by young activists.[24] The Communist party has, in some countries, come to look more like a conservative interest group, and its talk of the socialist revolution looks like nineteenth century rhetoric.

Castro himself, tempted though he may have been in October 1962, has remained loyal to the U.S.S.R. in the sense that he has expressed no support in public for China. The official Cuban attitude is one of distress that the conflict exists and an insistence that Cuba has its "own" position. Of course, the rigid hostility of China to the United States fits the demands of Cuban foreign policy better than peaceful coexistence. But signing the Nuclear Test Ban Treaty was regarded as a moral impossibility for a country that was still under attack by one of the signatories (the United States) and not as an act of defiance to the U.S.S.R., although presumably the lineup with Albania and China was not pleasing to Moscow.

Nevertheless, China simply cannot replace the Soviet Union as an economic prop. Castro and his government know this and act accordingly. Their first priority is the creation of a viable economy in Cuba. The continental revolution cannot be won if the "model" goes bankrupt. They now realize that the early programs of diversification in agriculture (i.e., the deliberate cutback of sugar) and industrialization were misconceived. Their immediate aim is socialism in one country. For this Russia is more useful than China, and other countries are a useful supplement to Russia. Hence the recent purchases of French and British equipment and the revision of the early notions of diversifica-

---

[24] For the tensions between old-style leaders and the new revolutionaries exploiting agrarian unrest in southern Peru, see Hugo Neira, *Cuzco: Tierra y Muerte* (Lima: Problemas de Hoy, 1965), written after this paper was conceived. In Ecuador I was told, "The leaders are all dancing the tango while we [the young revolutionaries] are doing the twist."

tion. In Leninist terms, the Cubans, though they would not recognize it, have become "economists."

What, then, is the balance of forces in Latin America? First, there is a tendency to overestimate the *short-term* chances of a Castro-type revolution and the opportunities which such a revolution, if successful, would open up for Communist penetration. It is true that the connection of Castro to Russia and to the Communist party is irreversible; the revolution is fiercely socialist and against any "third" solution in Latin America such as a Christian Democrat regime. Nevertheless, Latin American Fidelist revolutionaries feel that the degree of backing they may expect from the U.S.S.R. is limited by its interests as a Great Power. Old-line Communists do not take to the hills with the enthusiasm of students; like Russian Communists of today, their influence must generally favor the *via pacífica* as against the *via armada*. All that is important is not to find oneself caught out by events incapable of exploiting a revolutionary coup if it happens to be successful.

Castro's hopes that the "cordillera of the Andes" may turn into the "Sierra Maestra of the American continent" seem unfounded. The Cuban revolution was a model for *small* countries; its guerrilla technique will not work in large countries, where it might well create areas of discontent that would not "expand" into a national revolution. This is the case in Colombia and Brazil. In Venezuela the activity of terrorists looked as if it might upset the U.S. "model" of a "sensible" democracy that avoided blatant anti-Americanism. In fact, this has not happened, as the victory of the nonrevolutionary parties in the December 1963 elections proved. All that Castro could do was to declaim against an "electoral farce based on bloodshed and terror." Elsewhere (in Chile and Argentina, for instance) the Communists were committed to different tactics: the infiltration of labor movements and the utilization of Popular Fronts.

No large continental country seems in danger of a Communist takeover. In Brazil, in spite of serious political confusion and seemingly insuperable foreign exchange problems, there are forces that can thwart a social revolution.[25] Indeed, since Castro's revolution there has been no example of a comparable left-wing revolution elsewhere. On the contrary, in Castro's own words, "reaction progresses, right-wing military

[25] This was written before the revolution of April 1964, which resulted in the temporary elimination of any left-wing threat.

groups progress and the military coups follow one another with amaz-
ing speed . . . so-called democratic institutions clash with military
institutions."[26] The danger in Latin America is not a continent's drift
into Communism, but explosions in the *loci classici* of discontent in the
smaller countries—the Dominican Republic, Panama, Nicaragua. Latin
America is much less unstable than its student agitators make it look.
Increasingly, admiration of Castro is confined to a smaller section of
the left.

The United States (or at least its more alarmist politicians) thinks in
terms of a "sick" continent. Its task is to stop the spread of Castro-type
revolutions in this infirm body (biological metaphors are much in fashion). There are only two courses open on this analysis: either get rid of
Castro or remove the sickness that affects the continent. This cure is
seen fundamentally in economic terms, though it would be idle to deny
the humanitarian concern for poverty as such. Prosperity solves all.

As U.S. policymakers increasingly emphasize, Latin America must
save itself. It will not be saved by the present volume of U.S. investment. The Alliance for Progress will encounter many difficulties in its
attempt to release a "takeoff" in some countries or to revivify stagnant
economies elsewhere in Latin America.

What of the more drastic course, the elimination of Castro? As I have
argued (if a guess can be dignified with this title), "Castro" revolutions
will not spread to large countries, and U.S. politicians who believe that
the battle is lost if Castro lasts are perhaps confusing a local irritant
with a continental danger. How can he be brought down in any case?
Not by economic blockade. Even the allies of the United States will not
accept self-denying ordinances, and it can at least be argued that a
blockade by the United States and her continental allies alone probably
strengthens rather than weakens Castro's position and certainly drives
the whole economy into greater reliance on the Soviet bloc. There is
little that the United States can do about Cuba. There is a great deal
it can do about Latin America once it drops its Caribbean obsessions.

Finally, the present indications are that socialism in one country and
the need to import and export may force some moderation on Castro
himself insofar as this is compatible with the role of a second Bolívar
as set out in the Second Declaration of Havana (February 1962). This

---

[26] Speech of Sept. 28, 1962.

means that Cuba will have to seek relations with countries (e.g., France, Great Britain, and Japan) that can supply basic capital goods for a reformed economy based, for a time at least, on the transformation of local products. If the United States persists in isolating Cuba, it will find itself, not Cuba, being isolated. If Cuba persists in a policy of actively fostering revolution in Latin America, it will find its desired economic (and perhaps cultural) contacts outside the Socialist bloc difficult to establish.

LEON LIPSON, Professor of Law at Yale University, has directed
his specialized research toward Soviet law and Soviet
society.

Castro on the Chessboard of the Cold War*

LEON LIPSON

From Havana, now, Moscow still looks big. It is the Soviet Union that extends credits, supplies machinery, buys Cuban sugar
that it does not need, sends rockets, technicians, troops. It is the Soviet
Union that serves as Cuba's patron and protector in Cuba's running
quarrel with the United States. The Soviet Union has been said to furnish some of the inspiration and some of the guidance for Cuba's economic and administrative development under Fidel Castro. And it is
the Soviet Union that looms as the ambiguous sponsor of Dr. Castro's
chief allies and rivals in the leadership of the regime, the Cuban Communists. Dr. Castro proclaims himself a Marxist-Leninist, reviews Soviet military parades atop Lenin's mausoleum in Red Square, and has
pitched his tent firmly within "the Socialist camp." His government has
become more and more totalitarian. His expropriation of most foreign
and domestic ownership of Cuban industry is followed by amalgama-
tion of land holdings into state farms.

What could be clearer? From the observable behavior of Soviet leaders and their supporters throughout the world over forty years, and of

* This chapter has borrowed, too heavily for consistent footnoting, from several
highly useful sources: Theodore Draper, *Castro's Revolution: Myths and Realities*
(Praeger, 1962) and "Five Years of Castro's Cuba," *Commentary* (Jan. 1964); Boris
Goldenberg, "The Cuban Revolution: An Analysis," Ernst Halperin, "Castroism—
Challenge to the Latin American Communists," and Andrés Suárez, "Castro between
Moscow and Peking," in *Problems of Communism*, Vol. XII, No. 5 (Sept.-Oct.
1963); and Arnold Horelick, "The Cuban Missile Crisis: An Analysis of Soviet Cal-
culations and Behavior," *World Politics*, XVI, 3 (April 1964), 363-89.

178

the Soviet bloc of states over almost twenty, the pattern seems not very difficult to fill in. For many in the United States the pattern has been filled in, and Cuba presents them with the deplorable but familiar picture of a Soviet puppet state, sustained by the presence or the threat of Soviet military power, led by a demagogue whose path to Moscow it is not very interesting to explore, bent on the Communization of Cuban society and the subversion of the rest of Latin America or indeed of more distant neighbors. As the international lawyers say, why interpret that which stands in no need of interpretation?

Yet something about the stereotype is not quite right. Was Dr. Castro indeed a masked Communist when he took power, or has his evolution affected the Cuban present? How can the prescriptions of Che Guevara for revolution by guerrilla warfare be squared with orthodox Soviet doctrine? Is the recent priority on agricultural development consistent with Soviet (or with Marxist-Leninist) strategies of economic growth? What are the effects of Cuba's insular situation and great distance from Russia, of the recent changes in relations within the Soviet bloc, of the rise of China? What special advantages, and what special risks, does Cuba's partnership appear to involve for the Soviet Union? As other international lawyers say, you sometimes have to engage in a process of interpretation in order to decide whether interpretation is necessary.

Castro's Rule

Before asking whether the Cuban revolution was made by Marxist-Leninists, we may wonder whether it fitted Marxism-Leninism. If we limit our gaze to the early months of Castro's rule, we cannot find the impoverished proletariat of a highly industrial society overthrowing a capitalist ruling class. But then, the Russian Revolution of October 1917 also did not fit that pattern, nor did the installation of satellite Communist regimes in Eastern Europe on the bayonets of the Red Army. The suggestion that Dr. Castro came in as a Kerensky and was turned into a Lenin by the forces of history or the power of propaganda would be spurned alike by Castroites, Leninists, and Kerenskyites.

Neither did Batista's Cuba answer to the conventional requirements supposed now, in the looser theology of our day, to precede a Communist take-over in an industrially underdeveloped country. Cuba in 1958 was not a poor agrarian country with an archaic, semifeudal social structure but a relatively well-off country with a relatively strong and confident middle class, which furnished most of the leaders of Castro's movement. The processes of industrialization were neither so recent nor so disruptive as to cramp the economy and the social mobility of the people. The local Communist party was not the unchallenged vanguard of the workers, the master of the streets of the capital; and the urban proletariat itself was relatively passive by the standards of Marxist-Leninist strategy. The revolution against Batista was not even unmistakably "anti-imperialist," for there was not much difference between the leading supporters of the Batista regime and many of the men around Fidel Castro in their attitude toward foreign investment and influence.

To the Soviet Union, the doubtfulness of the foundling's parentage is no bar to adoption. Dr. Castro, like Lysenko, has benefited by the dogma that environment counts for more than heredity. If Castro was not a tempered Communist revolutionary, he could nevertheless be supported by the Soviet leaders and the local Communists for as long as was useful; and he could be educated; and in time, with good luck and management, the discrepancies of analysis could be smoothed over by the selective retrospection of tendentious official historians. Though Soviet doctrine is not yet wholly reduced to rhetoric, it knows its office is to wait upon events and policies. What counted, at first, for the Soviet leaders was that Castro had succeeded, and that he had succeeded where Blas Roca and the other open Cuban Communists had failed. He was worth using, even though, or because, he was not yet "their man."

It is still too early to call the score on the number and quality of Communists among Dr. Castro's bands in the Oriente. The difficulty of the task may exceed its importance. Some had ties of sympathy or training with the Cuban Communist party. Some may have aspired to a synthesis of socialism and democracy, though knowing and caring little about the extent to which the Soviet reality and the plans of the Cuban Communists departed from both socialism and democracy. Their own program and organization seem to have lacked coherence, but the verve of the Maximum Leader carried all before it.

Less than three years after taking power, Fidel Castro had moved a long way—so long that he saw fit to belittle the distance by relocating the starting point. As Theodore Draper has pointed out, Dr. Castro now claims too early a date for his attachment to Marxism-Leninism, and the claim is given credence by some of his enemies. His friends may be wiser. The bulk of the trustworthy reports of associates who have since broken with Castro accords with the hints to be found in the speeches and interviews given by men like Che Guevara and Blas Roca. At the outbreak of the revolution, Castro was no mere "agrarian reformer," but neither was he a "melon," green without and red within. He was a middle-class lawyer with a strong sense of injustice, a large head, great demagogic gifts, confused political ideas, abundant courage and presence of mind, and a sense of mission strong enough to overcome scruples of loyalty to persons or principles. He may be right in saying now that he would have had trouble in the early days if he had declared himself a Marxist-Leninist, for most of the leaders and most of the followers of the group that had succeeded to the vacuum left by Batista were not prepared to exchange a decaying tyranny for a vigorous one. Where he is wrong is in claiming that his declaration would have been truthful.

When we shift from men to measures, we find again a divergence in the interpretation. The initial or "humanist" phase of the regime can be dismissed, by confirmed Soviet-philes and -phobes, as a tactical precaution to deceive the opinion of the world, to defer drastic action on farm lands until the peasants could be cowed, to soften and weaken Castro's democratic allies within Cuban society. Or it can be explained as answering pretty closely to the current fluidity of Fidel's political philosophy while various groups wrestled for leadership in the government and for influence over Fidel.

Meanwhile the revolution made its own history. In June 1959 the Cubans attempted a conquest of the Dominican Republic in a smaller and still shabbier version of the Bay of Pigs invasion; it failed. In 1959-60 the planned reform of land holdings turned into what Boris Goldenberg has termed a "chaotic agrarian revolution." The Cuban Communists, better suited to the bureaucratic maneuvers of Havana than the rigors of the Oriente hills, won commanding posts in control of the press—in mass organizations in the machinery of propaganda and ideology. They provided a program and an organizational weapon with which Castro could meet the local opposition that his economic measures had aroused. The transformation to a totalitarian state (in the limited sense of a state that intervenes in a relatively large fraction of soci-

ety's functions and processes) has proceeded without a change of leaders but with changes in the leader and changes in the relations of his
lieutenants.

On the evidence now available it does not appear that, at the outset,
the Soviet Union sponsored Dr. Castro's movement. That conclusion
does not follow, however, from the well-known antagonism between
the Cuban Communists and some of Dr. Castro's followers, for the Soviet Union is not incapable of splitting its bets. Even the revelations in
the trial of Marcos Rodríguez Alfonso in March 1964, while significant
for other reasons, on this point tell us only that local Communists were
ready to betray non-Communist revolutionaries to Batista's police,
which is no novelty.

It looks rather as though the Castro government sought patronage
abroad and found it, not surprisingly, in the Soviet bloc. Though Dr.
Castro may be coloring the past when he says he was a Marxist-Leninist early in his rise, he probably assumed from the beginning that the
United States would not allow his revolution to survive and would
have to be checked by a powerful protector. His acquaintance with the
United States seems to have been primitive; he knew little of the diversity of viewpoints in American public opinion, even in the financial
community. The rejection of tentative United States offers of aid, in
1959, was accompanied by a "search for offers" elsewhere. In February
1960 the Cubans and the Soviet Union concluded a trade agreement,
and in May, during the Moscow visit of Blas Roca, formal diplomatic
relations were established. (The United States suspension of the Cuban
sugar quota came later in the year, after oil refineries in Cuba owned
by American and British interests had been taken over when they refused to process some Soviet crude oil.)

The prominence of official Communists in Castro's regime was not a
feature of the very first months after the downfall of Batista. As late as
May 1959, Dr. Castro accused the Communists in effect of instigating
counterrevolutionary disorders in Oriente. That would not have been
said in a thoroughly Communized regime, except in furtherance of a
more protracted masquerade than it would be reasonable to suppose.
Castro has been charged with using the Communists to put down the
revolutionary democratic wing of his supporters, and the Communists
have been charged with using him for the same purpose. Both may be
true. In any case, whatever opportunity the non-Communist left had

had to retain or retrieve influence over the regime was inhibited by the interplay of foreign and domestic factors: the pressure toward militancy in expansion of the Castroite movement over Latin America, the power and political attractiveness of sentiment against the United States, organizational successes of the Cuban Communists among labor and student groups, the pulls of Castro's most trusted advisers. By June 1959, the Cabinet was reshuffled so as to eliminate the "Plattists," and by early June the Partido Socialista Popular (PSP) had the satisfaction of knowing that Castro would not, for the sake of avoiding the label of Communism, himself press an attack on Communists.

It was still not certain whether the Communists of Cuba would hope to supersede Castro or only to dominate his staff and his policies. Perhaps the question is better phrased in terms of short and long range: For what period of time, in their opinion, would it be expedient to try to work through Castro pending his supersession? We must note that the answer given to a question of this sort by a local Communist party is likely to differ from the answer that Moscow would give in advising that party or in the conduct of its own foreign policy (the Egyptian Communists have learned that).

The events of 1960 and early 1961 seem to have persuaded the PSP that they could not soon dispense with Castro, who had superintended the relatively peaceful evolution of the regime to something like totalitarian tightness. And the events seem to have made clear to Dr. Castro that the PSP should enter and dominate the new Organizaciones Revolucionarias Integradas (ORI) coalition with the Revolutionary Directorate and the Movement of the Twenty-sixth of July. In April 1961— the month of the Bay of Pigs invasion, when we helped to vindicate Dr. Castro's caricature of the United States—he made his announcement on the "socialist context of our revolution"; in July, he reached an organizational agreement with the leaders of the PSP; in October, the five-man Cuban delegation to the Twenty-second Congress of the Communist Party of the Soviet Union officially represented the ORI but included (behind Blas Roca) the Cuban Minister of Labor (ORI) and the Cuban Ambassador in Moscow (Directorate). A year later, a pro-Communist French author reported with apparent pleasure that he had found it hard to distinguish "militants in the Directorate of March 13th or the Movement of the Twenty-sixth of July" and Communists: he "always had the feeling that he was meeting Communists." Dr. Castro, however, distinguishes with less difficulty, as the downfall of Aníbal Escalante and the replacement of some other old-time Communists seems to show.

From Moscow's viewpoint, then, Castro knocked at the door and, in more than one sense, was taken in. He professes himself a student of the science of Marxism-Leninism, and in some of his long orations he sheds indulgent ridicule on his earlier naïveté. He has made some lexical contributions to the technique of propagating Soviet institutions in a country whose population was not yet ready for them: he has relabeled commissar "revolutionary instructor"; agitator, "orientator"; kolkhozes, "agricultural societies"; schools of Marxism-Leninism," "schools of revolutionary instruction"; sovkhozes, "granjas del pueblo."

When we move from rhetoric to economic and social policy, we find that the lessons of Soviet experience were learned in Cuba not wisely but too well. According to Che Guevara, whose opportunities for observation commend his views to our attention, Soviet planning techniques were copied in unreflecting detail; an unrealistically high rate of growth was arbitrarily assumed as the point of reference for unrealistically high targets in specific industries; the planners emphasized the importation of factories without taking costs and scarcities of raw materials into account; the production of sugar cane was, at least at one stage, cut down with uneconomic swiftness; and some social services were expanded beyond the capacity of the economy to sustain their activity. A comprehensive appraisal of the social and economic policy of Dr. Castro's Cuba lies outside the scope of this chapter. In drawing a final balance, one would have to allow for the achievements bought at so high a price and to give credit for the rare initiative that led, in a Latin American country, to sins of commission. Enough has been said to establish Dr. Castro's credentials as a would-be follower of the Soviet pattern, with some adaptation, during a period in which that pattern was becoming increasingly diversified throughout the Soviet bloc.

In the United States the Castro claim that Cuba serves as a model and a staging area for the rest of Latin America is taken as seriously as it is put forward. How must it look to the Soviet Union? If the Soviet leaders acknowledge the importance of Dr. Castro's personal leadership, as well as other probably unique features of the Cuban situation in 1958-60, they do not expect an exact repetition of the Cuban experience in other countries of Latin America. Do they suppose that a repetition is expected by Latin Americans? Cuba receives substantial Soviet aid, but the Soviet Union probably does not expect the Latin American left to envy the Cuban situation on this score, for the aid evidently fails to make up what has been lost from other sources. And a second Cuba could not be confident of obtaining from the Soviet Union the equivalent of the aid being given to the first.

As a center for the organization of subversive movements in other Latin American countries, Castroite Cuba both supplements and competes with the Moscow-directed activity of local Communist parties. Though something is known from outside of the comings and goings of Communist leaders and Castro sympathizers, the information appears too fragmentary to justify conclusions about the place of Cuba in some alleged chain of command, subsidy, arms supply, or intelligence. Reports that a few of the leaders of the coup in Zanzibar in January 1964 had received training in Cuba are far short of proving that the Soviet leaders have delegated to Cuba the task of preparing insurrections in industrially less developed countries. Perhaps Cuba's relation to the Soviet Union in this respect is best described as one of competitive cooperation.

The content of Castroite strategy for insurrection not only fails to coincide with the line advanced by Communist leaders in Latin America; it smacks of doctrines to which prevailing Communist ideas of insurrectionary strategy have long been opposed. Here the most detailed and forthright pronouncements have come from Guevara, not Castro, and the possibility that the Maximum Leader has found it expedient to repudiate even Guevara cannot be ignored. But for the time being we may take Guevara's ideas as representing what Castroism stands for on this issue, especially in the polemics of the Latin American intellectual left.

Guevara's emphasis on guerrilla warfare placed the countryside above the cities and the peasantry above the urban proletariat, which Marxist-Leninist theory had held to be of first importance even in industrially backward countries. His proposition that revolutionaries must not wait till all "objective and subjective conditions" are ripe, but can create some of the needed conditions, diverges from orthodox Communist theory in two other ways: (1) More like Lenin than Leninism, it appears to accord relatively a greater weight to the will of the individual and the insurrectionary party, and a lesser weight to deterministic analysis; and (2) it implies an exhortation to advance D-day and a criticism of local Communist leaders for sluggishness excused by wrong theory. Thus, while Guevara criticized domestic Cuban policy for what he appeared to believe to be a harmful leftist deviation, on matters of continental political strategy he showed elements of both Maoist and Trotskyist influence. (There can be no better proof that the Communization of Cuba in the Soviet sense is incomplete than the continued prominence of Che Guevara, and no better proof that the Communization of Guevara is incomplete than the views with which he continues to be associated. It is too soon to tell whether his conspicuous but mysterious absence means that he has been unleashed, released, or leashed.)

There are some undeniable compensating advantages for the Soviet Union in this divergence of doctrine. First, because one side argues on behalf of a state that is allied with the Soviet Union and has after all furnished the one model of success in the Western Hemisphere, the debate takes on more life and immediacy and increases the possibilities of action by concentrating more attention on them. Second, in the somewhat more tolerant atmosphere of Communist polemic that many of the participants have tried to breathe in the past ten years, the existence of disagreement on strategy can, up to a point, serve to accommodate conflicting tendencies and thus broaden the base of the support given to the Communist leadership by the potential constituency among the intellectuals. Third, to the extent that the unorthodox doctrine does in fact come closer to a correct analysis of the situation, it may improve the strategic planning of the local leadership, whether or not the leadership expresses agreement with the doctrine. If the Soviet game were fixed only on the possibilities of revolution in Latin America, the Cuban rivalry with local Communist parties in other Latin American countries would seem useful so long as it continued to be manageable.

But Latin America is not the only focus of Soviet activity, and local advantages may be offset by broader considerations. The problems raised indirectly by Guevara's doctrines, and by Cuban dynamism in general, are those of global Soviet policy, in particular those of Soviet relations with China and the United States. We need not go so far as to call the Soviet Union a conservative power, or a "have" nation, to recognize the interest of the Soviet Union in preserving as much control as it can over the tempo of unrest in the industrially underdeveloped regions. That control is threatened by the existence of a strong pro-Chinese wing in or around the Communist parties of many Latin American countries. It is one thing for Soviet-controlled Communist parties to try to draw "national liberation movements" after them, patronizingly urging "revolutionary democrats" to step up their leftward march; it is another thing for the Communist parties to be hustled along by adherents of a more impatient doctrine, who themselves are encouraged by the Soviet Union's rival in the great schism.

This is apparent not only to the Soviet Union but also to Fidel Castro. The attraction of Communist China is compounded, it would appear, of the prestige of Mao's success in winning through to power after a long struggle in the countryside; the appeal of the doctrine that Communist revolution can be commenced before substantial industrialization; the enthusiasm for Communist China among Trotskyite and other groups on the Latin American left to whom the Cubans wish to appeal; the sympathy with another "victim" and enemy of the United States; the counterpoise that China can offer to the danger that inside Cuba the old PSP, supported by the Soviet Union, may smother Dr. Castro. In return for substantial Soviet economic aid and the Soviet capacity for rocket threats against the United States, Castro's primary loyalty must be to the Soviet Union for the time being, but the protégé of a powerful patron is often glad to be able to keep on good terms with his patron's rival. The Poles in jest acclaim Russia as their buffer against the Chinese; the Cubans cherish good relations with China lest the Soviet embrace hug too tightly. Castro's expressions of discomfort at the Sino-Soviet differences may be partly genuine and wholly prudent.

The course of the Sino-Cuban minuet has been traced by Andrés Suárez, writing in late 1963. Blas Roca stopped in Peking in March 1960, before his visit to Moscow in May, but he aligned himself and the Cuban PSP with the Soviet Union. Until December 1960, the Chinese public references described the Cuban leadership as that of a movement of national liberation, headed by democratic forces under Fidel Castro and the PSP. Castro pressed for Sino-Cuban friendship in order to keep some freedom of maneuver after he had invited Soviet assistance. Guevara, on a mission, got an offer of a trade agreement from the Chinese in October 1960, and two months later the Chinese began

188 LEON LIPSON

to acknowledge Castro's leadership in Cuba without the mention of the now firmly pro-Russian PSP.

The exacerbation of the Sino-Soviet conflict, so public since June 1963, has required the Castro regime (like other regimes aligned with the Soviet ex-bloc) to respond to the rivals' search for followers. Probably the Cuban decision to go along with Khrushchev owed less to any victory of Blas Roca over Guevara, or any discrediting of Guevara's policies, than to the plain fact that Castro's bread was buttered on the Soviet side. The Soviet-Cuban communiqués of May 1963 and January 1964 contained formulas that showed increasing Soviet pressure but still managed to avoid explicit condemnation of the Chinese.

Take, for example, the formula on the possibilities for "peaceful or nonpeaceful transition to socialism" (for which, in the current context, read "installation of an anti-United States regime without or with serious risk of a major war"). The Chinese, of course, have been stressing the duty to reckon with the possibilities of violence and not to shrink from them. The Russians have emphasized the superiority of the strategy of "peaceful coexistence." The May communiqué carried the same amount of water on both shoulders: ". . . the question of the peaceful or non-peaceful transition to socialism, in one country or the other, will be definitively solved by the peoples themselves and in accordance with the practical ratio of class forces and the degree of resistance of the exploiting classes to the socialist transformation of society." In January the emphasis had shifted slightly: ". . . conclusion on the utilization . . . of peaceful as well as non-peaceful paths in the struggle for the liquidation of the capitalist system." And the point was later underlined by a phrase on "the condemnation of factional and sectarian activity in the ranks of the Communist and Workers' Parties and in the international Communist movement."

The peak of Sino-Cuban official friendship probably came in late 1962 and early 1963, between the failure of the Soviet attempt to install intermediate-range ballistic missiles in Cuba (September-October) and the visit of Fidel Castro to the Soviet Union in the spring. The Chinese, who had supported Cuba warmly during the missile crisis, raged against the Soviet actions as adventurism followed by capitulationism. By September 1963 the Chinese had gone so far as to put responsibility for the specific crisis on the Soviet Union rather than the United States:

Although the tension in the Caribbean Sea stemmed from the U.S. imperialist policy of aggression against Cuba and although there has been a continuing danger of an invasion of Cuba by the U.S. imperialists, nevertheless, before the Soviet Union sent rockets into Cuba, there did not exist a crisis of the United States using nuclear weapons in the Caribbean Sea and of a nuclear war breaking out. If it should be said that such a crisis did arise, it was a result of the rash action of the Soviet leaders.[1]

Accusing the Soviet leaders of having, without consulting anybody, "wilfully embarked on a reckless course and irresponsibly played with the lives of millions upon millions of people," the Chinese professed to analyze the Soviet purpose as that of "political gambling" rather than that of defending the Cuban revolution. To the Soviet assurance that United States "aggression" against Cuba could be met by rockets launched from bases in the Soviet Union, the Chinese retorted:

That being so, why did you have to ship rockets to Cuba? . . . Anyone with common sense will ask: since the rockets were introduced, why did they have to be withdrawn afterwards? And inasmuch as the rockets were withdrawn afterwards, why did they have to be introduced before? According to you, there was a great deal of finesse in first putting them in, and then taking them out.[2]

By the time the Sino-Soviet schism had cut this deep, the Soviet-Cuban trade agreement of February 1963, the Soviet decision to turn weapons in Cuba over to Castro, and the Castro visit to the U.S.S.R. had repaired much of the damage done to the Soviet-Cuban relations by the denouement of the missile crisis. Even after agreeing to condemn "factional and sectarian activity," however, the Cubans apparently hoped to placate the Chinese by holding out against adherence to the treaty banning certain nuclear tests. The Soviet-Cuban communiqué of January 1964 went no further than to place the Cubans on record as considering "the successes achieved by the Soviet Union in the struggle for the cessation of nuclear tests and the agreement banning the orbiting of missiles with nuclear weapons a step forward in the direction of peace and disarmament." The Castro regime may like red, but they see no sense in painting themselves into a corner with it.

[1] "Statement of September 1, 1963, by the Spokesman of the Chinese Government: Comment on the Soviet Government's Statement of August 21," *Peking Review*, VI, 36 (Sept. 6, 1963), 7, 14.
[2] *Ibid.*

The Missile Crisis

Though in many ways the Soviet Union is still far from being a "have" nation, the Soviet leaders do "have" enough so that in the nuclear age they can no longer afford the luxury of casual provocation of the United States or of U.S. major allies. As Porgy's song says (better), possessions trouble your peace of mind and reduce your freedom of movement. Having a Cuban satellite is (chiefly because it appears to be) an important breach into the Western Hemisphere. But unless the satellite is firmly in hand, the Soviet Union runs the risk of being led into adventures at a time, and on a scale, for which it is not ready. What may be equally important, even with the shrunken distances of today's technology, Cuba is a remote and risky location for Soviet imperial maneuvering. That is one of the main lessons of the missile crisis of September-October 1962—the one time when the Cuban problem was thought by many to be capable of turning the cold war hot.

Why were the missiles sent to Cuba? The reason advanced in the Soviet Union was that deployment of the missiles in Cuba would protect Cuba against an attack, threatened by the United States. The Soviet move succeeded, says the Soviet apologia, for, in consequence of the withdrawal, the United States gave a pledge not to invade. That rationale has many defects. First, the Soviet actions exceeded what would have been fitted to that purpose. Second, the withdrawal came not when a pledge was given but when the United States implicitly threatened just such an attack as the deployment was supposed to have averted. Third, the pledge was not after all given, except upon the unfulfilled condition of international inspection of the Cuban bases. Fourth, the official Soviet rationale rests upon the major premise that the Soviet Union is a nonaggressive power, which, unless taken on faith, is subject to severe qualification; ordinarily one would not treat the sudden and secret deployment of missiles as an act of peace. Many of those who believe that Khrushchev deployed the missiles (and bombers) in order to force the United States to pledge not to invade Cuba have accepted this explanation in exchange for their early belief that he could not have deployed the missiles and bombers at all—just because he was a man of peace.

A second possibility was that the Russians had sent the missiles at the request of the Cubans. The Russians so hinted, at one point, and Jean Daniel's report of an interview with Fidel Castro in November 1963 goes part of the way toward corroboration. According to Daniel's report, Aleksei Adzhubei (Khrushchev's son-in-law, then editor of *Izvestia*) had been reminded by President Kennedy that the United States had not intervened in Hungary in 1956; Khrushchev took that statement to mean that Kennedy was warning the Russians against intervening in the event of an invasion of Cuba by the United States; Dr. Castro persuaded the Soviet leaders that a demonstration of Soviet support was necessary to deter the planned invasion; eventually the Cubans agreed to admit missiles.

This explanation, too, raises questions. Reports from Washington indicate that Kennedy had referred to Hungary to show by parallel Cuba's importance to the United States, but not in a context of intervention or nonintervention. Even if these reports are inaccurate, or if Adzhubei read the entrails wrong, the explanation by its own terms suggests that while it was the Cubans who asked for help it was the Russians who decided that the help should take the form of ballistic missiles. Finally, the account related by Daniel is in substantial conflict with the account of an earlier Castro interview (March 1963) with Claude Julien of *Le Monde:* "It was not in order to assure our own defense, but first of all to reinforce Socialism on the international scale. Such is the truth, even if other explanations are furnished elsewhere."

The interview with Julien came presumably at the height of Castro's disappointment at the Soviet withdrawal, determined (as it appears to have been) with a minimum of consultation with Castro himself. It would have been natural to fasten upon the Russians the major responsibility for a plan that had gone sour. The statement to Daniel, if the accuracy of the report be conceded, may well represent a more charitable but also a less scrupulous reconstruction that occurred to its author a year later, when the bitterness had receded and newer propagandistic themes had come to the fore.

One of the more wishful, though not necessarily less plausible, explanations for a Soviet initiative in pressing the missile shipments on Castro is advanced by an exile:

Instead of strengthening communism's beachhead in the western hemisphere . . . Castro, in the . . . Kremlin view, had been guilty of bungling and infantile political behavior which was damaging Cuba's usefulness as a base for the subversion of Latin America. The Cuban regime was shaky, vulnerable, jeopardized by internal uprisings and rebellion. The Kremlin saw but one alternative—to take over its Caribbean axis-partner entirely and convert Cuba into a puppet state.[3]

While Soviet motives for the missile deployment were probably mixed, the purpose of putting down unrest in Cuba is too limited to account for more than a small part of the decision. To risk a nuclear war with the United States required more important gains in prospect than cleaning up a local political mess in Cuba or even preventing the defection of Cuba as a Soviet "axis-partner."

Other interpretations have looked at broader issues. The strategic imbalance (the missile gap in reverse) between the United States and the Soviet Union in intercontinental ballistic missiles may, it is suggested, have persuaded Soviet leaders to try for a "quick fix" to improve the capabilities for shorter-range Soviet nuclear strikes against the United States while the buildup of the Soviet arsenal of ICBM's was going on. This explanation, by the way, impales the Soviet Union on one horn of the dilemma posed by the Chinese. It admits, as the Russians have hinted, that the strategic power based in the Soviet Union was not (as of early 1962) great enough to deter the United States from a first strike. But if Soviet missiles in Cuba were designed to play that role, the withdrawal must have come too early for the role to be fulfilled, for it can hardly be maintained that Soviet ICBM capabilities had improved fast enough between the decision to ship the missiles to Cuba and the decision to withdraw them.

Other explanations enjoying some currency in the West have attributed to the Soviet Union the intention of acquiring a pawn whose sacrifice could command a price. On this theory the withdrawal of missiles from Cuba could be traded off—not against a pledge not to invade, but against withdrawal from West Berlin, or against the dismantling of bases in Turkey. The Turkish exchange was indeed suggested, during one brief interval in the missile crisis, by Chairman Khrushchev. It still does not make sense.

In the first place, the time scales do not match. Removal of missiles from Cuba would have to take place quickly in order to be worth much to the United States. And disruption of the U.S.–Turkish military coop-

[3] Dr. José Ignacio Rasco, quoted in James Monahan *et al., The Great Deception* (Farrar, Straus, 1963), p. 200.

eration or (all the more so) abandonment of a basic, concerted Allied position on Berlin would require long and uncertain consultation, as the Russians must know.

In the second place, the categories do not match. In the Turkish case, the relevant frame of reference is not missiles here versus bases there, but missiles suddenly introduced into Cuba versus bases long established in Turkey and tacitly accepted by the Soviet Union. In the case of Berlin the lack of fit is even worse. No longer are the United States and the Soviet Union in a position (if they ever were) to swap allies, or to toss away commitments to allies, with the freedom of sultans exchanging concubines.

During the crisis, many expected the Russians to squeeze the Allies in Berlin in order to force a lifting of the "quarantine" or in retaliation for the "quarantine." Again, the categories did not match. A Soviet move on Berlin, to be tough enough to make the United States lift the "quarantine," would have had to be tough enough to trigger the nuclear retaliation that no one wanted. Despite recurrent unpleasantness, the "abnormality" of Berlin had lasted long enough for its dynamics to have become reasonably well understood. Upsetting the tacit balance there would have appeared less as a countermove in return for the "quarantine," more as a cumulative provocation on top of the deployment of the missiles to Cuba.

That this calculation could come out as unambiguously as it did is due in large part to the strategic efficacy of the means chosen by the United States. As Arnold Horelick and others have noted, the decisions were made promptly, the secrecy of the plans was adequately protected, and the means were nonviolent. Here we may recall a different parallel with Berlin. It might be fair to compare the "quarantine" in effectiveness, though not necessarily in moral or legal quality, with the building of the Berlin Wall in August 1961. In each case the power with overwhelming local conventional superiority took quickly and decisively a measure that could be upset only at the risk of incurring the grave international political odium of being known to have initiated violence. By setting up the "quarantine," the United States presented to the Soviet Union, which rightly declined to take it, the responsibility for escalation.[4]

[4] Thomas C. Schelling, *The Strategy of Conflict* (Harvard University Press, 1960) pp. 138-39, wrote: "This tactic of shifting responsibility . . . was nicely accom-

The Soviet move was probably based on too low an estimate of the probability of failure as well as of the political losses that failure would entail. Though the Soviet leaders appear to have miscalculated, it is highly likely that at least they calculated. They must have hoped to improve the missile balance. They probably had two other, less direct, objectives: One was to emphasize, especially to Latin America, the impunity with which, as they believed, hostile forces could be concentrated against the United States in an area that the world had come to think of as within the United States sphere of influence. Latin Americans would see dramatic evidence of Communist power close at hand. The other was to reassert, over the Castro government, the supremacy of Soviet interests and Soviet decisions on the biggest issues of common concern.

Both of these secondary objectives pertain to political rather than directly military strategy. Their attainment would not necessarily have brought a shooting war closer in any way easily foreseeable. Soviet influence and prestige in Latin America would almost surely have risen relative to the United States and to China. The weight of the Cuban Communists within the ORI and later the Partido Unido de la Revolución Socialista (PURS) would have increased. If you care for exact quantitative judgments, you may say that the prospect of a second Latin American state undergoing a pro-Soviet coup d'état would have been advanced by x years, or rendered y percent more probable, and you would be safe unless you filled in the numbers.

For the sake of balance we should recognize the view that the missile crisis ended in a Soviet victory and a defeat for United States plans. This view is shared by three groups: (1) some in the West who like to fear that in any confrontation the Russians always win or who like to hope that the United States always loses; (2) exiles who fear that the slight relaxation of tension that followed the missile crisis reduced the possibilities of their returning to Cuba under the aegis of the United States or of getting relatives, friends, and allies out of Cuba; and (3)

plished by Lieutenant Colonel (then Major) Stevenson B. Canyon, U.S.A.F., in using his aircraft to protect a Chinese Nationalist surface vessel about to be captured by Communist surface forces in his comic strip. Unwilling and unauthorized to initiate hostilities and knowing that no threat to do so would be credited, he directed his planes to jettison gasoline in a burning ring about the aggressor forces, leaving to them the last clear chance of reversing their engines to avoid the flames. He could neither drop gasoline on the enemy ships nor threaten to; so he dropped the initiative instead."

those who are inclined or compelled to believe the Soviet claims after the fact. One may agree with Group 2 that the possibility of an imminent change of regime has been diminished, and yet disagree with the appraisal of the outcome as regards the two major powers. As to Group 1, aside from noting that the actions of the three parties since the crisis do not bear out the hypothesis, one can only agree with Horelick's summary:

> . . . to regard the outcome of the Cuban missile crisis as coinciding in any substantial way with Soviet intentions or interests is to mistake skilful salvage of a shipwreck for brilliant navigation.

Group 3 deserves more consideration. It argues that the United States had planned to invade Cuba by means of Cuban and other Latin American mercenaries; that the United States hoped that the stir over the presence of offensive weapons would estrange world public opinion from sympathy with Cuba and furnish a pretext as well as the best occasion for invasion and destruction of the revolution; and that, instead, world public opinion disapproved of the "quarantine" and approved Soviet sobriety by contrast. The United States public was, on this view, made aware for the first time that nuclear war could hit home, and therefore it refused to support the extremists who favored an invasion. As the Soviet bases in Cuba, so the argument continues, were designed not to augment the strategic capability of the U.S.S.R. but to help defend Cuba against the threat of aggression, the missiles could be withdrawn without changing the relative positions of strength between the Soviet Union and the United States to an equal extent. This argument is, in principle, subject to verification; but the only solid evidence in its favor is that, as Theodore Sorensen and others have reported, some in the United States did vainly recommend going beyond a "quarantine." The other relevant facts point the other way. To those in Group 3 who adhere to an invariant major premise—that the Soviet Union is morally right and the United States morally wrong whenever their policies are in conflict—facts are never necessary and sometimes annoying.

Cuba among the Giants

The Cuban missile crisis, as has been noted, was a missile crisis between the Soviet Union and the United States that happened to involve a Cuban location. Though the crisis would not have occurred but for the fact that Cuba was available as a launching pad, it probably could not have been settled but for the fact that Cuba was to a large extent ignored by its protector when the moves toward settlement were taking place. From the United States standpoint, paradoxically, a nagging minor annoyance had proved intractable until the intervention of the Soviet Union presented a problem that, though large and urgent, was identifiable, familiar, and soluble. The physicians are baffled by the common cold but can cure the patient if the cold worsens to pneumonia. It still is true that no physician prescribes pneumonia for a cold; it is true also that one may catch pneumonia, or a cold, again.

Another improving moral that may be drawn for the future is that Cuba's sponsorship by the Soviet Union does not necessarily pose insuperable difficulties in the way of United States policy. The complications are more intricate; the stakes may be uncomfortably high from time to time; but the quality of the threat is not radically new except for the irrationally alarming proximity. The system of policy and alliance that found generally satisfactory responses to military threats in Greece and Malaya, political threats in France and Italy, and other initiatives led or followed by Soviet probing in many other parts of the globe cannot really be powerless to handle the Soviet side of the Cuban problem. To make the point even sharper, one might suggest that, if Americans are incapable of summoning the necessary ingenuity and patience with respect to their neighbor Cuba, they might learn something from the Finns.

That leads to a deeper and more disturbing question. Is it, in truth, the Soviet side of the Cuban problem that troubles the United States? Or is there some level of the American national mind at which Dr. Castro's ties to the Soviet Union are used as an excuse for avoiding unpleasant facts about the relationship of the United States to change, unrest, and underdevelopment throughout Latin America? The special involvement of the United States with Cuba has lasted more than sixty years. It is convenient to have a modern, fashionably geopolitical explanation for the latest manifestation of our difficulties. At the same time our indignation has a special edge, because we tend to think that Cuba has been our own little backyard problem, and the interest of the outsiders intrudes upon our proprietary sensibilities. We find it strange when the British or French contrast our relatively relaxed attitude to Mr. Nasser with our tense hostility to Dr. Castro. If the Soviet Union (and China too) were suddenly cut off from all contact with the Western Hemisphere, Fidel Castro the man and Castroism as a reflection of his demagogy might fall or grow dim, but the deep-seated social and political and economic difficulties that produced Castroism would remain. Unless met with more resolution and exertion than are now being devoted to them, these same difficulties would soon throw up a second Castro and a third (if not in Cuba, then in Argentina or Colombia or the Dominican Republic). And if the second Castro needed foreign support, which our blithe hypothesis had denied him from Russia or China, he could find it somewhere else.

Meanwhile, Russia and China are not cut off from the Western Hemisphere. Probably it is in Dr. Castro's interest as well as in that of the United States that if one of the two Communist great powers is to be involved the other should be also. Though China cannot now give Cuba effective military guarantees or economic aid, Dr. Castro will wish to keep on good terms with the Chinese as long as the Russians will let him. If the Sino-Soviet split becomes permanent and is acknowledged as final, Dr. Castro probably will not lose as much leverage in relation to the Soviet Union as will countries in Western Europe like Poland and Rumania.

The management of Cuba's relations with Communist China and the Soviet Union since the split became public requires skill and flexibility. For Cuba, the Soviet Union has the nuclear power and the foreign-aid funds. One estimate has Soviet aid to Cuba totaling $3 billion in 1959-65. Mainland China has the more attractive revolutionary zeal and the reassuring consistency of extreme, intransigent antipathy to the United States. At any one time, if domestic economic problems are uppermost in Cuba, the pull of Soviet aid must seem powerful; when the emphasis is placed on winning friends among the radical intellectual elite of Latin America, Maoism has more glamour. Though retaining his power in Cuba and expanding his influence in Latin America are to some degree interdependent, Dr. Castro must lean toward Russia when he thinks of the first objective and toward China when he thinks of the second.

Yet the choice may not be restricted to this alternative. First, Dr. Castro would rightly resist the assumption that a political movement in Latin America, inside or outside Cuba, must—in order to claim the epithets of Socialism, anti-U.S.-ism, or even Marxism—follow an Eastern model, however august and powerful its current exemplars happen to be. As he gains in confidence, he will claim more autochthonous origins for Castroist ideas and Cuban institutions, though his foreign policy may still agree closely with whatever overlap remains in the policies of his two largest sponsors. Second, Russia does not wholly lack influence among Dr. Castro's non-Cuban constituency; nor, on the other hand, is it easy to retain power in Cuba without making some moves on the local political scene that the Soviet Union would find it possible to accept but hard to applaud.

With the passage of time it must become necessary for Dr. Castro to shift from the demagogy of recurrent crises to durable political planning and maneuver, unless his friends or his foes oblige him by providing new crises. Perhaps it is this shift, and not increasing desperation, that we may infer from his entering negotiations to allow limited emigration to the United States and from the ostentatious withdrawal of Che Guevara. If the United States can tolerate harsh words, Dr. Castro may be prepared to offer some mild deeds. That course may, however, interfere with his ambition to lead the march of Communism in Latin America. If some Soviet satellites in Europe have had to pursue anti-American policies on Soviet insistence, in the Caribbean the question is whether local anti-Americanism can be restrained to suit the tactics of peaceful coexistence.

For the Soviet Union, Cuba is not a puppet but rather a friend, dependent, partner, and client, offering special advantages in Caribbean location and Latin culture. Yet Cuba is expensive and may be troublesome. Given the Soviet appraisal of the dangers of nuclear war, the Soviet-Chinese split, and the political rise of the underdeveloped nations, it is important to today's Soviet leaders to appear "responsible," sober, able to adapt to the possibilities of the environment. The projection of "responsibility" is complicated by the activities of ambitious minor partners eager for quick results and capable of some limited strategic exploitation of their own weakness. In a period of polycentrism this weakens the Soviet position in Cuba but affords an element of strength for the Soviet Union with regard to the United States. The Soviet problem is how to keep the Cubans in a state of controlled and limited irresponsibility—hostile to the United States but not pushing too close to the brink, and, above all, away from the friendly clutches of the Chinese dragon.

As the troubles of "empire" are presumed to be more readily bearable than the troubles that come from losing an empire, the Soviet Union presumably would rather keep its worries about the instability added by Dr. Castro to Soviet-U.S. relations, and about the controversies between Castroites and Communists in Cuba and elsewhere, than have no Castro. The loss of Cuba to neutralism, to the Free World, or (worst of all) to the Chinese camp would inflict on the Soviet Union different types of political losses in the less developed countries. But the United States would be wrong to suppose that Castro's positive importance for the Soviet Union is as great as Castro's negative importance for the United States. From Moscow, Havana still looks pretty small.

HANSON W. BALDWIN is military editor of the *New York Times* and author of numerous books and articles. He has written extensively on Cuba.

A Military Perspective

HANSON W. BALDWIN

What is the nature of the Cuban threat—if, indeed, there is any—to the military security of the United States and to the other countries of the Western Hemisphere? What is the significance of Cuba to the Western Hemisphere in strategic terms, in power balance, in military hardware?

In the years between 1898 and the advent of the Fidel Castro regime in Cuba in 1959, these questions were in the category of what the late President Franklin D. Roosevelt used to characterize as "iffy," or hypothetical, ones. Their very nature was ridiculous. Cuba, an underdeveloped island of about seven million people—many of them poor and uneducated—was tied to the United States by treaty, by friendship, and by economics. Its military power was negligible; its ruling political ideology, conservative. For more than half a century Cuba did not represent any kind of threat to the United States.

But prior to 1898, Cuba was owned by a European power—Spain, considered in the context of those times to be a major power though a decaying one. The Spanish-American War represented, in a strategic sense, a martial invocation of the Monroe Doctrine and a major change, in spheres of influence and balance of power, in favor of the United States. Cuba, the most important island in the Caribbean and the one closest to United States continental shores, was transferred from the strategic domination of Spain to the domination of the United States.

There was no doubt prior to, and during, the Spanish-American War that Cuba was considered a threat to the military security of the United States, because the island was controlled by a hostile, or potentially hostile, foreign power. Whether or not this estimate was a rational or an accurate one, in view of the fact that Spain proved to be a colossus with feet of clay, is beside the point. For it was widely accepted by contemporary military experts and by public opinion, as was demonstrated by the panic that gripped the Eastern seaboard when Cervera's fleet sailed from Spain for Cuba. And its acceptance changed history.

Today Cuba is aligned with a foreign power, an aggressive one frankly dedicated to the destruction of our way of life. Whether or not Fidel Castro was a card-carrying Communist when he overthrew Batista now has only academic pertinence. Today he is an admitted Communist, the head of a Communist police state which finds its primary military and economic support from foreign Communist governments, principally from Russia. Castro has built up a sizable indigenous military force. More important, Soviet military personnel numbered in four to five figures have been stationed on the island since 1962. And Soviet Russia has attempted—and is still attempting—to capitalize on the geographic position of the island to alter the global balance of power by neutralizing some of the strategic advantages the United States has enjoyed in overseas bases and missile strength.

Since 1898, the map of the world has been foreshortened by the technological revolution. Ocean-spanning missiles and jet aircraft have replaced Cervera's armored cruisers as the threat to national security. The United States is a colossus today as compared to the little nation newly emerging from hemispheric isolation a half century ago; it is, indeed, the leading power of the world. But it is faced, globally and in Cuba, by a power far stronger than Spain—indeed, the strongest power in the world next to the United States.

Questions concerning the military significance of Cuba, which for half a century would have been considered ridiculous, no longer appear so. In fact, the United States government considered Cuba to be a potential strategic threat twice in the administration of President Kennedy—once in the abortive and ill-managed Bay of Pigs episode and again in the fall of 1962, in the Cuban missile confrontation. That judgment has already altered the course of history. And it seems likely that the answers given tomorrow to the same questions will shape the future course of hemispheric, and perhaps even of global, history. A calm assessment of Cuba's military importance must now be a fundamental building block in the formulation of Washington's future Cuban policy.

Strategic Potentials of Cuba

Cuba's strategic importance—or lack of it—depends in the first instance on two interacting factors: strength and position.

Strength

The indigenous military strength of Fidel Castro's Cuba is built around hard-core armed services of about 75,000 to 125,000 rather well-trained and well-armed Cubans. A number of militia units apparently have been added to, and incorporated in, the regular armed forces, though without much additional training to date. The total full-time regulars, including these militia incorporations, may now approximate almost 200,000, the great majority of them in the land forces. These are supplemented by a part-time militia and defense battalions or home guard —totaling, on paper, 150,000 to 200,000 people. About 75,000 of these are lightly armed and imperfectly trained. To this must be added the paramilitary forces of a police state—the uniformed and secret police, numbered in five figures, supplemented by a well-organized block system of informers and spies.

To this numerically impressive force was added a new foundation in late 1963. Raúl Castro, Cuban Minister of the Armed Forces, announced that, for the first time in the island's history, compulsory military service would start in April 1964, covering the 17- to 45-age group. The announcement was both confession and portent: a tacit admission that the volunteer-army—militia—home-guard system had not produced the professional well-trained, well-organized forces that were envisaged; and a portent that the Cuban armed forces would probably in the course of time improve their state of readiness and strengthen their professionalism, if not their total numbers. However, the Cuban draft appears to have been initiated as much by economic as by military motives. For, according to Raúl Castro's frank speech, Cuba expects to save money through the draft by paying the draftees only some 84 pesos annually, as compared to the average annual pay of the present volunteer of more than 800 pesos. Moreover, during their three-year service Cuban draftees will follow the example set by the Red Chinese Army, and military labor will be utilized for three to four months to help cut cane and harvest the coffee crop.

The Cuban ground forces have plenty of excellent small arms of So- viet or Czechoslovak model, and Soviet-type mortars, field artillery, an- tiaircraft and antitank guns, rocket launchers, personnel carriers and tanks, communications equipment, and electronic gear of all types. Most of this is of post-World War II date. This type of conventional equipment is in such abundant supply that Castro felt able to ship con- siderable quantities (reportedly two shiploads) of tanks, small arms, and guns to Premier Ben Bella of Algeria, when Algeria became em- broiled with Morocco in border fighting in the fall of 1963. Small arms from Cuba have also turned up, in sizable amounts, in parts of the Western Hemisphere.

The Cuban Air Force, like the Cuban ground forces, is the most modern, and potentially the most powerful, in Latin America, at least as far as equipment is concerned. There are more than one hundred So- viet-type aircraft in Cuba, including more than forty modern superson- ic MIG-21 fighter interceptors. All planes probably are now flown by Cubans trained behind the Iron Curtain. The MIG-21, based on Santa Clara, Camagüey, and San Antonio, has a 400-mile range and can be variously armed with air-to-air missiles, cannon, or conventional bombs.

The Cuban Navy is small; in fact, it is the weakest element of the Cuban armed forces. It has virtually no capability for transporting con- ventional amphibious power—in other words, no real offensive power. One ancient and obsolete vessel (a so-called frigate), ten old former U.S. and Soviet coastal patrol craft, or subchasers, and twelve convert- ed Komar-type motor torpedo boats, plus some miscellaneous small craft provide very limited maritime power. The torpedo boats, equipped with anti-ship missiles of 10 to 15 nautical miles range, have a defensive value disproportionate to their size, if their missiles are well maintained and are accurate and reliable—sizeable qualifications.[1] Cu- ban tramp steamers and numerous fishing vessels provide bottoms fully capable of transporting—across the Caribbean and even to northern areas of South America—weapons, subversives, saboteurs, guerrillas, and small lightly armed parties of highly trained men.

Knitting together and backing up these forces is a modern—indeed, formidable—array of antiaircraft and coast defense missiles, radar sta-

[1] A Marine colonel has characterized these craft as "pocket gunboats mount[ing] a weapon capable of engaging a surface ship at main-battery gunnery range and with the striking power of a 14-inch projectile . . . strictly as a surface weapon . . . quite formidable."

tions, and ground-control intercept centers. How many of these are manned by Cubans, how many by foreign nationals, is unknown. Probably Cubans are manning most of these missile emplacements and radar sites, and they are learning fast.

At the end of 1963 about 200 radar stations lined Cuba's coasts. There are about 24 operational sites (some of these have been repositioned) and a total of about 500 missiles of the SAM (Surface to Air) I and II types, roughly equivalent to the U.S. Nike Ajax and Nike Hercules (minus the Hercules nuclear warhead). It was a SAM-II that shot down a United States U-2 flying at above 60,000 feet during the fall crisis of 1962. There are apparently four sites for coast-defense winged missiles, with ranges of 30 to 40 nautical miles, and enough missiles for fifteen more sites. Stored in warehouses, caves, and underground sites—immune from the prying eye of the aerial camera—are a variety of arms and equipment, details unknown.

The Cuban Army is organized in Western, Center, and Eastern sectors and ostensibly has units as large as armies and divisions, though these exist chiefly on paper. Except on paper, there is no evidence of any larger tactical unit than a battalion (800 to 1,200 men), and the Cuban military has a very low capability for combined arms operations (infantry, artillery, tanks, aircraft, etc.). However, one indication that Cuban military organization is becoming more formalized was the introduction in 1963 of normal officer ranks, up to and including full general, to replace the four officer grades that had prevailed since the revolution.

The will-to-fight and combat effectiveness of the indigenous Cubans remains an unknown quantity. Cuba could probably not be rated very high in any type of formal modern war employing large numbers of men or well-organized forces. Some of the Cubans make up in fanaticism what many of them lack in discipline and fighting spirit. In raids, covert warfare, individual feats of arms, or underground or guerrilla war, they might well be dangerous, if well led. Thus, except for its Navy, Cuba's armed forces are formidable in numbers and modern in equipment, particularly on the defensive within or around the home island. In numbers of men in uniform and quantities and variety of modern military equipment for land and air forces, Cuba is stronger than any other Latin American nation.

But the Cubans are not, unfortunately for Washington, the only fighting men in Cuba. Russian troops are still in the island. At one time, the Soviet forces probably numbered from 30,000 to 40,000 men, although the U.S. government never admitted, even inferentially, the presence of more than 17,000 to 22,000. Some of these troops were to emplace and operate the 2,200-mile IRBM's (Intermediate Range Ballistic Missiles) and the 1,000-nautical-mile medium-range mobile missiles that Premier Khrushchev sneaked into Cuba in 1962. Others were plainly employed as training cadres, engineering troops, and communications and radar specialists, to operate the Cuban electronic installations, to build military installations, and to train the Cubans. And some (the maximum number is in dispute) represented what has been called by intelligence experts a "Soviet expeditionary force." Some experts believe that this force once reached the proportions of a reinforced Soviet rifle division, or more than 13,000 men. Others think that the four highly mechanized and armored units that were its core, equipped with tanks and field artillery and FROGS (Free Rockets Over Ground), added up to no more than about 5,000 men.

The strength of these Soviet forces undoubtedly has decreased since the missile crisis of 1962. But just how many remain in Cuba is uncertain. Whether or not (or to what extent) the departing Russians have been replaced by troops from other Communist countries is also uncertain, although available evidence of Communist replacements from other nations is negative. A conservative estimate at the end of 1963 was that there were still at least 5,000—perhaps as many as 12,000— Soviet military personnel in Cuba.[2]

[2] Since 1963 the number of Soviet troops in Cuba probably has decreased sharply and may now be limited to advisers. The Cubans now fly most of their own aircraft and operate most of their military installations.

Intelligence experts have differed widely, ever since Soviet troops moved into Cuba, about the estimated strengths of the Russian forces in the island. The Senate Preparedness Subcommittee of the Senate Armed Services Committee, under the chairmanship of Senator John Stennis, studied the Cuban missile crisis, and particularly its intelligence aspects, intensively. In an interim report published on May 9, 1963, it stated that at that time the current estimates of Soviet strength in Cuba were 17,500, and that some estimates were as high as 40,000. These figures are in sharp contrast to published administration statements of the time. The committee said, "We conclude that no one in official United States circles can tell, with any real degree of confidence, how many Russians are now in Cuba." Privately, some well-informed intelligence sources supported the committee's figures. Since the release of this report, Russian strength in Cuba has declined, but again, according to some intelligence experts, not to the degree announced by the White House. The difficulty of estimating numbers of troops accurately has often been illustrated in the history of warfare. During World War II, for

As of December 1963, all that can be said with reasonable certainty is that Soviet personnel apparently still operate most of the radars and the antiaircraft missiles, still are training the Cubans, and still retain an independent, though relatively small, ground-combat capability.

Position

The strategic importance of any area or position depends upon a complex of geographic, economic, and political factors. The position may have strategic global importance, or it may have tactical local significance. Cuba has both, despite its inherent limitations as an island. Its global importance is chiefly positional and political-psychological, although these assets came dangerously close to being transformed into a military asset of the first importance in the missile crisis of 1962.

Probably the chief strategic advantage of the United States in the world conflict with Communism has been its positions overseas, including its friends, its allies, its bases around the Eurasian rimlands close to the heartland of Soviet Russia. The U.S.S.R. possesses allies in the indigenous Communist parties of virtually all the nations of the world, but Moscow has had, until Fidel Castro ruled Cuba, no bases that its troops (or allied Communist troops) could openly use in the Western Hemisphere. A Communist Cuba—where Russian armed forces are still based only 90 miles from our shores—means that Moscow has taken the first step in its long and continued efforts to emulate, or compensate for, the great advantage the United States has hitherto enjoyed—the advantage of bases overseas.

This outpost, thousands of miles from Russia, implies for the Russians some grave liabilities as well as assets, as Premier Khrushchev found out. Cuba is so close to the continental United States, and is separated from Soviet Russia by so many thousands of miles of sea and air that it could be blockaded by superior U.S. forces (as was shown in the fall of 1962) and overwhelmed in an actual shooting war. Cuba has so few resources itself that its military and economic strength must be supplied by transfusions from without—a wasting process to the donor. In a conventional shooting war Cuba would represent at best a diver-

example, the Navy's estimates of Japanese garrisons in some of the Pacific islands were far less than the actual numbers. The disguise of camp sites or the removal of uniforms (some of several concealment measures employed in Cuba) makes the current cold-war task even more difficult than in wartime.

sion and an irritant that would inevitably be eliminated. But the elimination would be costly in terms of both effort required—a minimum of
three to six divisions—and casualties.

Nevertheless, modern nuclear war (the war of missiles and jet aircraft) makes even an isolated and exposed base like Cuba highly attractive to Russia. As a missile or air site, Cuba offers the advantage of dispersion. It provides a launching site close enough to the United States
to permit Russia the use of short-range or intermediate-range missiles,
which are far cheaper, less complex, and, because of the shorter range,
more accurate than ICBM's. The Cuban missile crisis demonstrated
that it was quite possible, with stealth and cunning and secrecy, to
transport nuclear-tipped missiles that could ravage America across
thousands of miles of ocean, and to emplace at least some of the missiles
within a few score miles of our coast before we knew much about it.
Because even short-range missiles based in Cuba could have devastating consequences if nuclear war ever came, the island has assumed a
role of major geographic and strategic importance within the context of
a quick one-shot war.

This potential—the consequence of geographic position and modern
technology—is, however, less important than the political and psychological significance of a Communist base in the Western Hemisphere.
The specter of Communism—and particularly the presence of Soviet
armed forces in the Caribbean—has had two contradictory effects in
Latin America. It has caused fear; at the same time it has generated respect for Castro's defiance of the United States and for Russian power.
In the United States, many Americans believe that a Communist Cuba,
backed by Russian uniformed personnel, is a dangerous precedent and
a violation of the Monroe Doctrine (for decades an important item in
U.S. foreign policy). The political and psychological repercussions in
the future of the hemisphere are unpredictable.

In a tactical, or local, sense—within the context of the Caribbean—
what is Cuba's importance?

In the pre-air-power, premissile age of Alfred Thayer Mahan, in the
age of short-legged naval vessels, Cuban coaling stations were regarded as of key importance in enabling our naval forces to control the
Caribbean and its adjacent waters.

The geographic position of Cuba still gives the island importance today in the exercise of control over the Caribbean, despite changes in weapons, ranges, and fuel. The island dominates the most important shipping routes from the North Atlantic into the Caribbean Sea and the Gulf of Mexico, and to the Panama Canal. The oil, iron ore, bauxite, tin, and copper of South America are transported to the United States in close proximity to Cuban coasts.[3] Cuba lies squarely athwart the most direct air routes to the Panama Canal and to northern South America. In some exercises, troop-carrier aircraft bound for the Canal Zone have had to be detoured around the island, to the consequent loss of payload or range. Electronic aids for navigation, communications channels, and missile tracking and guidance systems also crisscross the Caribbean. Many of these invisible "beams" pass in close proximity to Cuba, and some of them could conceivably be jammed or distorted by Cuban-based transmitters.

As in Mahan's time, Cuba is still the most important island, from the point of view of size and geographic position, in the Caribbean area. But this importance is less, relatively, than in the age of short-legged weapons. The Florida Straits, the Windward Passage, other passages between the Atlantic and Caribbean, and the Caribbean Sea itself can be patrolled, and to a major degree controlled, from the U.S. mainland and from Puerto Rico, Trinidad, the Canal Zone, and other bases, without dependence upon Cuba itself (Guantánamo Bay). The use of Cuban bases, and a friendly Cuba, would simply make the job of controlling the Caribbean's sea-air communications much easier.

Cuba's Military Operational Utility

Strength and position give Cuba an important strategic potential, in both a global and a local context. Whether or not this potential can be utilized (and, if so, in what way) is another question. Strength and posi-

---

[3] "A Communist power astride the Windward Passage is a major strategic danger," a high-ranking officer has said. "Since about two-thirds of all the Atlantic traffic entering and leaving the Caribbean goes through the Windward Passage, it has much the same strategic significance to our Western-Hemisphere Mediterranean (as Mahan called the Caribbean), as the Straits of Gibraltar do in Europe. . . . during World War II our Navy had to convoy more shipping through the Windward Passage than through any other sea area under U.S. control except the approaches to New York harbor. People don't fully realize what a strategic chokepoint the Windward Passage is, and I think this represents an important element in the Communist threat from Cuba today."

tion are static factors; their ultimate importance depends entirely on how they are used.

The United States

From the perspective of the United States, what military operational utility does Cuba have?

The United States Naval Base at Guantánamo Bay, known to generations of Americans as "Gitmo," is a 45-square-mile $76,000,000 investment. It has two airstrips, including an 8,000-foot strip for jets, one of the best naval anchorages in the Caribbean, and 1,400 buildings. Normally about 6,000 Americans are stationed there (the Marine garrison is now somewhat strengthened), and another 4,000 to 5,000 are aboard ships of the fleet operating from Gitmo, while almost 1,600 civil service employees work in the shops.[4]

Since the Spanish-American War, the base at Guantánamo has been developed into perhaps the most important naval facility outside our shores in the Western Hemisphere. The base has liabilities. The army of civil workers who operate its facilities and the 24 miles of fence line and 10 miles of seacoast make the base's internal security problem a complex one. Sabotage and terrorism would be difficult though not impossible to meet. The base has no fresh-water supply of its own. Water had been piped from a pumping station on the Yateras River, four miles outside the reservation, to tanks on the base. In early 1964 this supply was cut off by Castro. Washington reacted by cutting the Yateras River pipeline permanently, importing water by tankers, and ordering the base to make itself self-sufficient in water supply by construction of a desalinization plant and other means. The base in the future will be fully prepared to get along without the Yateras River supply. Finally, high Cuban hills outside the reservation dominate parts of the base. If Soviet-type anti-ship missiles or long-range artillery were emplaced on these hills, it might well make the airstrips unusable and the anchorage in the Bay untenable for ships.

Again, this theoretical advantage to Castro is more than compensated for by the liabilities that would be incurred if this gambit were actually

[4] Including domestics and unskilled laborers, about 2,115 Cuban workers were still employed on the base in March 1964. Almost 900 of these live on the base; the rest commute through the gates and by water taxi to their homes in Cuba. The Cuban work force was reduced by 748 persons after Castro interrupted the base's supply of water.

used. Denial of the use of the base to our ships and planes could be no more than temporary and would mean open hostilities, which would immediately expose Cuba to massive (conventional) assault. As a matter of fact, the Marine garrison at Guantánamo has long had plans to seize the dominating hill masses close by if Castro should press the button.

So much for the military limitations of Gitmo. Its military assets are of three types.

It is an important training base used by all ships in the Atlantic at one time or another for shakedown and refresher training. A Fleet Training Group, Atlantic, under the Commander in Chief, Atlantic, is based at Guantánamo to aid ship training. As a training base it is complemented by the newer base at Roosevelt Roads, Puerto Rico (and nearby Vieques). Modern missile ships use the longer-firing ranges available outside Roosevelt Roads. Guantánamo is, of course, replaceable as a training base, but it has many facilities that Roosevelt Roads presently lacks, and these could be duplicated in Puerto Rico only at high cost.

In addition to its training and fleet support role, Guantánamo Bay has logistical or supply importance. It has naval and air supply and repair facilities unavailable at any other Caribbean base, and it offers a staging base for fighter aircraft, or troop-carrying or cargo aircraft, en route from the United States to Latin America.

Guantánamo's strategic location makes it an extremely useful (though not indispensable) base in any limited war or for the basing of reserve power in any crisis or quasi-war situation (similar to the crises of 1963 in the Dominican Republic and Haiti). Its usefulness would vary, of course, depending upon the area of crisis. In World War II, it was a convoy port, where Atlantic and Caribbean convoys made up and sortied. Antisubmarine and shipping surveillance patrol planes of the Navy still base intermittently at Gitmo. Guantánamo Bay is one of the links in a chain of bases including Florida, Roosevelt Roads (Puerto Rico), and Chaguaramas (Trinidad). In a time of limited war, this chain would permit the United States to control the Caribbean–Gulf of Mexico area, maintain surveillance of all shipping in the area, and protect the Atlantic approaches to the Panama Canal.

In nuclear war, Guantánamo Bay would have little utility except as a dispersal port for U.S. naval power. Like the Panama Canal, for which it acts as a link in the Atlantic defenses, the base would play virtually no role in an all-out nuclear interchange. (The Canal itself, for that matter, could be blocked or hopelessly wrecked by one well-placed nuclear warhead). Potentially Gitmo could be useful as a ballistic-missile early-warning station if the need should arise to establish such stations to cover the southern approaches to the United States. However, other more favorable locations might be found for the giant radars required. The base could also be used to provide early warning of enemy aircraft and as a link in the undersea sound-detection system, which may someday provide early warning of the approach to our coasts of enemy missile submarines.

Guantánamo's usefulness as a base is thus of optimum importance in limited war situations or in cold war crises, particularly in situations involving conflict, or the risk of conflict, in any of the Caribbean countries. Since the political stability of these countries is at best dubious, and since Washington seriously considered armed intervention in two of them during 1962 and 1963, this consideration is of obvious importance.

Finally, Guantánamo Bay has a political importance to the United States that transcends its military usefulness. The treaty (last reaffirmed in 1934) that governs our use of the base, is remarkably similar to the treaty that underlies our rights in the Canal Zone. We enjoy in the area of the base "complete jurisdiction and control"—or the *de facto* exercise of sovereign rights—over almost 29,000 acres of land and water. "Ultimate sovereignty" (not defined in the treaty) is Cuban, but our "complete jurisdiction and control" continues indefinitely unless the U.S. "abandons" the base or formally agrees with Cuba to revision of the treaty terms. The treaty cannot be revised or abrogated by Cuba alone; it requires mutual consent.

Revision of the treaty terms for Guantánamo will inevitably lead to revisionism elsewhere—in Panama, in Trinidad, globally. What happens to Guantánamo will profoundly influence what happens to the Canal Zone, to our base in Trinidad, and, indeed, to our bases all over the world, and particularly to our position in Latin America. United States power and prestige are involved in Gitmo, whether we like it or not.

But Cuba, to the United States, is more than a naval base at Guantánamo Bay. The "presence" and cooperation of a friendly government in Cuba has major military implications in Latin America. Some Latin American leaders are openly ambivalent; they publicly decry the Castro leadership but privately admire the man who has successfully defied the majesty and power of the United States. Cuba can be an example, a bellwether. The political importance of Cuba is obvious, but the military implications of a friendly government there are too often overlooked. A friendly government means the denial to any potential enemy of the military and political advantages (many of them potential, some actual) that now accrue to such an enemy through the Fidel Castro regime. The cooperation of a friendly government in Cuba would mean elimination of a base for a hostile power.

The U.S.S.R.

What are the possible military uses to the U.S.S.R. of a Communist Cuba? There are six primary uses:

1. *Missile base.* First and most important, in the global equation of power, is the potential utility of Cuba as a missile and/or aircraft base. It would be a mistake to overestimate this importance, but it would also be a mistake to underestimate it.

Cuban missile bases alone could not possibly neutralize the present tremendous nuclear delivery superiority of the United States. Our superiority in strategic power is now too great, and is likely to remain too great, for at least a decade. Missiles launched from Cuba could have no effect upon the hundred or so Strategic Air Command (SAC) bombers, armed with nuclear weapons, that are always in the air; nor could they knock out the nation's Polaris submarine fleet hidden submerged in a waste of waters or the Navy's aircraft carriers or ships. Nor would Cuban-based missiles, likely to be limited in numbers and warhead power, be capable of eliminating all, or even most, of our hardened below-ground silo sites. (Accuracy, warhead yield, and reliability all influence greatly the strategic calculation of missile capability. The Russians might have an 80 percent "confidence factor" that two seven-megaton warheads might destroy one Minuteman silo. But to increase this "confidence factor" to 95 percent might require [as a hypothetical example] twenty seven-megaton warheads.)

But Cuban missile sites would provide Russia an easy way of counterbalancing to some degree, but only to some degree, the present U.S. superiority in nuclear delivery capability. The United States excels in long-range ICBM's; the Russians have specialized in the cheaper and easier-to-build medium-range (1,000-mile) and mobile missile and the fixed-site 2,200-mile missile. Probably some five hundred of these land-based types are today in position on Communist soil in Western Russia and Eastern Europe capable of reaching U.S. European bases, but with insufficient range to reach the United States.

Missiles of these types emplaced in Cuba in 1962 accomplished a number of purposes:

They were emplaced on our southern periphery, where radar and missile early warning were weak or completely lacking.

These emplacements brought within enemy firing range most of SAC's bomber bases, many of our air defense installations, and many of our land-based missile sites. Their presence, even though they were never fired, tended to alter, though not to overturn, the balance of strategic power by neutralizing *some* of these sites.

The nation's great cities were brought within easy missile range by the Cuban sites. Some of these cities were already threatened by the few operational Russian-based ICBM's. Our cities thus became double hostages to Moscow, even though Moscow itself would have been doomed by the long-range power of the United States.

Cuban-based missiles and, to a lesser extent, long-range aircraft with atomic bombs made our defensive task more difficult. Above all, they brought a sharp new awareness of terror and threat to the American mainland—an awareness of nuclear danger that had not existed in the public mind to anything like the same degree before the Cuban missile crisis.

What of the future?

Most intelligence agencies and military men believe (though they cannot provide 100 percent proof) that the Soviet nuclear-tipped MRBM's (Medium Range [mobile] Ballistic Missiles) and IRBM's (Intermediate Range Ballistic Missiles) that produced the 1962 missile crisis were actually removed from Cuba.

But caves on the island are known to be packed with military equipment of various sorts, and if missiles are not included in these below-ground inventories today, it is perfectly possible that they may be tomorrow. All the missiles that played their brief role in the limelight of world crisis in 1962 were liquid-fueled missiles. Liquid-fueled missiles require a relatively long countdown and must be supported by fairly complex fueling trucks and facilities. The 2,200-mile missile requires permanent installations and lengthy construction. But the Soviet

1,000-mile mobile ballistic missile was described by Secretary of Defense Robert S. McNamara as capable of being moved from one site to another and reemplaced within six days. Other sources have since estimated that these mobile Russian missiles—like the German V-2, which could be launched from any hard, flat, and level area—might be emplaced in 16 to 18 hours.

Even if these estimates represent an exaggeration, it is certain that future generations of Soviet mobile missiles will, like our own, be fueled by solid propellants. Solid fuel reduces the time for countdown and also eliminates a complex of fueling trucks, volatile liquids, and pumping systems. It makes the missile more mobile, easier to conceal, and far easier to move about and to emplace. If such solid-fueled missiles, with their simplified supporting equipment, were transported to Cuba and carefully hidden, it is quite conceivable that they could be removed from concealment under cover of darkness and erected ready for firing in predetermined positions by the following dawn or soon after. This rather dreadful potentiality, it should be emphasized, is *not* an actuality today, but it is well within the capabilities of Soviet military science in future years.

Cuban missile sites would provide other benefits from the Russian point of view. They would increase geographic dispersion of Communist missile bases and oblige the United States to allocate some of its nuclear-deterrent forces to neutralize them. They would be so close to U.S. shores that some of the fallout from our own counterattacking weapons might be disseminated in the United States. And, since accuracy is, to a degree, a factor of range, the closeness of Cuban missile sites to their targets would ensure more hits.

All these advantages might be nullified, in a strictly military sense, in some future time, by technological developments. When Russia has acquired a large fleet of nuclear-propelled, missile-firing submarines and has constructed many heavily protected easily concealed launching sites for solid-fueled ICBM's on her own soil, the cost-effectiveness equation (particularly the difficulties of logistics) might dictate the permanent abandonment of Cuba as a potential Soviet missile site. But this time is not yet at hand, and it is not likely to be until, at the earliest, the latter part of the 1970's.

Soviet bombers based in Cuba would offer less of a threat, though a tangible one. Bombers are harder to conceal than missiles. Even if underground hangars were available (at great cost), long adjacent air-

strips would be necessary for takeoff. Surprise by air attack based on
Cuba is entirely possible,[5] but our defense against piloted aircraft is
well developed, and speed and altitude limitations of the plane would
make this threat a far less dangerous one than that of the missile.

A mobile strike force of conventional ground forces, with their para-
phernalia of equipment—tanks, artillery, rockets, and perhaps tactical
nuclear weapons—would have very little chance of achieving surprise,
or even of moving beyond Cuba's limits. The necessary concentration
of troop-carrying aircraft or of amphibious and naval shipping required
to transport the troops beyond Cuban waters would signal any attack
far in advance.

Thus Cuba, as a potential missile base, still offers to Russia some important military advantages—particularly in some future time when
Russian nuclear delivery capability might have approached more closely to parity with the United States. Until such time, the actual utilization of this potential by Moscow would probably be considered by the
Communists to involve unacceptable political and military risks, unless
there was virtual certainty in Moscow that the missiles could be secretly transported to, and concealed in, Cuba pending the time when they
might serve a political or psychological or even a military purpose on
the chessboard of world conflict.

Thus, in sum, utilization of Cuba as a missile base by the U.S.S.R.
would clearly be within the future military and technical competence
of the Russians, but missiles in Cuba would imply a willingness on
Moscow's part to accept the risks of global nuclear war.

2. *Naval base.* The second, and probably far more likely, utilization
of a Communist Cuba by Russia is as a naval and submarine base or
refueling and replenishment station. Announcement has already been
made, though without many details, that Soviet Russia would aid Cuba
in the development of a port and facilities for fishing fleets.[6] Russian
trawlers, as well as Cuban fishing vessels, are using Cuban ports. About

---

[5] Light planes from Cuba have already penetrated our radar screen, some of
them undetected.

[6] The U.S.S.R. has been negotiating, apparently with some success, to obtain
trawler and fishing-boat repair and replenishment facilities at Veracruz, Mexico,
deep in the heart of the Caribbean. This represents to some officers an "ominous"
penetration of our home waters. This may be an overstatement. Nevertheless, the
far-ranging activities of the Soviet fishing fleets have important military implications, as well as economic and political consequences. The utilization of the
Japanese fishing fleets prior to, and during, World War II in an auxiliary naval
role provides some instructive lessons to those inclined to minimize the activities of
the Soviet fleet.

a dozen Soviet trawlers are intermittently based on the island. During the missile crisis of 1962, there was a considerable concentration of Soviet submarines off Cuba, and there have been persistent but unconfirmed reports since then that one or more Soviet destroyers or submarines were to be transferred to the Cuban Navy.

A fueling facility for submarines, trawlers, and small craft, and machine shops capable of making minor repairs (the shops in the U.S. Naval Base at Guantánamo Bay are the best on the island) is an entirely feasible development and could be mutually beneficial, both economically and militarily, to the U.S.S.R. and Cuba. Such a "base" would permit Soviet vessels to remain on station in Western Hemisphere waters for far longer cycles than if those vessels were limited to Soviet mainland bases or to refueling tankers at sea.[7]

3. *Intelligence center.* The third potential importance of a Communist Cuba to Russia is as an intelligence base, or center, for the open and secret collection of information of all sorts about the United States and the Caribbean. Cuba is ideally situated for such a purpose. Vital shipping lanes skirt its shores, and visual reconnaissance from Cuba can easily check the types, nationalities, and sizes of ships that pass. Nearby are Cape Kennedy and the U.S. Atlantic Missile Range, used for both military and civilian earth satellite and space shots and for missile testing of Polaris, Minuteman, and other military missiles. Electronic monitoring of the extensive radio and radar transmissions needed for such a range has undoubtedly been conducted from Cuban-based "listening" stations for some time. Indeed, the Russians could, if they wished, erect a large radar in Cuba that would provide them with much the same type of information about missile launchings, trajectories, and ranges that is provided the United States by giant radars in Turkey and the Aleutians. Soviet trawlers with electronic equipment have long been prowling the Florida coast and, indeed, the entire Atlantic coast. These are equipped with recording devices that transcribe all military

---

[7] Suggestions that the Russians may be sharing command and control of the arms they have furnished to Cuba have more political than military importance. The Cubans already operate and use many of these weapons; the Russians may operate the more advanced weapons systems, but there is no evidence of a truly unified joint command. However, the Russians might choose, with Castro's cooperation, to establish their version of a multilateral naval force based, in part, on Cuban ports. Missile-firing submarines jointly manned and operated by Soviet-Cuban crews would have a major political and psychological effect in the Western Hemisphere and might, in time, have some military importance.

electronic transmissions from United States radar or radio stations and detect the "pulse rate," frequency, and location of such stations. Some of these trawlers are based in Cuba. Aircraft based in Cuba are capable of overflying parts of the American southeast and of photographic reconnaissance. (Soviet commercial flights to Cuba already skirt our coasts.) Finally, Cuba offers an ideal base for the infiltration of intelligence agents or "spies" of various kinds (mixed, for instance, among legitimate refugees) to the United States mainland, to Puerto Rico, to other Caribbean islands, or to Central and South America. Cuba is being used actively as a Russian intelligence outpost today; unquestionably, its most important intelligence function is the monitoring of U.S. missile-range transmissions and of U.S. military radio and radar stations.

4. *Tracking station.* Another possible use of the Cuban island position by Russia is as a site for instrumentation, control, and communications equipment for Soviet space shots. Heretofore Russian monitoring and control stations have either been entirely within the boundaries of the Soviet Union or based aboard ship. Today, Russia is building a space tracking station in Cuba.

5. *Base for subversion.* As a Communist base in the heart of the Western Hemisphere, a Cuba is useful to Russian Communism as a base for the export of subversion, propaganda, sabotage, and guerrillas. The island has already been used as such a base in a small degree; the troubles in Venezuela and, to a far lesser extent, in Bolivia, Chile, and Panama can be traced in part to influences emanating from Cuba. As such a base, Cuba represents a threat to the unstable regimes and poverty-stricken volatile masses of the Caribbean islands and Central America in particular, and to all of Latin America in general. With its inadequate sea power and its proximity to the overpowering sea and air power of the United States, Cuba poses little danger of a formal large-scale or organized invasion of another country. But a tramp steamer or a submarine or a fishing vessel or a plane can easily carry a platoon of men. There is no possible way, short of complete blockade and "seizure-and-search," to prevent the infiltration of other Latin American countries by small groups of hard-core Communists, highly trained in the specialities of sabotage and subversion, of propaganda and guerrilla war, and of inciting revolution and overthrowing governments. Nor is there any way to stop gunrunning from Cuba, as a base,

to other countries of the hemisphere. Today, Cuba is serving this Russian purpose well. It is a training base for many Latin American specialists in revolution and ferment—a staging base, to be used when needed, for the expansion of Communism in the Western Hemisphere. (See Tad Szulc's chapter, pp. 69–97, for a discussion of Cuba as a base for subversion in Latin America.)

6. *Military diversion.* There is finally for Russia the military diversionary value of Cuba. This would be of most importance were Cuba to become a well-developed missile base, for in such a case it would be absolutely essential for the United States to earmark a sizable part of its strategic power to eliminate the Cuban missile sites before their missiles could be launched. In limited war, or in times of mobilization for crises elsewhere, Cuba could divert a sizable portion of our ready strength long enough to "foul up" time schedules and influence other operations. Even with no imminent crisis in sight, and all missiles supposedly removed, Cuba today diverts fractional but important elements of our military strength in many different forms.

Surveillance by maritime patrol aircraft of all shipping bound to and from Cuba requires the more or less constant use of at least one (sometimes several) U.S. naval patrol plane squadron (twelve planes to a squadron). It also necessitates a careful global reporting system that tabulates, when known, the cargoes and ports of call of all Soviet-bloc ships that call at the island.

Photoreconnaissance—in the absence of on-the-spot inspection, which neither Fidel Castro nor the Russians have ever granted—is obviously of vital importance, as the missile crisis of 1962 showed. Photorecon flights have, however, certain limitations and liabilities. Comparative chronological photographs of the same areas can reveal unusual activity, or new installations on the surface, sometimes even if camouflaged, but they cannot reveal what is stored underground, or carefully hidden in warehouses, buildings, or dense forests. In view of the rapidity with which modern missiles can be erected, frequent flights would be required if Washington were to guard itself fully against another nasty surprise similar to that of September and October, 1962. For no one flight, even at high altitude, can possibly cover the entire island of Cuba. Repeated and frequent flights are necessary for full coverage. Thus Cuba as a Russian base diverts the efforts of the Strategic Air Command's high-flying U-2 photoreconnaissance aircraft, which make what the Pentagon euphemistically calls "periodic" flights near, and over, the island. To provide the low-level photos that are essential to accurate interpretation of any telltale signs the high level mosaics may yield, about three squadrons of Navy, Marine, and Air Force high-speed jet photorecon planes must always be available. These planes have not been used over Cuba for months.

There is a political liability and increased risk in the use of low-level flights: Our aircraft would fly within easy range of Russian and Cuban antiaircraft guns, and would be so obvious to Castro's armed forces that he would probably charge aggression. An even greater disadvantage has, so far, prevented the utilization of night photoreconnaissance missions. Photo flash bombs or flares, utilized at night for picture-taking from aircraft, would illuminate large areas, and the flash and the boom would almost certainly prod Havana into charging Washington with "bombing." Despite these political and psychological liabilities, low-level and night reconnaissance may, at some future time, be necessary, if intelligence estimates indicate that Russia has developed very mobile quickly-emplaced solid-fueled missiles.

Because of the political and psychological liabilities of too thorough photoreconnaissance, the United States must supplement in Cuba its "seeing eye" aircraft with what is probably the most intensive intelligence effort mounted by this country against any single objective. This must take many forms: electronic intelligence; monitoring of all radio and radar transmissions from Cuba; raids by refugees or agents; operation of spies or agents within Cuba; and infiltration by small parties of armed men, with intelligence, sabotage, or guerrilla missions, into Cuba. The Central Intelligence Agency and the armed services are thought to participate in these activities—the former on what may be a substantial scale, with its own "fishing vessels," speedboats, and aircraft.

Since Fidel Castro came to power in Cuba, and particularly since Russia began to utilize Cuba for military purposes, the United States has constantly maintained a naval amphibious squadron with a reinforced Marine battalion landing team (about 1,700 men) in the Caribbean or close to it. The Marines are either aboard ship cruising within a few hours of Cuba, or at Vieques, an island near Puerto Rico. This force can be useful, of course, as contemporary history has shown, in any trouble spot in the Caribbean, but its focus is Cuba. The garrison of Guantánamo has also been somewhat strengthened. Behind these first-line units the Army, the Navy, and the Marines maintain ready alert forces for quick transportation by sea or by air to the Caribbean area. And along the Florida coast, particularly from Key West to north of Miami, radar stations and air defense facilities have had to be strengthened, and some of the nation's best fighter interceptors have been assigned to the area.[8]

What the collective manpower total and dollar cost of all these precautions amount to is the Pentagon's secret. But even measured against the gargantuan yardstick of a $52-billion defense budget, it is not insignificant. Cuba as a Russian-equipped base costs us many millions annually, and it demands a diversion of a sizable fraction of our most specialized and skilled forces to what is essentially a static, defensive task on our own doorstep.

The most discouraging and ominous part of this military equation from the American point of view is that Russia, with very little additional effort (perhaps even feigned effort) can force the United States to raise the ante considerably. A sudden increase in the number of Soviet ships sent to Cuba, unusual engineering work in Cuba's mountains, overt displays of strengthened military power, the threat of new missiles, and the eruption of trouble fostered by infiltrators trained in Cuba, in other Caribbean islands, or in Central America, would immediately necessitate the allocation of additional United States military power for the Caribbean area. In this game Russia holds the cards. Moscow can play it hard or soft and force our effort to ebb or flow with her actions. We cannot—and must not—forget that in the fall of 1962 some forty odd missiles and perhaps (at a maximum) 40,000 Russians forced the mobilization and concentration by the United States of more than half a million soldiers, sailors, marines, and airmen.

[8] Some indication of the diversionary drain that Cuba represents is given by testimony presented to congressional committees by Maj. Gen. W. R. Shuler, U.S. Army, and others on the 1964 military construction appropriations bill. The total Army Air Defense requests for new construction approximate $22,560,000. An estimated $14.4 million of this amount is earmarked for "facilities and land acquisition for air defense in the Homestead-Miami area and in the Key West, Fla., area . . . to meet a new requirement which has grown out of the . . . Cuban crisis last Fall." Four Nike-Hercules and four Hawk antiaircraft missile batteries have been emplaced in temporary sites (to be made permanent with the moneys requested) in the Homestead-Miami area, and four Hawk batteries are in position in the Key West area.

The Castro Regime

The viability of Cuba and the continuation of his government is Castro's first concern. The island itself must be secure before foreign adventures are attempted. Thus Castro's prime military objectives have been couched essentially in defensive terms; his A1 policy has been to strengthen the island against any U.S.-supported invasion. But Cuba is also useful to Castro, as it is to the U.S.S.R., for the export of subversion and of small covert, or overt, military forces.

Most observers agree that in most countries of Latin America the bloom is off the rose as far as the popularity of Castroism is concerned. But it still has a hold, particularly among extremist fringes. But what makes Castroism a potential strategic threat to the hemisphere is the backing of Soviet power. Castroism and Communism today must be considered as synonymous in military, if not in political, terms. But this may not always be so. Fidel Castro has already shown signs of impatience with Moscow's habit of domination. He has discarded some of the old-line Cuban Communist leaders. He has indicated his intentions of recognizing Albania, sole European satellite that has chosen the Chinese, rather than the Russian, way. These signs of "independence" could have significant military implications in the future, but it would be unwise to expect Castro and Moscow to come to a break. Castro appears to be maneuvering for position, for greater flexibility—as nearly all the satellites are attempting to do—but he knows that Red China can at best help him with limited physical means and moral and psychological support, and that the economic and military fortunes of Cuba for the immediate future, at least, are tied to Moscow.[9]

From the military point of view, Cuba without Russian support would eventually become merely a nuisance to the hemisphere, chiefly annoying in its capacity for fomenting trouble and encouraging revolution. Cuban military strength would wither on the vine, though slowly. If all Russian military support were withdrawn from Cuba, the strategic significance of the island would be minor in the equation of global power.

---

[9] According to some observers, Cuba has imported, by devious routes, rice, ready-made clothing, modern medicinal products, and even some machinery from Red China.

Summary

All this suggests that the island of Cuba, by virtue of geography (and recently by virtue of the Russian transfusions of military power), is of long-term and continuing importance in Caribbean, hemispheric, and global strategy.

The Cuban position alone, even if exploited as fully as possible by Moscow, could not alter the global balance of power. The superior power position of the United States does *not* depend upon what happens in Cuba. But a Cuba developed as a Soviet base could be one important element in the world equation of power. A strong Soviet military position in Cuba could divert sizable segments of U.S. military strength, could neutralize some of our nuclear retaliatory capability, and could thus become an important political pawn in, for instance, another Berlin crisis.

Cuba is not vital to us as a base. But unless future U.S. security is to suffer a continuous and unpredictable series of retreats and alarms, it should be denied as a base to any potential enemy. Under certain circumstances—the discovery of Soviet long-range missiles on the island, for instance—immediate military invasion by the United States might be necessary. Other circumstances, such as a major increase in the export of arms, saboteurs, and terrorists to Latin America, might require less stringent, but definite, action, such as a partial blockade. In any case, as long as Soviet Russia uses Cuba for its purposes, statesmen and military planners in the United States will have nightmares.

BAYLESS MANNING is Dean of the School of Law at Stanford University. He served from 1960 to 1962 as Chairman of the Latin American Studies Program at Yale University and from 1962 to 1963 as Special Assistant to the Undersecretary of State.

An Overall Perspective

BAYLESS MANNING

The intensity of American reaction to the Cuban situation baffled most foreign observers. The chapter contributed by Raymond Aron and Alfred Grosser reveals its authors to be at heart puzzled by the sharpness of our response despite their deep and sympathetic familiarity with the United States. The Aron and Grosser position, though critical of United States policy, represents the segment of European opinion that is most favorably disposed toward us in this matter. Opinion in Latin America is more diverse; some elements, particularly in nearby Caribbean countries, condemn the United States for not using its military power to blot out Castro, other elements decry at United States interference in the sovereign life of Cuba, while majority opinion probably holds a simultaneous distaste for the Castro regime and for United States reaction to it.

Of course, the foreign policy of the United States is not determined by majority vote of other governments. Nor should it be. The fact that others hold a view of the Cuban situation different from that held by the United States is not in itself terribly important. But the widespread incomprehension of the reaction of the United States to the Castro regime is important. In nuclear international politics, nothing is more dangerous than misunderstanding of the temper and disposition of any of the major participants. Khrushchev's misassessment of the facts very nearly blew up the world. It is well worth while, therefore, to identify

223

some of the special factors that combined to generate the persistent heat that arcs across the narrow waters between Cuba and the United States.

In truth, the wonder is not that we shied. The miracle is that we did not bolt. Events of the last six years in Cuba could hardly have been more jarring to the people of the United States if they had been expressly planned for that purpose.

To the American public at large Cuba has been *terra incognita*. Probably most Americans have thought of Cuba, if they have thought of it at all, as a vague affiliate of the United States, as a client dollar area (all but physically attached to Florida) holding some sort of special preference in the sugar trade, as the site of a primary United States naval base, and as a faintly exotic center of beach and night life for United States tourists. The stormy history of Cuban-American relations over the last 150 years, set out in Henry Wriston's chapter, has not been a familiar story to the American public. A century and a half of trouble and difficulty over the island should have conditioned us to expect more of the same. But that conditioning did not come about, for the facts were not widely known. Cuba's political history in the present century and its long struggle to find its independence and itself were also not known. Few Americans had heard our role in the Spanish-American War presented in the Cuban version—as American intervention designed to steal Cuba's freedom at the very moment when its patriots had finally won it from Spain. Who in the United States recalled the Platt Amendment, either its beginning or its ending? We were ignorant—almost willfully ignorant—about Cuba. While knowledge of facts does not guarantee intelligent decisions, intelligent decisions are difficult to make without knowledge of facts. And we had almost none. If Hawaii had overnight been transformed into a hostile power, we would hardly have been more astounded than we were by the sudden snarl and show of teeth in Castro's Cuba.

Our ignorance of the Cuban situation was merely a particular instance of our long-standing national disinterest in Latin America as a whole and our lack of knowledge about it. American companies and government offices looking for experienced men to work in Latin America find the task almost impossible. Every educational institution vainly seeking to locate scholars of Latin American history, culture, politics, or sociology knows that in these resources the United States is an under-developed country. Whether the political optical equipment of each nation has a preferred focal length I do not know. But the United States seems clearly to have one. Events in Europe and Japan seem to be at our proper focal range and are observed with reasonable clarity. Events in Africa and most of Asia are somewhat out of range and are seen only if on a galactic scale. Events on our own borders—in Canada and in Latin America—fall inside our focal range and are virtually invisible regardless of their size. From every rational standpoint—political, military, and economic—one would have expected the United States to have developed a vast and widely held expertise on matters Latin American. But that did not occur—still has not occurred. To the people of the United States it did not seem credible that serious political difficulty could flare up so close at hand as Cuba, lying inside the range of our historical political vision.

We were, moreover, nationally unprepared for the Cuban affair in another sense. As to Latin America, we have been ethnically and culturally arrogant. The railing heard in some Latin American circles about United States gunboat diplomacy, economic imperialism, materialistic viciousness, and callous exploitation of Latin America's human and natural resources may mostly be dismissed as politically motivated and uninformed. The record of the American business community in Latin America is on the whole at least as good as the corresponding record of the business sectors of other countries and better than the records of the Latin American countries themselves. And the sporadic resort by the United States to power diplomacy over the last century compares favorably with the persistent practice of such techniques by the other major powers of the world. The United States need not apologize for its general performance in Latin America, and it can rightfully claim to have done much good. But in our national attitude toward Latin America, we have been culturally arrogant.

Profound historical forces have shaped this attitude. Weaned on English tales of the defeat of the Armada, and on tales of the doughty Drake, we are taught in grade school that the Spaniards came to plunder while the English came to colonize and that Spanish power was eventually and inevitably smashed in Florida, in Texas, and in California. Predominantly Protestant, the United States has, despite its own record of internal religious tolerance, tended to be suspicious of Latin

America's Catholicism. Since the Reformation, Spain has been for us the symbol of medieval despotic monarchy, the Inquisition, and reaction. In addition, the general citizen of the United States has held a low estimate of the capacity of the Latin American to govern himself stably, to do hard work, or to organize group endeavor, and he attributes the lower state of economic development of the Latin American countries to these alleged deficiencies. Though our knowledge has increased somewhat in recent years, the American public has in the past had almost no awareness of Mexico's economic growth, of Argentina's industrialization, of Chile's governmental stability, or of Brazil's urbanization. Altogether the United States has tended to feel itself superior, and has made no effort to conceal that feeling.

Cultural *hubris* is an old story in the history of man. It led Hellas to consider all non-Greeks, and Cathay to consider all non-Chinese, barbarians. Such *hubris* is dangerous. It invariably leads to miscalculations of the environment; makes it difficult to perceive the desires, activities, and motivations of others; generates resentment; and eventually leads to costly blunders. While the eyes of the United States were firmly riveted on matters it considered important (that is to say, events lying in the national focal range), such as the Berlin confrontation with the Soviet Union or the Suez crisis, the nation was wholly unprepared by history or by attitude for the possibility that Cubans on their little island could suddenly precipitate international crisis for us on our doorstep.

Correspondingly, the American citizen is proud of his nation's accomplishments—the success of the United States in achieving a reasonable balance between order and personal freedom, the world's highest standard of living, and a reputation for getting things done. In general, he anticipates the voluntary deference that is owed to the mighty and the successful. Further, the United States citizen typically considers his nation a benefactor, helping the less fortunate with technical and economic aid, carrying the main defense burden against the enemies of the Western Hemisphere, and providing the economic motive power for all the countries of North, Central, and South America. And he considers his country to be a symbol of revolutionary freedom, standing steadfastly for democracy and the rights of man. From this perspective, the American public was completely incapable of understanding, and shocked by, the news in 1958 that Vice President Nixon had been stoned in Lima by students at San Marcos University. And it was equally un-prepared for the violent anti-American line taken by the Castro regime —a line which, in turn, appeared to generate substantial sympathetic resonance among much of the Latin American populace.

Hanson Baldwin's chapter, offering a military perspective of Cuba, provides insight into another important aspect of the American re-sponse to the Castro regime. Americans are not accustomed to looking down gun barrels that are not firing. Long secure between two oceans and two unarmed frontiers, the United States has not had to endure the anxieties of watching potentially hostile troops massed provocatively on its borders. Englishmen may have become accustomed to continen-tal warships in the Channel, and Frenchmen even numb to German ground maneuvers across the Rhine, but the American public has not undergone a similar experience. To the American public, a report of foreign submarines off our coasts or troops in battle dress nearby can only mean a preliminary to all-out assault upon us, and we will be strongly tempted to jump first. Most of us today are living in the cross hairs of intercontinental missiles locked on United States targets some-where in the vastness of the Soviet Union. But few of us know that. And besides, as we are reminded by Norman Mailer's patrol that was more afraid of bees than of bullets, the mind of man reacts to the lesser threat while repressing the greater as less credible. To have Soviet troops "only 90 miles away" may seem fairly humdrum business to many Europeans. But it does not seem so to the American public.

And then there is the Canal. Always riding near the top of the polit-ical and military consciousness of the American people, there is the Pan-ama Canal. If there had to be trouble in one of the Latin American countries, why did it have to be one that lay directly athwart the ap-proaches to the Canal? Three generations of Americans have taken as unchallengeable that the Canal is a main artery in our national corpus and an essential link in our defense perimeter. We built it; we keep it going; it is part of our national organic structure. Yet, unaccountably, the Canal seems not to be really ours, seems to lie exposed to the ele-ments and in the hands of others. To what extent the presence of an un-friendly regime in Cuba actually affects the defensibility of the Canal is a matter to which Mr. Baldwin addresses himself in his chapter. For present purposes, the expert answer is not the important consideration.

The significant fact is that the American public believes that the presence of the Castro regime in Cuba places the Canal in military jeopardy. And that, in American eyes, is a matter of deadly seriousness.[1]

Our great naval base at Guantánamo presents still another aspect of Cuba seen in military perspective. If there had to be a serious political explosion in a country of the Western Hemisphere, did it have to occur at the focal center of our naval training and defense operations in the Caribbean and South Atlantic? Holding Guantánamo under a long-term treaty with the Cuban government, the United States has poured millions of dollars and sixty years of work into developing the base. Three generations of Navy men have trained at Gitmo, and in two major world wars it has been the pinion of the defense of the Canal, the hemisphere, and the eastern sea frontier. Its functions have changed over the years, and, as Mr. Baldwin observes, modern marine technology has reduced its former critical role as a coaling station. But Guantánamo has been and remains an integral part of the operations of the United States Navy. As seen by most Americans, a threat to Guantánamo is a knife at the national jugular.

In addition to the special military significance of Guantánamo to the United States, the events of the Cuban affair also had a special political backdrop in the Monroe Doctrine. Few Americans have a clear idea of what the Monroe Doctrine is, how it came about, or what its limits are. Fewer have a knowledge of the Roosevelt Corollary to the Monroe Doctrine, either by name or by content. But the average American citizen holds two ideas about the Monroe Doctrine firmly and sharply in his mind. As to the substance of the Doctrine, he carries the general impression that the United States has sworn forever to use its full

[1] There may be another, nonmilitary, aspect to the matter of the Canal that is worth noting. Most Americans are aware, in a general way, that Theodore Roosevelt acquired control of the Canal area by uncomfortably direct methods, and though these Americans are sufficiently tough-minded to insist that our national interest requires us to maintain control of the only passage through the Isthmus, few of them are sufficiently tough-minded to live entirely at ease with the history of the case. In a United States not yet much experienced in the jungle world of international affairs, there are more practitioners of *realpolitik* than believers in *realpolitik*. Roosevelt and Wilson each stand in one of the main currents in our political heritage. When these currents cross, they produce a kind of defensive anxiety. Our conviction of the essentiality of the Ditch to our national interest coexists with a vague disquietude of conscience about it. We are correspondingly touchy on the subject.

resources, if necessary, to prevent any nation that is not in the Western Hemisphere from holding a position of political influence in the Western Hemisphere. The other clear point in his mind is that, whatever the details of the Monroe Doctrine may be, it is a keystone of our foreign policy, has been since the early days of the nation, and is unchallengeable. Any American who would fail to enforce the Doctrine, who would retreat from it, who would qualify it, is certainly a weakling and probably a traitor. The Doctrine's special history and significance are set forth in Mr. Wriston's chapter. But for present purposes, it is less important to know what the Doctrine is than to know what the American people believe it to be.

In the American view, the Latin American countries appear as weak, divided, and unstable, and the United States appears as a strong and beneficent protector. The United States citizen assumes that the other countries of the hemisphere want to keep European and Asian political influence out of the New World and that they welcome United States help in the job. He believes that, in turn, it is a moral duty of the United States, given its strength, wealth, and military might, to assume the defense of the New World for its own protection and as a matter of *noblesse oblige*. To this end he is willing to spend vast sums of American money and sacrifice the lives of American troops. And he is further willing to waive any claim against the rest of the countries of the hemisphere for his country's serious contribution to this endeavor. He sees the cause as just, the motives benevolent, the commitment unwavering.

As Kalman Silvert's analysis of our general Latin American policy points out, the Latin American countries often do not view the Monroe Doctrine this way at all. They are apt to feel that they are patronized by the United States. They argue that as sovereign powers they should be free independently to choose their friends and associates from among all the participants of the world community, whether in or out of the Western Hemisphere. They do not like to be reminded constantly that their external defense lies in the hands of another power. They have become paranoiac on the question of United States "intervention" in countries of the hemisphere—paranoiac to a point where it sometimes seems that in the Latin American scale of values no national objective is as important as the elimination of American "interventionism." And to many in Latin America, the Monroe Doctrine has become a symbol of that interventionism. Of all this, most United States citizens know quite literally nothing.

The American public awakened one day to find that Cuba had entered into a series of trade and military alliances with the Soviet Union and that there were Soviet military and political personnel basing themselves in Cuba. Quite apart from the actual military threat implied by this event, and more important than the military threat, the sudden Russian presence in the Western Hemisphere was taken by most American citizens as an overt provocation. It was taken as a deliberate challenge to the most cherished single principle of tested American foreign policy—the Monroe Doctrine, a century and a quarter old.[2] Seen from the American public perspective, the Soviet Union's action could only be interpreted as throwing down the gauntlet, as a deliberate effort to pick a fight. It is not a part of American tradition to turn down that species of invitation. And it was not turned down.

The American business sector, and certain national attitudes about it, also played a significant part in the unhappy recent years of United States–Cuban relations. In the past, much of what the American populace has known of foreign relations and foreign countries has filtered in from the American investorate. There is much truth in the observation heard in Latin America that in the nineteenth century, and well into the twentieth, the diplomatic corps of the United States operating in Latin America was chiefly engaged in the business of claims adjustment on behalf of the American business community. And a significant component of Theodore Roosevelt's foreign policy in this area involved the use of American political power to aid in the collection of debts owed to American investors. This seems quite right and natural to the American public. The American taxpayer works hard and pays his debts, including his taxes to the United States government; other people should work hard and pay their debts as well, particularly when they are the beneficiaries of United States capital investment and of various kinds of aid paid out of American tax dollars. So long as the only significant conduit between a Latin American country and the American public is through American investors, it is inevitable that the

---

[2] The other great historical principle, President Washington's parting injunction against entangling alliances, had, after 1940, quietly melted away under the rays of America's rising political power and the compression of a shrinking world.

pattern of communications will be long periods of silence when things are going "normally," punctuated by sudden flurries of headlined awareness when a shift in local conditions abroad suddenly makes it difficult to collect debts, to protect property, and to do business as usual. As a result, the average American tends to think of Central America as a place where bananas come from and where periodic inexplicable revolutions suddenly disrupt business operations for a time.

From the perspective of a Latin American country in which a United States firm invests, the company may appear as a titan, able to rock an entire national economic and political framework with a sneeze. In the roar of America's giant pluralistic economy, a sneeze or even a death rattle of the same company would hardly be audible. The communications silence about a country that spells "normalcy" to the American public may well be accompanied within the country by a dangerous buildup of tensions. When the lid goes off, the American investors in that country suddenly become vocal and turn to the American public and government for help. Whenever the United States government responds favorably to such an appeal, it is simply a further proof to many Latin Americans that Washington, D.C., is in the vest-pocket of a handful of American companies with interests in Latin America—a proposition that the American public finds so palpably absurd as to be blinded from perceiving why so many Latin Americans think it is so.

Relations between the American business community and the Cuban economy are discussed by J. Wilner Sundelson and in portions of Robert F. Smith's and Henry Wriston's chapters. With rare exceptions, American business investors in Cuba in the 1950's felt snug and comfortable, warmed by Cuba's sun and by Sergeant Batista's effective concern with order and stability. The American people heard nothing. If some businessmen saw trouble on the horizon, they did little to bring it to the attention of the American people or of the State Department. As Mr. Sundelson points out, as late as 1956 the Department of Commerce issued an inviting tract on investment in Cuba that makes no mention of the sources of social discontent and political instability that were to make it possible in November 1958 for Castro to depart from the Sierra Maestra and walk into Havana on January 1, 1959, to the salutes of a virtually unanimous nation. The American people heard nothing, or substantially nothing, of the growling of the lava until one day the whole top of the Cuban mountain blew off. Shock and surprise were inevitable.

The business community is always a tempting target for criticism and often a whipping boy, in part because it seems sometimes to be actively competing for the role. But the performance of those elements in the United States that may loosely be lumped together as "liberal" was, in the case of Cuba, little more helpful than the performance of the business sector in preparing the American public for the Cuban situation. Accurately perceiving what the American business community did not perceive—the weakness and viciousness of Batista's regime and the popular appeal of the *barbudos* in the hills—the American liberals fell back in stunned amazement as, step by step, Castro's supposed commitment to liberal democracy dissolved when once he had come to power and his regime moved to the extreme of antiliberal totalitarian left socialism. Batista's enthusiasts, both on the island and in the United States, had said all along that Castro was a "Communist." But how could they be persuasive about that analysis when they were so transparently unperceiving of the general political condition of the island, of the corrupt gangsterism of the Batista regime, and of the impossibility of its continuation? Those who denounce a Catiline a day in defense of a palpably untenable status quo do not long maintain public confidence in their prophecies. But neither do those who find a saint in every social critic and a savior in every young revolutionary. By 1961, when, as Mr. Smith's chapter points out, the Marxist character of the Castro regime had been made manifest, the forces of liberalism within the United States fell into disarray. When the time came for the Bay of Pigs, an untried President found himself with an inherited operation already under way and two groups of advisers—a tongue-tied group of liberals who had completely misassessed Castro and a strident group of American business interests who had completely misassessed the rot in Batista's Cuba. The wobbly performance of the government of the United States in the Bay of Pigs affairs was an almost inevitable consequence.

Finally, in this catalogue of factors that, taken together, make comprehensible the last six years of Cuban-American relations is the cold war. Here, both Leon Lipson and Tad Szulc provide insight—one on the confrontation with the U.S.S.R. and the other on the course of Castroite subversion in Latin America. Again, the scenario of events in

Cuba could not have been more inflammatory from the standpoint of the American public. Any foreign presence in Cuba would have been received with alarm in the United States for the many reasons given earlier. When that foreign presence was a Communist country and our major antagonist in the cold war, the public temper rose above boiling. The results were twofold: one complicating, but the other, in its own way, helpful.

The complication, of course, was that the Cuban situation, already fraught with consequence for the whole of America's hemispheric policy, was transformed into a sub-arena of the worldwide struggle between the United States and the Soviet Union. Cuban policy had become Cuban policy plus Latin American policy plus overall cold war policy. Decisions of the government of the United States vis-à-vis Cuba had now to be weighed not only against domestic and Latin American reaction, but also in the context of repercussions on the Berlin situation, nuclear test ban negotiations, NATO, Indian-Chinese border fighting, and the fearful prospect of worldwide nuclear war. No President, perhaps excepting Lincoln, has had to face so confounding a situation as that which descended upon President Kennedy.

Still, Russia's overt entry made one invaluable contribution. Overnight it substituted an approximate national unity for the splintered irresolution abroad in the land at the time of the Bay of Pigs. All the factors reviewed here were brought to a clear focus in the minds of the American public, and all factors pointed in one direction. The United States would not, under any circumstances, tolerate a major Soviet military base in Cuba even if it should prove necessary to destroy the Soviet Union and much of the United States in order to prevent it. Khrushchev apparently had no inkling whatever that this would be the response of a unified American will. The world can only be grateful that the United States had a President who was able to put the point across and that, at the last minute, Khrushchev was able to perceive that the Americans were serious beyond serious. The people of the United States had no very clear idea of how to cope with the Castro problem, but from fifteen years of experience in the cold war they had learned much about how to cope with the Soviet Union.

Every possible circumstance that could have pressed us to precipitate action seems to have been present in the Cuban case as it developed from 1959 to 1963. Perhaps we should simply have marched into Cuba and destroyed the Castro regime, as we could have on any weekend. That is how the Russians would have reacted; indeed, it is how they did react in Hungary in 1956. It is what the French Empire and the Spanish Empire and the British Empire would have done, and what they have done when they have felt themselves and their national interests to be threatened, often in far less degree than when we felt ourselves to be threatened in Cuba. But one may not think with another's head nor play by another's style. The Bay of Pigs may have made analytic bad sense and military bad sense, but it may not have made political bad sense. In a democracy, halfway measures were consonant with a halfway state of the public mind. In the 1960 presidential campaign Cuba was on every tongue, and, as is the custom in the language of American politics, there was much talk of the Cuban "issue." But there was really no Cuban "issue" in the election. There was a Cuban problem and an acute sense of public alarm about it, but, except for a small minority who argued for all-out invasion or the unleashing of the Strategic Air Command, there were no clear alternative policy programs offered to the American people or voted on by them. Both Kennedy and Nixon made clear their deep concern about the Cuban situation, implied that they would do something about it that would be fairly tough, but stopped well short of committing themselves to an assault by United States armed forces. In retrospect it would be hard to say what difference there was between the positions of the two candidates on the matter, and the hairbreadth victory achieved by Kennedy in the election simply blurred the situation further. In a democracy, leaders must lead, but the range of tolerance in which they may move is severely limited. The ultimate sources of America's foreign policy toward Cuba, its bumbling at Playa Girón, and its brilliance during the missile crisis lay in the shift in the perception and unity of the American people.

WITH THE MISSILES DISMANTLED, and the most immediate Russian threat removed from the island, the world turned with a shudder of relief to other things, and the rapid currents of international politics swiftly cast up new facts, new problems, and new personalities. Within a year Kennedy was gone, and within two years Khrushchev was ousted from power. In those two years governments also changed hands, peacefully or otherwise, in England, Germany, Italy, Holland,

Turkey, Venezuela, Brazil, Argentina, Chile, Mexico, India, Colombia, Bolivia, Peru, and the Congo, to name but some. The Nuclear Test Ban Treaty was signed; the Chinese exploded a nuclear device; de Gaulle slammed the door on the apparently certain entry of England into the Continental economy; schism rived Communist orthodoxy as Christianity suddenly moved toward unity; Indonesia, born out of the United Nations, stalked out of its membership; the American Negro leaped a generation forward; birth control became table conversation; the U.S.S.R.–United States race to the moon took on a weird Oxford-Cambridge competitive quality; and Vietnam emerged as the next spluttering fuse of the cold war. But Castro remains in Havana.

His efforts to export his revolution seem stalled. As reviewed by Mr. Szulc, Castroite subversionary efforts against other Latin American governments can have serious disruptive effects where the insurrectionary atmosphere is receptive, and have been a complete failure where the environment is not already at the ignition point. Riots in the Panama Canal Zone are traceable in part to the activities of Castro agents but have their deeper source in the history of United States-Panamanian relations. The blatancies of Cuba's antagonism to the established governments of Latin America have led one after another to cut off diplomatic relations until only Mexico, with its own special revolutionary history, remains in regular diplomatic contact with Havana. Vigorous anti-Castroite forces have moved into control in Peru, Brazil, and Argentina, while Venezuela and Chile turned in stunning performances in the democratic process with the election of Presidents Leoni and Frei. Guantánamo remains secure, though harassed, while the Canal, operating on a renegotiated basis somewhat more favorable to Panama, may be on its way to being joined before long by a parallel artery built at sea level and for that reason less vulnerable to attack. The United States government remains vigorously opposed to the Castro regime and the Castro government remains vigorously opposed to the United States. In this sense, neither is following a policy of "coexistence." But they are in fact both existing, and it has to be true that each day of actual coexistence increases the credibility that they can coexist. There seems little enthusiasm in the United States today for invasion of the island. And Fidel in turn seems not anxious to invite certain disaster by marching on Guantánamo.

There are too many variables in prospect to make specific speculation about the future in Cuba a profitable exercise. A single assassin's
bullet, fired at Castro in anger over a trivial job appointment, could
throw Cuba into chaos, for it is far from clear that any substitute could
be found for his personal leadership. Serious faction among those seeking Castro's ear could reduce the regime to impotence. If the Soviet
Union should shift, or be forced to shift, its line and cut off the flow of
oil and machinery to Cuba, the regime, already hard pressed to maintain its economy, could be brought under irresistible pressure to renegotiate its relations with the Western Hemisphere, or to make way for
a government that will do so. The Castro regime appears to be moving
into its period of difficulty with the Cuban equivalent of the kulak, and
while it is difficult to believe that a group of cultivators of middle-sized
farms can overthrow the regime, it remains to be seen whether a Cuban
Communist government has the stomach for the Stalinist solution—
mass starvation and execution—and whether, if it pursues that solution,
it can sustain the domestic political consequences.[3]

Economic pressure as such will probably never lead to a collapse of
the government in Cuba. Cuba appears to be far from a starvation
economy, and even under starvation conditions the history of man
would indicate that a unified political military power can maintain itself almost indefinitely despite progressive enmiseration of the people. But poor performance of the economy restricts the resources of the
regime, introduces a soggy public apathy in place of the revolutionary
fervor the regime requires to move it forward, and saps the attention
and focus of the leadership. It is also not impossible that the regime
may eventually be able to turn the Cuban economy around and put it
on a more stable basis than it has at present. Its adolescent experiments
at wholesale industrialization having been abandoned, the Castro government has announced that it will be returning to an emphasis on sugar
production, in which it enjoys a substantial natural advantage. There is
no reason why the regime may not also reverse itself and undertake to
restore the formerly promising cattle industry, which it almost deliberately destroyed. No one seems to have figured out a way to operate a
socialist economy without heavy human cost, without substantial

---

[3] For a discussion of the general economic problems of the Castro regime, in
particular of the middle-sized farm, see Theodore Draper, *Castroism: Theory and
Practice* (Praeger, 1965), Chap. III.

inefficiency, and without a pervasive gray monotony. But the system can be made to work and, after initial chaos has been replaced by a degree of order, can provide for some growth in social services and economic productivity. Given enough time, enough luck, enough stability, enough help from the Soviet Union, enough political restraint of its leaders, enough patience on the part of the Cuban people, and enough willpower to succeed in the economic sphere, the Castro regime may ultimately turn the corner. But to do so would require all its energies, all its resources, and all its time. There will be nothing left for crusading, exportation of revolution, or military adventure.

Thus it is possible to conceive of a Castro indefinitely in power on his island but indefinitely frustrated in his efforts to expand his political base outside the island. But the character of the man does not seem to fit him well for this role. It is difficult to summon the scene of a gray-bearded Fidel Castro at the age of seventy-seven delivering five-hour speeches to an enthralled nationwide Cuban audience on the glories of the ninth five-year agrarian reform plan. It is also difficult to envision a Soviet Union that will indefinitely pour a million dollars a day subvention into a political outpost, which, it now knows, the United States will never permit it to use to full political and military advantage unless, perhaps, it is forced to follow that course by Peking's competitive pressure. It is difficult to envision a Cuba seeking, decade after decade, to subvert the other governments of Latin America and remaining decade after decade diplomatically isolated from them. One is tempted to think that time, in the long run is against Fidel, as it always is against the red-eyed zealot. One suspects that eventually Castro will either be inspired to do something foolish that will lead to his violent destruction or will find himself forced to renegotiate his way back into the Western Hemisphere at a considerable price. If this analysis is at all correct, the United States is today following the right general course of action. That policy consists of an inflexible posture vis-à-vis Guantánamo; a clear and unwavering defense of the Canal, coupled with exploration of proposals for an alternative route to reduce the vulnerability of the waterway; steady diplomatic and economic pressure to the extent (which will be increasingly limited) that we can persuade others to cooperate with us; the closest possible collaboration with the other countries of Latin America to forge a whole new environment in the hemisphere through the Alliance for Progress; a clear, steady signal to the Soviet Union to stay out of the Caribbean; and a stiff policy of containment against Castroite subversion in other parts of Latin America.

If the Castro regime were in some way to be unseated, the political consequences would be very uncertain. Some of the problems that would result can, however, be anticipated.

1. The first thing that is clear is that there will be chaos, that the United States will be called upon by many to step into the breach to restore order and civil administration, and that the United States should not do that except in the most extreme circumstances. Another round of patron-client relationship in the history of the United States and Cuba would most likely prove self-defeating in the long run. If some kind of externally imposed order is necessary until a new Cuban government can be formed, it should be established in collaboration with other countries of the hemisphere, probably through the Organization of American States.

2. There will be a clamor from Cuban exile groups and former American investors in Cuba to restore to them such of their former properties as still exist on the island, and to require the successor government to agree to make full dollar compensation for property lost. But any new Cuban government will have an exceedingly difficult time under the best of circumstances as it attempts to reorganize the society and the economy. It will need to continue to make use of much of the present socialized economic structure, without incurring the losses consequent upon a disruptive effort to dismantle it, and return quickly to a full private-enterprise economy. One can imagine an extended period in which the new government extricates itself step by step from uneconomic operations, doing its best within its domestic political limits to allocate to private groups the properties released. The successor government should not be required to commence its precarious life with a million-party litigation to sort out the original eggs that have gone into the Cuban socialized omelet. And any new democratic government must be free to fashion its own economic ideology, picking and choosing on an experiential and political basis from among the operating programs inherited from the Castro regime. In the matter of property claims, the United States could play a Teddy Rooseveltian role and throw its full political weight behind the claimants and against a feeble disorganized government. Or it could withhold its direct political sup-

port and leave the claimants to pursue the new government as best they can. Neither of these policies recommends itself. Conceivably, the United States could be instrumental in developing a multilateral international claims procedure that would first seek to draw into a single pool all foreign claims and then seek to negotiate with the new government a long-term plan of payment, or, more realistically, partial payment. To the extent that the United States government could bring together in its own hands the claims of American citizens, it would be better prepared to act rationally if the day should come when the problems of launching a new Cuban government are immediate problems. Most Cuban property claims that have not already been paid, or recouped through tax write-offs, will probably never be paid now, no matter what happens. History cannot be turned back. And revolution is a haphazard and costly affair—one of the periodic risks of life to which man in an organized society is exposed.

3. The United States should do whatever it can to make possible a satisfactory trade and export posture for the successor government. That means buying Cuban sugar. Without sugar exports Cuba is without foreign exchange, and without foreign exchange it cannot operate its economy and manifestly cannot pay foreign claims of any kind. Cuba's former sugar quota has been allocated to other sugar producers, including domestic producers within the United States. It may be expected that any effort to reintroduce Cuban sugar into the American consumer's market will encounter sharp resistance from those favored under the present arrangements. But a market must be found in spite of that resistance. If Cuba is not to be brought directly into the United States as a state (statehood was suggested by Jefferson, and others have since often resuggested it), America's best hope lies in a progressive, prosperous, independent, democratic Cuban government. We should go far to help bring about that long-range result.

4. The United States should stand ready to provide technical assistance, if requested by the successor government, to help restore the smooth functioning of social services, industrial plant, and economic infrastructure throughout the island.

5. A particularly difficult problem will be presented by the fact that for a period of years the Cuban people will have been submerged in a sea of Soviet and Communist propaganda and will be substantially out of contact with much of their true environment. As we have learned in

Japan and Germany, mass reeducation to a democratic way of life can be achieved with substantial success, but it calls for great skill, much work, and intelligent preparation.

6. American business firms will probably not reoccupy the dominant position in the Cuban economy that they once held. Nonetheless, there will be a need for capital, and there will be new marketing opportunities as the regime changes. The private American business sector, perhaps with a measure of special support from the United States government, will have a significant role to play in regenerating the Cuban economy.

What lessons may be drawn from the Cuban experience? Every party involved can, if it will, learn much from the last few years in Cuba.

Let us begin with the Soviet Union and the Communist world generally. These people seem to need regular and recurrent reminders that the United States, though slow to move, can be exceedingly tough. It is regrettable that the lesson does not seem to stick. Stalin learned it in Iran and in Berlin, Mao in Korea and now again in Vietnam, and Khrushchev in Cuba. Let us hope that Mr. Kosygin will not force us to make the same point again. The Caribbean is *Mare Hemisphericum—* or, taking *nos* to mean the countries of the Western Hemisphere, *mare nostrum*. From that position there will be no retreat. On that point there will be no negotiation. The missile crisis should have made that vividly clear to the entire world.

To Europeans, both before and after the missile crisis, the Cuban situation seemed either no problem at all or at most some peculiar local problem bothering the United States. Accustomed to living with their own domestic Communist parties, most of which have lost their revolutionary drive, conditioned to Soviet proximity, relaxed in their defense posture because of their secure conviction that the United States will provide the necessary military cover if called upon to do so, the West European countries have been exasperating allies at best in America's struggle with the Cuban problem. In the heat of the missile crisis, they saw what was at stake and stood firmly with us. For the rest, they have never appreciated the American perspective, have thought it ludicrous that the great United States should be so upset by an idiosyncratic ideologue on an insignificant island, and have accepted the opportunity to pick up Cuban trade opportunities no longer available to American businessmen. French and British coolness toward our Cuban policy found some of its source, too, in the disapproving stance the United States government took toward the French and British invasion of Suez in 1956. The Bay of Pigs fiasco produced a certain *Schadenfreude* in British and French hearts as they recalled the finger-shaking of the United States at the Suez fiasco. As a practical political matter, the European countries, firm allies on the big issues, are unlikely to become seriously engaged in the Cuban situation. Their concerns are elsewhere, and their analysis differs too profoundly. But the Cuban affair can remind them of the way even a post-Stalinist Soviet Union may work if given an opening.

The nations of Latin America had an enormous amount to learn from the Cuban case, and there is evidence to indicate that they are learning it. Overnight, the missile crisis made the cold war a reality for the first time for most of the Latin American countries. Russia and China had seemed light-years away. Local Communist parties in Latin America, while sometimes violent in language, were mainly populated by weary old functionaries and idealistic students, who were a nuisance but not a significant political threat or force. The Castro movement in Cuba had had a deep and obvious appeal to many Latin Americans. Castro, the man, was cast to their tastes, in the classical Spanish heroic mold: individualistic, personally courageous, emotional, eloquent, and messianic. They rather enjoyed the prospect of a Latin American country, any Latin American country, standing up to the United States, regardless of the issue. They tended to sympathize with Castro's thesis that American business interests had dominated the economy long enough—and Latin American capitalists were nearly as apt to share that view as Latin American left-wingers. Moreover, most Latin Americans felt that what happened in a small, historically unstable country was really not terribly important anyway; in the universe of Latin America, Cuba was hardly a significant actor. Finally, most Latin Americans had been nursed on the belief that the dominant problem in the conduct of hemispheric foreign affairs was United States interventionism. They felt that, whatever their estimate of the merits of the Castro regime, the important thing was to see to it that the Cubans were able to follow their own course and that the United States would not interfere. And then it all fell apart.

Castro's eloquence was found to be a mask for mendacity, as he announced himself a Marxist, shaped his regime in the pattern of Soviet-style socialism, and dropped all pretense of a free press and the elements of constitutional democracy. Then, in a clumsy, overt way, the Castro government began to meddle in the internal affairs of other governments of Latin America. Cuban diplomatic representatives abroad were found to be operating espionage rings and propaganda mills, working in conspiratorial support of local groups seeking to overthrow the government, and, at least in the case of Venezuela, providing direct armed support to insurrectionary forces. "Interventionism" suddenly assumed two new facets. This interference was Cuban, and intervention was no longer viewable as a United States monopoly. And, for the first time, the Latin American countries were asking themselves whether they too ought to do some intervening in order to keep the Castro situation in hand. They responded through the OAS and then, with the exception of Mexico, by cutting off diplomatic relations with Havana.

When Soviet missiles began to arrive in Cuba, bringing into range not only the cities of the United States but those of Latin America as well, and bringing, too, the visible presence of Soviet troops drilling in the public plazas of Havana, a new chapter in Latin American political thinking opened. It became clearer still that there is intervention and intervention. It turned out to make quite a difference who was intervening with whom, in what way, and for what purposes. Suddenly, too, the much maligned Monroe Doctrine took on a different aspect, and the willingness and ability of the United States to assume the major hemispheric defense responsibility against the Soviet presence in Cuba had a newfound appeal. In the eyes of Latin Americans, the United States diplomatic position over the preceding fifteen years had at last become plausible. For the first time the cold war entered their lives as they saw a skirmish fought out in their very midst.

Finally, Castro's socialist regime provided a showcase to Latin Americans. The example has done much to educate politically inexperienced, idealistic Latin Americans who had been inclined to take it for granted that socialism is the solution to the growth and distributional problems of their own economies. They may now see in Cuba an absolute dictatorship, a conscript labor force in uniform, rationing of food in a land where it has always been plentiful, the failure and abandonment of forced draft industrialization, and an economy that would not run at all if it were not for Soviet subsidy. They may see, too, some pluses: governmental leaders who are personally honest; wider availability of housing, medical care, and schools; and an improvement in former patterns of racial discrimination and privilege. One can see the record— what has been gained, what has been lost, and what it has cost. Latin Americans of good will, eager to develop their countries, are now forced to ask themselves whether it is truly necessary to impose a police state in order to secure an honest government, to conscript labor in order to get work done, to stifle democracy in order to produce apparent consensus, to extirpate the professionally trained in order to provide professional services, to smash the small farmer in order to raise food, to attack one's neighbors in order to vindicate a claim to be free from attack, and to lie to the people out of fear of their reaction if they knew the truth.

The Cuban case over the last seven years offers to Latin Americans an instructive, sometimes painful, lesson in international politics, in domestic politics, in the realities of running a modern economy, and in the human and ethical values that are at stake in the contest between democracy and totalitarianism. Some Latin American countries may still conclude that if they are to move into the economic order of the twentieth century they must follow in Castro's footsteps. But after witnessing the Cuban experience, these countries can no longer be in ignorance of the terrible costs entailed, and the prospect will deter many.

Finally, there is the United States. What may we learn from our Cuban experience?

At the first level of superficiality, there are a number of things we should have done long ago and will need to do tomorrow. Our people have long been poorly educated about Latin America. Public apathy and misinformation about this important neighbor have been the norm. Correction of the situation through our schools, our magazines, our newspapers, and our government education programs should be assigned high priority. Communication to the public through the business community is not enough, for the source is too narrowly based and the transmission too intermittent and selective. Cuba is but a chapter in the history of a continent undergoing violent change. Any Tuesday morning may find us confronted with a crisis in Brazil, in Chile, in Ecuador, in the Dominican Republic, or anywhere else. To cope with it, we will require all the data and educated judgment we can bring to bear.

The American business community should have learned much from

its brush with Castro. Mr. Sundelson has made the point well; re-
pressed silence in a foreign society committed to the *status quo* is not
"normalcy." American businessmen may not have considered themselves
in the business of political analysis while they were operating at home,
but they would do well to gain some proficiency in that field when they
operate abroad, especially in emerging countries.

Our automatic liberals, in turn, might learn from their observation of
Fidelism that it is not wise to become enamored at the first sound of a
sweet voice. The fact that the forces of reaction brand every reformer a
Communist does not excuse viewing every revolutionary leader as
"just an agrarian reformer." Both reactions are conditioned reflexes, operating independently of the facts. When the next hero figure of reform
appears on the horizon, we can be less hurried and less enthusiastic in
our acclaim until more of the record is in.

For Americans generally, it is time to learn that paternalization of
the Latin American countries is not a winning policy for the United
States. Whatever its motivations, it arouses resentment and, in the long
run, trouble. Cultural arrogance is even more inexcusable and costly.
Wriston, Smith, and Sundelson make the point that American cultural
attitudes toward the Cubans and American economic business domination of the Cuban economy have returned to haunt us. Precisely because the Latin American countries are not as economically developed,
not as politically organized, not as militarily powerful as we are, it is
essential that special care be accorded their independent sovereign positions and the dignity of their citizens. And the literate Latin American
living in a sophisticated urban culture, considering himself as much a
part of the Western World as any North American, knowing his country to be older in time and in culture than the United States (how many
North Americans know that the University of Córdoba in Argentina
and San Marcos University in Lima are older than Harvard?), seldom
finds a North American who recognizes these facts or is especially interested in learning about them. We have thought that because we
were strong and rich and big, the Latin American countries should follow us deferentially on all issues and in all contexts. That day is gone.
The democratic leadership that is emerging in many of the Latin American countries today must be expected to move and act independently
of telephone calls from Washington. If the dreadful experience with
Castro has awakened us to the fact that we are entering, and are already in, a new era of Latin American relationships in which Latin

Americans must be treated as partners and not clients, it will have produced a great dividend.

As regards the cold war, Cuba provided us another important lesson, though many knew it already. Used in a discriminating way, a hard foreign policy line is apt to be the right one and the most effective one in dealing with the Communist world. Only a small minority of Americans suffer from the suicidal yearning to leap to their nuclear scabbards and "have it out" with the Russians and Chinese. A somewhat larger group leans the other way, concluding over and over again, as each incident in the cold war occurs, that we should sit down at the table with the Russians like reasonable fellows and negotiate out a fair middle position. The Cuban incident should have made it clear, as other incidents have also made it clear, that the Communist powers will interpret quiet reasonableness as weakness—as Khrushchev did in the Vienna meeting with President Kennedy—but that they will respect a solid surface pressing against their noses. One wishes it were a better world that we live in, one that was free of periodic tests of political will. But it is not a better world than it is, and it will be considerably worse if we are not realistic about it.

The Cuban experience should also have taught us something further about the relationship between economic development and politics. The thesis of many (not all) proponents of economic aid to developing countries is that economic development is the answer to political instability, that revolutionary Communism erupts where economic and social development is retarded, and that the safety of the democratic process rests ultimately in the hands of the middle class. The facts in Cuba read interestingly on this thesis. Castro, Guevara, Dorticós, Roa, and all other leaders of the revolutionary movement in Cuba are from the educated middle class. When revolution came to Cuba, it was the fifth most literate country in Latin America, and it had the best-developed communications and transportation infrastructure of any country in Latin America. Per capita income in Cuba, while low, was high enough to make it the fourth highest among the Latin American countries.

The Cuban revolution must be seen as a political event, brought about mainly by political causes. It had the advantage of able political leadership, grew out of political protest against the decadence of the incumbent regime, and rested more deeply still upon the pride of the Cuban people and a desire to express their nationalism. Political consciousness and political will made the big difference, not economic underdevelopment. Deprivation of schooling or medical care produces complaints, but revolution requires a degree of deprivation plus a sense of moral or ethical outrage at the deprivation, plus a political sense that something can be done about it, plus political leadership. Man in organized society will sacrifice great economic benefits in order to gain, or seem to gain, psychic benefits measured in political coin. The modern social revolutionary looks upon his revolution as an event in the history of moral action and, like Castro, continually calls upon the people for rededication to the grand principles and mystique of the revolution.[4] Only in the most superficial way is the process economic in character. Even expropriations of the lands and properties, carried out in the name of economics and socialist organization, tend to be mainly motivated by a spirit of normal retribution against those who are considered to have exploited the people and those who have rejected the dogma of the revolution. To judge from the Cuban case, politics is mainly about politics. Economic growth rates and the provision of public services do not make—or prevent—revolution.

The consensus of the writers in this symposium is that there is probably nothing that the United States could have done within the last few years to prevent the Castro revolution or something like it. One may always play the idle game of reconstructing history, speculating for example on what Cuban history might have been if the United States had taken it in as a state at the turn of the century. But the forces at work are very long range, and when one walks on stage at any given time his freedom of action is severely inhibited by what has gone before. We Americans have insufficient familiarity with the long flow of history. We tend to believe that where there is a problem one can simply step into the middle of it and solve it. This view is far preferable to the view, common abroad, that nothing can be done to solve anything. Often the Americans have found answers, or at least partial answers. Nonetheless, the American people must be brought to realize that in the field of international politics, particularly in the century of total change, there are situations that cannot be controlled, that there are deep and old forces at work that are not within the power of the United States government significantly to alter, and that most situations defy statement in terms of either-or. We have made considerable

---

[4] Che Guevara is, for example, reported to have said in an interview with Jean Daniel, "For me, it is a question of doctrine. Economic socialism without Communist morality does not interest me." *L'Express,* July 25, 1963, quoted by Theodore Draper, "Five Years of Castro's Cuba," *Commentary,* 37, 1 (1964), 31.

progress in this comprehension in the years since World War II. The cold war itself has begun to teach us something about patience and living daily with a problem. The public is slowly coming to accept the inevitability that a great world power is likely to be continuously under pressure and skirmishing at some point or points around its perimeter.

Change today is constant and quick. It is also bewilderingly multiple, and we have not yet figured out how to react to this multiplicity. Revolution breaks out in a new country, formerly a European colony. We accurately identify nationalism as a powerful force in the movement, and, looking back upon our own anticolonial history, we react sympathetically. The revolution begins to get rough; men are shot without procedural amenities; office is exercised without electoral proceedings; men who are in a hurry and think they have far to go move quickly, and we begin to hear of individuals who are trampled on in the process. Our sympathy drops off. Then we learn that the predecessor regime was corrupt, brutal, and wholly unconcerned with the social welfare of its people. The new regime, though a little quick with the rope, is made up of idealistic young men, tends to be honest, and is concerned with the general welfare of its people. Humanitarian reform, with which in our own minds we are clearly historically identified, is seen as being on the march, and we regain enthusiasm for the movement. Then the economic order of the revolution begins to emerge. This being the latter half of the twentieth century, that economic order is invariably located somewhere along the spectrum of socialist planning, involving social mobilization and allocation of economic resources. Why this should be so the American citizen does not fully understand. The American public associates its own mixed economic system, which it calls private enterprise, with the remarkable achievements of the American economy; it has no significant indigenous left-wing political movement; and it identifies socialist economic solutions with the Soviet Union's plans for world domination. It has little or no awareness that its most treasured symbols of liberal democracy and free enterprise have historically been perverted in many of the emerging countries to the uses of the traditional ruling elements against whom the revolutionary effort is directed. Nationalist rebellion the American people understand well; democratic revolution to establish free speech, religious freedom, and equality of opportunity and education it understands well; social and economic revolution in the mode of the twentieth century it has not experienced. When, as has now happened several times, a revolution that began with American sympathies moves on into violent social revolution, and Communist forces make their presence felt, the United States finds itself ranged against the revolutionary movement, and many conclude that affairs might after all have better been left in the hands of the Batistas, the Diems, or the evicted European colonial power.

Probably we shall have to learn over the next generation or so that there is no consistently successful United States policy that can be brought to bear on these rapidly moving, unstable, revolutionary situations in the less developed countries. Maintenance of the status quo, support of the Batistas, is out of the question. It can only make enemies for the United States, and besides it will fail. Forced prolongation of such regimes in office will merely intensify the explosion when it comes. On the other hand, revolution, once begun, tends to run its course, and nothing will alter the fact that the political coloration of most revolutionary leaders in the latter half of the twentieth century will be some hue or shade of socialism. As each new situation emerges, the United States will have to try to pick and choose its way, shunning impulsiveness, making as few mistakes as possible, concentrating on its long-range objectives, and expecting the transition to be stormy and long. It will have to learn to do so against the pressures of those of its own citizenry who softheadedly embrace every movement of social change and the pressures of those who woodenheadedly believe that the only alternative to the status quo is the bomb. When revolution erupts in developing countries, the United States will seldom have an opportunity to choose the participants, dictate the circumstances, or select the timing. We can do what we can to try to support the democratic elements in the revolution. We can do what is necessary to protect American citizens and, to the extent possible, American property. And, when our national interest is sufficiently clear, as it is in the Caribbean, we can go much further and take greater risks to see to it that particular limited consequences divertly adverse to our security interests will not occur. These things we can do and should be able to do successfully, albeit at a cost. But beyond this there will be occasions when, however little we like it, the course of revolution will take a turn not to our liking but beyond our control. When that happens, we shall have to live with the discomfort until the tides of history roll forward into another phase, submerging old problems and casting up new ones.

Bibliography

ABEL, ELIE. *The Missile Crisis.* Philadelphia: Lippincott, 1966.

ARÉVALO, JUAN JOSÉ. *El anticomunismo en América Latina.* Buenos Aires: Editorial Palestra, 1959.

ARON, RAYMOND. "Social Structure and the Ruling Class," *British Journal of Sociology,* I, 1 (June 1950), 132-35.

ARRENDONDO, ALBERTO. *Cuba: Tierra indefensa.* Havana: Editorial Lex, 1945.

ASSOCIATION OF THE BAR OF THE CITY OF NEW YORK. *The Inter-American Security System and the Cuban Crisis.* (Hammarskjöld Forums, New York, November 19, 1962.) Dobbs Ferry, N.Y.: Oceana Publications, 1964.

BERLE, ADOLF A. *Latin America: Diplomacy and Reality.* New York: Harper & Row, for the Council on Foreign Relations, 1962.

BRINTON, CRANE. *The Anatomy of Revolution.* New York: Random House, 1960.

BUELL, RAYMOND L., *et al. Problems of the New Cuba: Report of the Commission on Cuban Affairs.* New York: Foreign Policy Association, 1935.

BURKS, DAVID D. "Cuba Seven Years After," *Current History,* 50 (January 1966), 38-44.

————. "Soviet Policy for Castro's Cuba," in John J. TePaske and Sydney Nettleton Fisher, eds., *Explosive Forces in Latin America.* Columbus: Ohio State University Press, 1964.

CAMPO, C. DEL. "La Revolución Guatemalteca," in A. Rumianstev, ed., *El movimiento contemporánea de liberación nacional y burguesía nacional.* Prague: Editorial Pazery Socialismo, 1961.

CARTIER-BRESSON, HENRI. "An Island of Pleasure Gone Adrift," *Life* (March 15, 1963).

CASUSO, TERESA. *Cuba and Castro.* New York: Random House, 1961.

249

CRANE, ROBERT D. "The Cuban Crisis: A Strategic Analysis of American and Soviet Policy," *Orbis*, 6 (Winter 1963), 528-63.

CUEVAS CANCINO, FRANCISCO. "The Foreign Policy of Mexico," in Joseph E. Black and Kenneth W. Thompson, *Foreign Policy in a World of Change.* New York: Harper & Row, 1963.

DALLIN, A., ed. *Diversity of International Communism: A Documentary Record, 1961-1963.* New York: Columbia University Press, 1963.

DANIEL, JEAN. "Boycotting Cuba: Whose Interest Does It Serve?," *The New Republic* (December 28, 1966), pp. 19-22.

DEWART, LESLIE. *Christianity and Revolution: The Lesson of Cuba.* New York: Herder & Herder, 1963.

DRAPER, THEODORE. *Castroism: Theory and Practice.* New York: Praeger, 1965.

———. "Five Years of Castro's Cuba, *Commentary*, XXXVII, 1 (January 1964), 25-37.

DREIER, JOHN C. "The OAS and the Cuban Crisis," *S.A.I.S. Review*, V, 2 (Winter 1961), 3-8.

ECONOMIC AND TECHNICAL MISSION TO CUBA. *Report on Cuba.* Washington, D.C.: International Bank for Reconstruction and Development, 1951.

EKMAN, PAUL, et al. "Coping with Cuba: Divergent Policy Preferences of State Political Leaders," *Journal of Conflict Resolution,* 10 (June 1966), 180-97.

FAGAN, RICHARD R. "Charismatic Authority and the Leadership of Fidel Castro," *Western Political Quarterly,* 18 (June 1965), 275-84.

———. "Calculation and Emotion in Foreign Policy: The Cuban Case," *Journal of Conflict Resolution,* 6 (September 1962), 214-21.

FITZGIBBON, RUSSELL HUMKE. *Cuba and the United States, 1900-1935.* New York: Russell & Russell, 1964.

FONER, PHILLIP. *A History of Cuba and Its Relations with the United States.* New York: International Publishers, 1963.

FRANCO, VICTOR. *The Morning After.* New York: Praeger, 1962.

GERMANI, GINO. *Política y sociedad en una época de transición.* Buenos Aires: Ed. Paidós, 1962.

GERMANI, GINO, AND K. H. SILVERT. "Politics, Social Structure and Military Intervention in Latin America," *Archives Européenes de Sociologie,* Vol. I, No. 2 (1961).

GIL, FEDERICO G. "Antecedents of the Cuban Revolution," *Centennial Review,* 6 (Summer 1962), 373-93.

GIMENEZ, ARMANDO. *Sierra Maestra: La revolución de Fidel Castro.* Buenos Aires: Editorial Lautaro, 1959.

GIRARD, ALAIN, AND RAUL SAMUEL. *Situación y perspectivas de Chile en septiembre de 1957.* Santiago de Chile: Ed. Universitaria, 1958.

GLICK, EDWARD B. "Cuba and the Fifteenth UN General Assembly: A Case Study in Regional Disassociation," *Journal of Inter-American Studies*, 6 (April 1964), 235-48.

GOLDENBERG, BORIS. *The Cuban Revolution and Latin America*. New York: Praeger, 1965.

GRABER, D. A. *Crisis Diplomacy*. Washington, D.C.: Public Affairs Press, 1959.

GREENE, GRAHAM. "Return to Cuba: The Revolution Is Still Alive," *The New Republic* (November 2, 1963), pp. 16-18.

GRUPO CUBANO DE INVESTIGACIONES ECONÓMICAS. *Un Estudio Sobre Cuba*. Coral Gables: University of Miami Press, 1963.

GUGGENHEIM, HENRY. *The United States and Cuba*. New York: Macmillan, 1934.

HAGAN, ROGER, AND BART BERNSTEIN. "Military Value of Missiles in Cuba," *Bulletin of the Atomic Scientists*, Vol. 19 (February 1963).

HAYWOOD, RICHARD M. *The Myth of Rome's Fall*. New York: Crowell, 1958.

HEALY, DAVID F. *The United States in Cuba, 1898-1902*. Madison: University of Wisconsin Press, 1963.

HENNESSY, C. A. M. "The Roots of Cuban Nationalism," *International Affairs*, 39, 3 (London, July 1963), 345-59.

HIRSCHMAN, ALBERT O., ed. *Latin American Issues: Essays and Comments*. New York: Twentieth Century Fund, 1961.

HORELICK, ARNOLD L. "The Cuban Missile Crisis: An Analysis of Soviet Calculations and Behavior," *World Politics*, 16 (April 1964), 363-89.

JACKSON, D. BRUCE. "Whose Men in Havana?," *Problems of Communism*, 15 (May-June 1966), 1-10.

JESSUP, PHILIP. *Elihu Root*. New York: Dodd, 1938.

JOHNSON, LELAND L. *U.S. Business Interests in Cuba and the Rise of Castro*. Santa Monica, Calif.: Rand, 1964.

KENNAN, GEORGE F. "America and the Russian Future," *Foreign Affairs*, XXIX, 3 (April 1951), 351-70.
———. *American Diplomacy*. Chicago: University of Chicago Press, 1951.

LEUCHSENRING, EMILIO ROIG DE. *1895 y 1898: Dos guerras cubanas, Ensayo de revaloración*. Havana: Sociedad Cubana de Estudios Históricos y Internacionales, 1945.

LIEUWEN, E. *Arms and Politics in Latin America*. New York: Praeger, for the Council on Foreign Relations, 1960.

LINCOLN, FREEMAN. "What Happened to Cuban Business?," *Fortune*, LX, 3 (September 1959), 110-12.

MCDOUGAL, MYLES S. "The Soviet-Cuban Quarantine and Self-Defense," *American Journal of International Law*, 57 (July 1963), 597-604.

MACGAFFEY, WYATT, AND CLIFFORD R. BARNETT. *Cuba: Its People, Its Society, Its Culture.* New Haven, Conn.: HRAF Press, 1962. (Also published in paperback under the title *Twentieth Century Cuba: The Background of the Castro Revolution.* Garden City, N.Y.: Doubleday Anchor Books, 1962.)

MATTHEWS, HERBERT L. *Return to Cuba.* Stanford, Calif.: Bolivar House, Stanford University, 1964.

MEYER, KARL ERNEST, AND TAD SZULC. *The Cuban Invasion: The Chronicle of a Disaster.* New York: Praeger, 1962.

MINTZ, SIDNEY W. Foreword to Ramiro Guerra y Sánchez, *Sugar and Society in the Caribbean.* (Caribbean Series No. 7.) New Haven, Conn.: Yale University Press, 1964.

MORGENTHAU, HANS J. "The Impotence of American Power," *Commentary,* XXXVI, 5 (November 1963), 384-85.

NEIRA, HUGO. *Cuzco: Tierra y Muerte.* Lima: Problemas de Hoy, 1965.

NELSON, LOWRY. *Rural Cuba.* Minneapolis: University of Minnesota, 1950.

O'CONNOR, JAMES. "Cuba: Salvation through Sugar," *The Nation* (October 12, 1963), pp. 212-14, 226-27.

OLSON, MANCUR, JR. "Rapid Growth as a Destabilizing Force," *Journal of Economic History,* XXIII, 4 (December 1963), 529-52.

ORTEGA Y GASSET, JOSÉ. *Invertebrate Spain.* New York: Norton, 1937.

ORTIGUEIRA, ROBERTO. "La Desintegración, Estado Normal de Paises en Desarrollo," *Journal of Inter-American Studies,* V, 4 (October 1963), 471-94.

PACHTER, HENRY M. *Collision Course: The Cuban Missile Crisis and Coexistence.* New York: Praeger, 1963.

PAZOS, JAVIER. "Was a Deal Possible in '59?," *The New Republic* (January 12, 1963), pp. 10-11.

PHILLIPS, R. HART. *The Cuba Dilemma.* New York: Obolensky, 1962.

———. *Cuba: Island of Paradox.* New York: McDowell, Obolensky, 1959.

POPULAR SOCIALIST PARTY OF CUBA. *The Cuban Revolution.* New York: New Century Publishers, 1961.

PORTELL VILÁ, HERMINIO. *Historia de Cuba en sus relaciones con los Estados Unidos y España.* Havana: Jesús Montero, 1938-41.

PRATT, JULIUS. *A History of United States Foreign Policy.* Englewood Cliffs, N.J.: Prentice-Hall, 1955.

PUIGGROS, RODOLFO. *Historia crítica de los partidos políticos argentinos.* Buenos Aires: Editorial Argumentos, 1962.

RAMÍREZ GÓMEZ, R. "El Informe Prebisch," *Cuadernos Americanos,* Vol. CXXXI, No. 6 (Mexico, 1963).

RAVINES, EUDOCIO. "La estrategia comunista en América Latina," *Estudios sobre el comunismo* (Santiago de Chile, 1954).

REAL, JUAN JOSÉ. *Treinta años de historia argentina.* Buenos Aires: Ediciones Actualidad, 1962.

ROCA, BLAS. "El desarrollo histórico de la revolución cubana," *Cuba Socialista,* Vol. IV, No. 29 (1964).

ROOD, HAROLD W. "Military Operations against Cuba," *Claremont Quarterly,* 10 (Winter 1963), 5-18.

ROSTOW, W. W. in F. M. Osanka, *Modern Guerrilla Warfare: Fighting Guerrilla Movements, 1941-1961.* New York: Free Press, 1962.

ROVERE, RICHARD H. "Letter from Washington," *The New Yorker,* 37 (May 6, 1961), 139-46.

RUSK, DEAN. "The Alliance in the Context of World Affairs," in John C. Dreier, ed., *The Alliance for Progress: Problems and Perspectives.* Baltimore: Johns Hopkins Press, 1962.

SAUVAGE, LEO. *Autopsie du Castrisme.* Paris: Flammarion, 1962.

SCHELLING, THOMAS C. *The Strategy of Conflict.* Cambridge, Mass.: Harvard University Press, 1960.

SCHNEIDER, R. M. *Communism in Guatemala, 1944-1954.* New York: Praeger, 1958.

SEERS, DUDLEY, *et al. Cuba: The Economic and Social Revolution.* Chapel Hill: University of North Carolina Press, 1964.

SILVERT, K. H. *Expectant Peoples: Nationalism and Development.* New York: Random House, 1963.

———. "Peace, Freedom and Stability," in William Manger, *The Alliance for Progress: A Critical Appraisal.* Washington, D.C.: Public Affairs Press, 1963.

SMITH, EARL E. T. *The Fourth Floor.* New York: Random House, 1962.

SMITH, ROBERT F. *Background to Revolution: The Development of Modern Cuba.* New York: Knopf, 1966.

———. *What Happened in Cuba: A Documentary History.* New York: Twayne, 1963.

STOKES, E. S. "National and Local Violence in Cuban Politics," *Southwestern Social Science Quarterly,* XXXIV, 3 (September 1953), 57-63.

SZULC, TAD. *The Winds of Revolution: Latin America Today—And Tomorrow.* New York: Praeger, 1963.

THOMAS, HUGH. "The Origins of the Cuban Revolution," *The World Today,* 19 (October 1963), 454-56.

TORRIENTE, COSME DE LA. "The Platt Amendment," *Foreign Affairs,* Vol. VIII, No. 3 (April 1930).

U.N. ECONOMIC AND SOCIAL COUNCIL, ECONOMIC COMMISSION FOR LATIN AMERICA. *Economic Survey of Latin America, 1959 Preliminary Report.* New York: United Nations, 1960.

U.S. DEPARTMENT OF COMMERCE, WORLD TRADE INFORMATION SERVICE. *Economic Developments in Cuba, 1957.* (Economic Reports, Pt. I, No. 59-42, Pt. II, No. 58-25.) Washington, D.C.: Government Printing Office, 1958.

U.S. DEPARTMENT OF COMMERCE. *Investment in Cuba: Basic Information for United States Businessmen.* Washington, D.C.: Government Printing Office, 1956.

U.S. DEPARTMENT OF STATE. *Cuba.* (Publication 7171, Inter-American Series.) Washington, D.C.: Government Printing Office, 1961.

VELIZ, CLAUDIO. "The New Cuban Industrial Policy," *The World Today,* 19 (September 1963), 371-74.

———. "Obstacles to Reform in Latin America," *The World Today,* Vol. 19, No. 1 (January 1963).

WHITAKER, ARTHUR. "Cuba's Intervention in Venezuela: A Test of the OAS," *Orbis,* 8 (Fall 1964), 511-34.

———. *The United States and Argentina.* Cambridge, Mass.: Harvard University Press, 1954.

WINDASS, G. S. "The Cuban Crisis and World Order," *International Relations,* 3 (April 1966), 1-15.

WOHLSTETTER, ALBERT AND ROBERTA. *Controlling the Risks in Cuba.* (Adelphi Papers, No. 17.) London: The Institute for Strategic Studies, 1965.

WOOD, BRYCE. *The Making of the Good Neighbor Policy.* New York: Columbia University Press, 1961.

WRIGHT, QUINCY. "The Cuban Quarantine," *American Journal of International Law,* 57 (July 1963), 546-65.

ZEITLIN, MAURICE, AND ROBERT SCHEER. *Cuba: Tragedy in Our Hemisphere.* New York: Grove Press, 1963.

Index

Index